Production Studies

2 8 APR 2025

WITHDRAWN

"Behind-the-scenes" stories of ranting directors, stingy producers, temperamental actors, and the like have fascinated us since the beginnings of film and television. Today, magazines, websites, television programs, and DVDs are devoted to telling tales of trade lore—from on-set antics to labor disputes. The *production* of media has become as storied and mythologized as the *content* of the films and TV shows themselves.

Production Studies is the first volume to bring together a star-studded cast of interdisciplinary media scholars to examine the unique cultural practices of media production. The all-new essays collected here combine ethnographic, sociological, critical, material, and political-economic methods to explore a wide range of topics, from contemporary industrial trends such as new media and niche markets to gender and workplace hierarchies. Together, the contributors seek to understand how the entire span of "media producers"—ranging from high-profile producers and directors to anonymous production assistants and costume designers—work through professional organizations and informal networks to form communities of shared practices, languages, and cultural understandings of the world.

This landmark collection connects the cultural activities of media producers to our broader understanding of media practices and texts, establishing an innovative and agenda-setting approach to media industry scholarship for the twenty-first century.

Vicki Mayer is Associate Professor of Communication at Tulane University. She is author of *Producing Dreams, Consuming Youth: Mexican Americans and Mass Media* as well as *Below the Line: Producers and Production Studies in the New Television Economy* (forthcoming).

Miranda J. Banks is Assistant Professor of Visual and Media Arts at Emerson College.

John Thornton Caldwell is Professor of Film, Television, and Digital Media at UCLA. He has authored and edited several books, including *Televisuality: Style, Crisis and Authority in American Television*, *New Media: Digitextual Theories and Practices*, and *Production Culture: Industrial Reflexivity and Critical Practice in Film and Television*.

Production Studies

Cultural Studies of Media Industries

Edited by
Vicki Mayer
Miranda J. Banks
John T. Caldwell

 Routledge
Taylor & Francis Group

NEW YORK AND LONDON

First published 2009
by Routledge
711 Third Avenue, New York, NY 10017

Simultaneously published in the UK
by Routledge
2 Park Square, Milton Park, Abingdon, Oxon OX14 4RN

*Routledge is an imprint of the Taylor & Francis Group,
an informa business*

© 2009 Taylor & Francis

Typeset in Perpetua by Keyword Group Ltd

Library of Congress Cataloging in Publication Data
A catalog record has been requested for this book

ISBN 13: 978-0-415-99795-9 (hbk)
ISBN 13: 978-0-415-99796-6 (pbk)
ISBN 13: 978-0-203-87959-7 (ebk)

Contents

Introduction

Production Studies: Roots and Routes

Vicki Mayer, Miranda J. Banks and John T. Caldwell

Consider the following scenes drawn from popular media narratives of film and television "producers" at work:

> Cruise glitzy LA with Ari, Vince, Drama, Turtle, and Eric. Swerve into the Hollywood fast lane and hit LA hot spots with the *Entourage* gang. Give your comments and reviews on all of the locations featured in the show or add some of your own favorite haunts.[1]

> "The realtor did say something about the house having been shown in the opening shots of each episode of *The Mary Tyler Moore Show* and that this was where Mary supposedly lived." […] The woman who lived there when the show was first broadcast "was overwhelmed by the people showing up and asking if Mary was around," Ms. [Mary Tyler] Moore said. When the producers returned for fresh footage several seasons later, she said, the owner "had by way of retribution draped huge 'Impeach Nixon' signs all over the house."[2]

> George Lucas returned to the United States after principal shooting in Tunisia and Britain and almost immediately checked himself into a hospital because he thought he was having a heart attack. Lucas was unhappy with the work of the film's original editor in Britain, and had to scrap his work entirely.[3]

> Ann Donahue, executive producer of *CSI* and *CSI: Miami* [in a public event]: "Sleep when you're dead. [crowd applauds] Because you only get this—and we know this—you only get this once. And it's what you wanted to do your whole life."[4]

We frequently come to know about media producers and their work, ironically, through the representations they make. From the "making of" videos that cull DVD customers to entertainment television tabloids that "report" on the excitement on the sets, the non-fiction portrayals of production often reflect the drama of some of their producers' best-known fictional works.[5] To wit: conflict and chaos frequently precede teamwork and collaboration, leading ultimately to creativity and commercial success in recitations of how production occurs. These stories have filtered their way through the popular press and trade lore, and even into the annals of scholarship, attracting researchers and students alike to look "behind the scenes" of the films and series that they encounter in daily life. It could be said, at first glance, that the off-screen production of media is itself a cultural production, mythologized and branded much like the onscreen textual culture that media industries produce.

This collection of essays hopes to dig deeper into this notion of production as a culture. To do so, we are interested in how media producers make culture, and, in the process, make themselves into particular kinds of workers in modern, mediated societies. We want to look up and down the food chains of production hierarchies, to understand how people work through professional organizations and informal networks to form communities of shared practices, languages, and cultural understandings of the world. We assume that directors and editors, lighting technicians and storywriters, contract casting agents and full-time studio caterers are all cultural actors, too. They shape and refashion their identities in the process of making their careers in industries undergoing political transitions and economic reorganizations. Production studies scholars, as contributors to a field of interdisciplinary inquiry, draw their intellectual impetus from cultural studies to look at the ways that culture both constitutes and reflects the relationships of power; or in the words of Nicholas Garnham, they examine "the cultural producers, the organizational sites and practices they inhabit and through which they exercise their power."[6]

This is obviously not an objective unique to cultural studies, but an objective that transformed the study of media across academic disciplines, forming its own field of study. From their beginnings in propaganda studies in the 1930s to auteur analyses of the 1950s, media researchers have typically distinguished their objects of study as unique from all others. The reach of mass media texts, the celebrity of particular professionals, the infiltration of media commodities into daily life, and the economic resources marshaled by media industries and concentrated in a handful of global cities provide easy alibis for why studying media production is different from other production realms. Indeed this has justified to us why this very book is needed given the long literatures on labor and industrial production. Even research into the production processes of making film or television content, a tradition found in communication and organizational sociology, sought to declare media production as an exception to other forms of production.[7] The now staid phrase for explaining media production as "creativity within constraints" captures the balance that media researchers strike between describing media workers as the creators of popular culture and as functionaries in the service of capitalism.[8] These works are foundational to be sure, highlighting difference in the study of media producers and their practices, but this difference also deferred other questions about media production raised in parallel studies of cultural identities, meaning, and representation. We briefly cite a few trends that we would add to the roots of media production studies.

The cultural turn in the social sciences and the ethnographic turn in the humanities over the past three decades have pushed researchers to look at cultural production with new eyes. No longer restricted to sites of deviance and difference, exoticism and Orientalism, sociologists, anthropologists, and geographers have sought out shopping malls, industrial zones, and virtual games as "spaces" where people actively make meanings through their consumption habits, active bodies, and ritual activities.[9] Meanwhile, literary critics and historians added fieldwork and focus groups, oral interviews and memory analyses to their methodological toolbox, recognizing the ways people generate stories in the contexts of their lived realities.[10] Together, these trends have shared a concern with texts, the active role of language and narratives in constructing the real, as well as the relationships between the speakers and receivers of these texts. Ethnomethodologies, while multiplying the possible stories about how people make meaning in societies, have also complicated the generalizing claims that scholars used to make about the unique role of media in the world. What seemed like the mass appropriation of media technologies and their contents was actually distributed unequally through societies and communities organized along fault lines of class, gender, race, and a host of other cultural distinctions.[11]

One place these academic strands weave together more complex tales about media is in the study of consumers and audiences as interpretative communities. Treating television viewers or romance book fans as "producers" of meaning, audience studies have mined the ways that people talk about their consumer practices as formative of their identities as well as how identities shape ways of consuming and talking about consumption.[12] Studies of club cultures and computer classroom cliques have illustrated the ways that places, with their shifting power hierarchies, affect consumer dynamics.[13] In this expansive body of work, we see that even the objects of consumption are sites of cultural production as consumers adopt, modify, and re-purpose the cultural meanings of domestic tools and media technologies.[14] Situated frequently as participants in the communities they researched, critical scholars have had to reflect on their own positions, relationships, and, ultimately, authority in theorizing consumption.[15] The inductive insights of these studies of media viewers and consumers have set a new standard for studies of producers, their interpretative communities, and the conjuncture of contexts within which they produce meanings.

At the same time, production studies scholars face challenges not frequently confronted in the study of media consumption and audiences. Whereas these forerunners frequently framed consumption in terms of the politics of pleasure, production studies need to conceptualize practices within the political economy of labor, markets, and policy. The convergence of media might open productive potentials for users, but they also introduce anxiety and uncertainty into the work worlds of those charged with making those interactive and "empowering" media.[16] Short-term and seasonal contracts, deskilling and self-surveillance, outsourcing and multitasking are the new buzzwords of a "new international division of cultural labor" driven by runaway productions, synergistic sales, and the push towards a niche media economy dedicated to the wealthiest one percent of media consumers.[17] To the degree that media systems globally have been or have become commercially driven, state policies that focus on national cultures, indigenous expressions, or simply media contents have not similarly protected media workers.[18] The paradox of the media worker is that the promise of autonomy, creativity, fame, or wealth still oversupplies the labor market, allowing media industries to control the mise-en-scène (setting and action) of production narratives.

In the process, production studies borrow theoretical insights from the social sciences and humanities, but, perhaps most importantly, they take the lived realities of people involved in media production as the subjects for theorizing production as culture. Production studies gather empirical data about production: the complexity of routines and rituals, the routines of seemingly complex processes, the economic and political forces that shape roles, technologies, and the distribution of resources according to cultural and demographic differences. Two research questions follow this careful data compilation. How do media producers represent themselves given the paradoxical importance of media in society? How do we, as researchers, then represent those varied and contested representations? The crisis of representing producers, their locations, industries, and products is the burden of representation for production studies. Articulated from various disciplines as grounded theory, lay theory, action theory, and so on, production studies privilege but also interrogate research methodologies that place the researcher in dialogue with subjects usually charged with representing us.[19] This dialectic leads production studies toward grounded and inductive, even if partial, conclusions.

Our Scope in this Collection

Drawing on the broad trends that have shaped the study of cultural production in the past, every essay in this collection offers its own approach to studying media production. In the process, they open new inquiries into the questions of authorship and authority, structures and subjectivities, and representation and reflexivity that cut across our respective disciplines, namely: anthropology, communication, cultural geography, film, and sociology. Some of these authors come to production studies after establishing their careers in other arenas, importing the queries central to their discipline to production studies and enriching the scope of the field beyond a narrow focus on cultural industries. Other authors began their careers thinking about media industries and its employees. Their work has become required reading for anyone interested in studying producers as cultural communities. For them, this book has been an opportunity to reflect on the theoretical and methodological issues in hindsight of their signature research projects. Still others in this collection were media professionals, having unique work resumes—from journalism and broadcasting to independent video and music—that preceded their research agendas. The autobiographical memories of production work may be "gossamer walls" between our authors, their subjects, and their readers.[20] All of these modes of participant-observation have helped raise questions here about access, rapport, and collaboration in the research process. We welcome these questions as part of our research agenda.

Supporting our scholarly project, we have integrated historical and materialist accounts of cultural industries, work practices, and organizational formations as the columns upon which we construct well-rounded investigations of production cultures. We concur with the familiar calls to move beyond the unproductive segregation of cultural studies and political economy.[21] Rather, we see how national policies and global markets shape, sometimes dramatically, the local sites studied by the contributors of this book. In addition, our focus on contemporary production practice embeds longer histories that fall outside of the scope of this volume. Fortunately, our academic colleagues continue to inform our inquiries with their thorough research into the archives, oral histories, and empirical remains of production history.[22]

The scope of this book encourages boundary crossing at two borders. First, we want to alert social scientists to the cultural histories of the contemporary media institutions they are analyzing and entering as field researchers. As various chapters that follow suggest, the ignorance of longstanding trade languages, personnel networks, and rifts over resources can be the surest route to a short meeting, unreturned phone calls, or even failure to achieve research goals. Even a cursory visit by scholars to a field site, whether a producer's office, a studio set, or a runaway film location will inevitably involve confronting discourses and practices that have been defined by convention over decades. Second, by contrast, humanities scholars need to acknowledge the slippery social nature of labor practices that social scientists excel at recognizing and accounting for in their work. One must be mindful that all texts, whether found in an archive or one's own field notes, are constructions, versions on the real that may serve different roles in a production studies project, from corporate branding and spin, to the personal reflections of an outsider looking in. To these scholars, we suggest a healthy dose of skepticism and reflexivity as components of the research process and presentation. Our interdisciplinary scope is thus prescriptive, recommending a balanced approach to production texts as sociocultural constructions, and production activities as cultural texts.

As an attempt to stake out the contours of this field, the essays presented here also reference classical works in sociology, anthropology, film and television studies, cultural geography, and communication that have looked at media production. This has not been an exercise of canon-building to reify the field, but rather an effort to point out works that have inspired our authors in their own studies of production as culture. Standing on the shoulders of figures we have found compelling, we intend to show that production studies, as we are conceiving of them, existed well before their consolidation into anything as formalistic as a field. Towards interdisciplinary production studies, we have added a bibliography at the end of this volume.

We admit there are still many gaps to fill. The case studies presented here focus almost exclusively on film and television production in the predominantly English-speaking world. Given the ubiquity of video in modern media cultures, we recognize the importance of these industries, while realizing that their institutional dependencies, for example on electronics industries, and far-flung professional networks implicate far more industries than we present here.[23] Were we to claim comprehensiveness over production studies, we would cast a wider net over more media industries, from music labels to video game programmers, over a larger geography of the physical world. It is perhaps a limitation of studying media in a global economy that we still lack multisited and collaborative projects, which would allow us to compare the ways production resonates differently to working communities given divergent contexts and historical conditions.[24] To this, we hope that future scholars will contribute their own disciplinary roots and routes to this emerging body of intellectual inquiries.

Histories of Media Production Studies

As indicated in our introduction to this volume, production studies mine theories and methods drawn from a diverse set of disciplines that, to date, have rarely been brought into dialogue. Lacking a historical tradition of our own, we as production studies scholars have traded our reference lists and syllabi, trying to fill the gaps in our knowledge of media industries, labor practices and communities, and regulatory and legal policies. Works that academics have all but forgotten in their respective disciplines have become our signposts, guiding us as to what has been done and what remains to be done. The chapters in this first part address but a few of these early works, presenting their value both historically and for future researchers.

Each of the four chapters in this part offer two objectives that have driven production studies in the past, namely: to accurately describe industries from the ground up, and, second, to use these descriptions in the formulation of social theory. To the latter end, Vicki Mayer's "Bringing the Social Back In" and John Sullivan's "Leo C. Rosten's Hollywood" offer the contexts that drove early production scholars Hortense Powdermaker and Leo Rosten to study Hollywood as a social system with broad theoretical implications. Mayer takes on alienation as a theoretical concept that informed these scholars, and, drawing on a case study of reality television casting, shows how production studies might re-theorize alienation in light of current working conditions. Sullivan similarly demonstrates that early production studies aimed to build upon the reigning social theories of the day through careful analysis of Hollywood's production personnel as power brokers. More than just a guidebook to the egos that drove film studios, Rosten's work sets the stage for future studies of the ways producers and their personnel exert power, according to Sullivan.

These early theoretical explorations relied on careful descriptions of the film industry, its economics and politics—central components of the study of production industries and labor today. Amanda Lotz's "Industry-Level Studies" offers Todd Gitlin as one of the forefathers of critical industry studies, a field focused on the negotiations between people within media industries. Gitlin's ability to get inside the industry to show the process of production has set the standard for other scholars, including Lotz, who look at creative production processes and their structural constraints. In contrast, Matt Stahl's "Privilege and Distinction in Production Worlds" presents a new historiography for the study of production through the legal definitions of authorship and work for hire. Drawing on judicial precedent and contractual relations to define employment categories, copyright, and intellectual property, Stahl argues that the study of creative production in media industries must encompass critical and comparative legal analysis. Together, the chapters in this part use the hindsight of history to investigate media industries and their personnel in light of contemporary industrial trends, from the multiplication of new media, technologies, and niche markets, to the segmentation of labor struggles and worker solidarity.

Producers: Selves and Others

Production studies interrogate the term "producer" as one that identifies a specific category of media practitioners, while also marginalizing other practitioners in the production process. Grounded in organizational hierarchies of media labor, and reinforced by "auteur" studies of film and television producers as the "authors" of their creative projects, the notion of authorship is one of both subjective identification and outsider objectification. The authors of the chapters in this part address the subjective, and often self-reflexive, identities of media practitioners as they represent themselves and their communities. At the same time, these authors are mindful of the hierarchies throughout work worlds that bear upon and evaluate these practitioner identities.

In the "auteur" tradition, Denise Mann and Christine Cornea investigate the people at the apexes of production hierarchies. In "It's Not TV, It's Brand Management TV," Mann challenges notions of creative authorship through a redefinition of the role of the showrunner as television's key producer in Hollywood. Working to produce high-concept, big-budget blockbusters for the television networks, the showrunner has become an entertainment brand manager in the corporate bureaucracy. Mann's case study, the television series *Lost* (2004–), reveals the financial considerations and pressures involved in making cross-platform hit content. Cornea has also seen these market-driven measures, though on a different scale. Responding to Mann's US-based perspective, Cornea explores the transnational role of the writer–executive producer in "Showrunning the *Doctor Who* Franchise."

Whereas Mann and Cornea shine light on the mostly-male environs of the present-day auteurs, Laura Grindstaff and Miranda J. Banks look to the largely female work forces that buttress the work of producers, as traditionally defined. In "Self-Serve Celebrity," Grindstaff questions the idea of "ordinary" people who participate in daytime talk and primetime reality television genres. Through an analysis of the means of production, rather than the ends, she holds a mirror to the emotional labor of televisual performance, and, in the process, sees her own labors as an ethnographic fieldworker. Banks' "Gender Below-the-Line" complements this consideration of labor and emotion with her look into the feminized work force of costume designers. The devaluation of her subjects' careers as "women's work" pushes Banks to articulate a new agenda for feminist production studies, one that brings feminist film and television studies to the industry's numerous female production communities.

Production Spaces: Centers and Peripheries

The third part of the book invites us to pay particular attention to the physical, cultural, and symbolic locations of media production. It was not long ago that studies of film and television production limited their geographic considerations to the space of a studio set or the places where media capital was most concentrated, i.e., Los Angeles, California. These chapters draw on recent scholarship about how space and place affect media production, both in terms of production processes and practices, and in terms of the academic practices that research these myriad locales.

Of the four chapters in this part, only one is set primarily in California, and all are transnational in geographic scope. Candace Moore's "Liminal Places and Spaces" examines the spaces where producers conduct events for fans of the premium cable and DVD series *The L Word* (2004–). Integrating Victor Turner's notion of "liminality" with Nick Couldry's articulation of a "media ritual," Moore describes the active involvement of series producers in the maintaining of a lesbian fan community through choreographed parties; thus transforming viewer expressions into market research. Shot in Vancouver, British Columbia, the binational production of

The L Word parallels in some ways the binational production of film and television scholarship addressed in the chapter by Elana Levine. Based in the US, Levine reflects on questions of identity raised in studying the production and distribution of a Canadian television series in "Crossing the Border." Much as in her case study *Degrassi: The Next Generation* (2001–), Levine had to cross borders, physical and cultural, in comprehending producers' dualistic pride in the series' national setting and its presumed appeal to American teen audiences.

Research questions about location do not evoke easy answers, as revealed in Jane Landman's "Not in Kansas Anymore" and Serra Tinic's "Borders of Production Research." Considering the assumption that the "New International Division of Cultural Labor" underscores the dominant position of the US in international co-production, Landman found much evidence to the contrary in the production of *Farscape* (1999–2003), an Australian–US series that tried to experiment within the sci-fi genre. Landman's interviews with producers and research into local input into the production process suggest that the series is better described as a "co-venture" and as a creative collaboration, rather than as piecework production under the tight fiscal and creative control of US interests. Similarly, Tinic considers the "situatedness" of all production studies in influencing scholars' questions and assumptions in fieldwork. Written as a response to Levine's chapter, Tinic places the case study in a Canadian-based context of national policy and global aspirations. The chapters in this part remind us of the importance of pursuing multisited production studies, while cautioning against taking our interpretations for granted as objective.

Production as Lived Experience

Production studies should not be undertaken without paying particular attention to the lived experiences of the producer and the scholar alike. As its title suggests, this final part culls out key lessons that are largely implicit in many of the preceding chapters: first, the ways that life's everyday experiences impact, inform, and influence the practical and creative work of the people they study; and second, the ways that critical, cultural, and ethnographic studies of production inevitably involve and animate complex, and sometimes problematic, relations between researchers and their human subjects. These chapters might be considered groundbreaking in their attempts to blend registers and cross scales in setting an agenda for production studies as studies of culture.

Ethnographic methods challenge researchers to reflect on the ways lived experience and everyday knowledge are themselves symbolic representations. Sherry Ortner's "Studying Sideways" offers a way of theorizing these methods, not in terms of studying up or down power hierarchies in the field, but rather studying across. Drawing comparative insights from past fieldwork and a current project on Hollywood producers, Ortner demonstrates that the problematic affinities and sometimes testy interchanges between producer and scholar result from their shared economic and/or intellectual capital. Even so, a producer will frequently present themselves as the more authoritative member of the dyad. In "Audience Knowledge and the Everyday Lives of Cultural Producers in Hollywood," Stephen Zafirau draws on his experiences observing film producers as they publicly justify, rationalize, and explain their career choices. By showing how producers self-represent as either removed from the audience or as part of the audience, Zafirau grounds industries' need for audience knowledge in the producer–researcher interaction. Together these two authors underscore the risks of an unreflexive acceptance of producers' discourses.

Conversely, researchers need to broaden their reach in production studies to producers' impacts on their social environments. In an entreaty to prioritize producers' actions over political and economic structures, Oli Mould explains the use-value of French sociologist Bruno Latour's "actor-network theory" in his chapter "Lights, Camera, but Where's the Action?" By placing Australian film director Robert Connolly in a network of social relations, Mould shows how Connolly's actions animated the production technologies and objects, such as the script, in the making of a single film. This attention to practice is echoed by John Caldwell in "Both Sides of the Fence," a triad of interviews with scholar-practitioners who study and work in their own production fields. Addressing practical issues of gaining access to closely guarded communities; the impact of professional identities on types of disclosure in the field; and the "trade-offs" between research and work, Caldwell's interviews consider the lived experiences of those who move between the industries of media and scholarly production. His interviewees will, without doubt, become future articulators of production studies.

Notes

1 "*Entourage* Guide to Los Angeles," HBO Productions, http://entouragewiki.hbo.com/page/Entourage+Guide+to+Los+Angeles, accessed September 22, 2008.
2 Neal Karlen, "The House That's So, So Mary," *The New York Times*, January 12, 1995.
3 Todd Jatras, "Gallery: The Making of *Star Wars*," *Wired*, April 23, 2007.
4 "Show Creators and Showrunners: Women Who Create Today's Innovative Programs," official transcript of Academy of Television Arts and Sciences, Los Angeles, CA, December 3, 2003.
5 John T. Caldwell, *Production Culture: Industrial Reflexivity and Critical Practice in Film and Television* (Durham, NC: Duke University Press, 2008).
6 Nicholas Garnham, "Political Economy and Cultural Studies," *Critical Studies in Mass Communication* 12, no. 2 (1995): 65.
7 See, for example, William T. Bielby and Denise D. Bielby, "Organizational Media of Project-Based Labor Markets: Talent Agencies and the Careers of Screenwriters," *American Sociological Review* 64, no. 1 (1999): 64–85; Muriel Cantor and Cheryl Zollars, eds., *Current Research on Occupations and Professions: Creators of Culture*, vol. 8

(Greenwich, CT: JAI Press, 1993); Paul DiMaggio, "Cultural Entrepreneurship in 19-Century Boston: The Creation of an Organizational Base for High Culture in America," *Media, Culture & Society* 4, no. 1 (1982): 33–50; Philip Elliott, *The Making of a Television Series: A Case Study in the Sociology of Culture*, ed. Jeremy Tunstall (London: Constable, 1972); Paul Hirsch, "Cultural Industries Revisited," *Organization Science* 11, no. 3 (2000): 356–361; Joseph Turow, "Learning to Portray Institutional Power: The Socialization of Mass Media Organizations," in *Organizational Communication: Traditional Themes and New Directions*, eds. Robert McPhee and Phillip Tompkins, *Sage Annual Reviews of Communication Research* (Beverly Hills: Sage, 1985), 211–234.

8 D. Charles Whitney and James S. Ettema, "Media Production: Individuals, Organizations, Institutions," in *A Companion to Media Studies*, ed. Angharad Valdivia (Oxford: Blackwell, 2003), 157–186.

9 Patrick Brantlinger, "A Response to Beyond the Cultural Turn," *The American Historical Review* 107, no. 5 (2002): 1500–1511.

10 Faye Ginsberg, "Ethnography and American Studies," *Cultural Anthropology* 21, no. 3 (2006): 487–495.

11 See, for example, Faye Ginsberg, Lila Abu-Lughod, and Brian Larkin, eds., *Media-Worlds: Anthropology on New Terrain* (Berkeley: University of California Press, 2002); Eric Rothenbuhler and Mihai Coman, eds., *Media Anthropology* (Thousand Oaks, CA: Sage, 2005); Kelly Askew and Richard Wilk, eds., *The Anthropology of Media: A Reader* (Malden, MA: Blackwell, 2002).

12 See, for example, Will Brooker and Deborah Jermyn, eds., *The Audience Studies Reader* (London: Routledge, 2003).

13 Examples include: Sarah Thornton, *Club Cultures: Music, Media and Subcultural Capital* (Middletown, CT: Wesleyan University Press, 1996); Sunaina M. Maira, *Desis in the House: Indian American Youth Culture in NYC* (Philadelphia: Temple University Press, 2002); Marie Gillespie, *Television, Ethnicity and Cultural Change* (London: Routledge, 1995); Ellen Seiter, *Television and New Media Audiences* (Oxford: Oxford University Press, 1999).

14 Two recent works in this area are: Stewart Hoover, Lynn Schofield Clark, and Diane Alters, *Media Home and Family* (New York: Routledge, 2004); Roger Silverstone, *Media, Technology and Everyday Life in Europe: From Information to Communication* (Hampshire, UK: Ashgate Publishing, 2005).

15 This tendency towards self-reflexivity was part of feminist and postcolonial agendas in studying interpretative communities. For example, see: Laura Grindstaff, *The Money Shot: Class, Trash and the Making of TV Talk Shows* (Chicago: University of Chicago Press, 2002); Elizabeth Bird, *The Audience in Everyday Life: Living in a Media World* (New York: Routledge, 2003); Purnima Mankekar, *Screening Culture, Viewing Politics: An Ethnography of Television, Womanhood and Nation in Postcolonial India* (Durham, NC: Duke University Press, 1999); Lila Abu-Lughod, *The Audience in Everyday Life: Living in a Media World* (Chicago: University of Chicago Press, 2004).

16 Diana Crane, *The Production of Culture: Media and Urban Arts*, ed. Garth S. Jowett, vol. 1, *Foundations of Popular Culture* (Newbury Park, CA: Sage, 1992); David Hesmondhalgh, *The Cultural Industries* (London: Sage, 2002).

17 Toby Miller et al., *Global Hollywood 2* (London: BFI, 2002); Dan Schiller, *Digital Capitalism: Networking the Global Market System* (Cambridge, MA: MIT Press, 2000).

18 Justin Lewis and Toby Miller, eds., *Critical Cultural Policy Studies: A Reader* (Malden, MA: Blackwell, 2003); Toby Miller and George Yúdice, *Cultural Policy* (London: Sage, 2002).

19 These terms are discussed in greater detail in Barney G. Glaser, *Doing Grounded Theory: Issues and Discussions* (Mill Valley, CA: Sociology Press, 1998); Ladislav Valach et al., *Action Theory: A Primer for Applied Research in the Social Sciences* (London: Praeger, 2002); Seiter, *Television and New Media Audiences.*

20 Andrea Doucet, "'From Her Side of the Gossamer Wall(s)': Reflexivity and Relational Knowing," *Qualitative Sociology* 31, no. 1 (2008): 73–87.

21 Eileen Meehan, "Commodity, Culture, Common Sense: Media Research and Paradigm Dialogue," *Journal of Media Economics* 12, no. 2 (1999): 13. See also, David Hesmondhalgh, *The Cultural Industry*, 2nd ed. (Thousand Oaks, CA: Sage, 2007).

22 For those exploring these histories, we recommend: Geoffrey Nowell-Smith, ed., *The Oxford History of World Cinema* (Oxford: Oxford University Press, 1999); Michael Curtin, *Playing to the World's Biggest Audience: The Globalization of Chinese Film and TV* (Berkeley: University of California Press, 2007); Robert Kolker, ed., *The Oxford Handbook of Film and Media Studies* (Oxford: Oxford University Press, 2008); Ben Goldsmith and Tom O'Regan, *The Film Studio: Film Production in the Global Economy* (Lanham, MD: Rowman and Littlefield, 2005); David Puttnam and Neil Watson, *The Undeclared War: The Struggle for Control of the World's Film Industry* (London: HarperCollins, 1997); Vanessa Schwartz, *It's So French! Hollywood, Paris, and the Making of Cosmopolitan Film Culture* (Chicago: University of Chicago Press, 2007); Sarah Street, *British National Cinema* (London: Routledge, 1997); Jonathan Rayner, *Contemporary Australian Cinema* (Manchester: University of Manchester Press, 2001); Shohini Chaudhuri, *Contemporary World Cinema: Europe, the Middle East, East Asia and South Asia* (Edinburgh: Edinburgh Press, 2006); Elizabeth Ezra and Terry Rowden, eds., *Transnational Cinema: The Film Reader* (London: Routledge, 2006); Christopher E. Gittings, *Canadian National Cinema* (London: Routledge, 2002); Chris Anderson, *Hollywood TV* (Austin: University of Texas Press, 1994); Tino Balio, *Hollywood in the Age of Television* (New York: Unwin-Hyman, 1990); Michele Hilmes, *Only Connect: A Cultural History of Broadcasting in the U.S.* (Belmont, CA: Wadsworth Publishing, 2006); Denise Mann, *Hollywood Independents* (Minneapolis: University of Minnesota Press, 2008); Steve Neale and Murray Smith, eds., *Contemporary Hollywood Cinema* (London: Routledge, 1998); Derek Kompare, *Rerun Nation* (New York: Routledge, 2005); Thomas Schatz, *The Genius of the System* (New York: Pantheon, 1989); Lynn Spigel and Jan Olsson, eds., *Television After TV* (Durham, NC: Duke University Press, 2004); Justin Wyatt, *High Concept* (Austin: University of Texas Press, 1994).

23 See critiques of the objects of study for film and television studies in Laura Grindstaff and Joseph Turow, "Video Cultures: Television Sociology in the 'New TV' Age," *Annual Review of Sociology* 32 (2006): 103–125.

24 We accept this critique so cogently elaborated against ethnographic projects specifically in Michael Burawoy et al., eds., *Global Ethnography: Forces, Connections and Imaginations in a Postmodern World* (Berkeley: University of California Press, 2000); and against cultural studies in general in Cameron McCarthy et al., eds., *Globalizing Cultural Studies: Ethnographic Interventions in Theory, Method and Policy* (New York: Peter Lang, 2007).

Part I

Histories of Media Production Studies

Figure 1.1 Intellectual Property/WGA Strike. Photo by Miranda Banks, 2007.

Chapter 1

Bringing the Social Back In

Studies of Production Cultures and Social Theory

Vicki Mayer

As a field of study, "production studies" captures for me the ways that power operates locally through media production to reproduce social hierarchies and inequalities at the level of daily interactions. Production studies, in other words, "ground" social theories by showing us how specific production sites, actors, or activities tell us larger lessons about workers, their practices, and the role of their labors in relation to politics, economics, and culture. It is this connection, between the micro contexts and the macro forces, which illuminates the social implications in an otherwise narrow case study and modifies the grand claims that have become commonplace regarding the role of media in society. It is also this connection between macro and micro that is so frequently lost in the efforts to describe the current media landscape, its interconnected industries, and its networks of professionals. It is ironic that as media industries continue to aggregate and dominate larger labor markets and audience shares, fewer production studies have actually addressed the real ways that local communities construct their subjectivities in the face of these consolidations of media capital and reconfigurations of media work.

Social theory was not always divorced from local realities. From the 1930s to the early 1950s, a series of international scholars, many of whom published in the United States, tried to envision how media workers experienced the growth of a cinematic industrial complex based in Hollywood, and its attempts to harness and control labor power. Written at a time when many Americans were already deeply skeptical about the growing commercialization of culture and the threats of propaganda, both political and economic, these early foci on producers and production belie the desire for a holistic sense of how production and consumption intertwined in the lives of real people. They documented how alienation, a Marxist concept found in his *Economic and Philosophical Manuscripts of 1844*, operated to estrange people from the value of the things they made. For Marx, the bigger and more economically powerful a product was after its production, the more the workers who made it suffered. In the process, their work was devalued, erased by the value of a product they had no control over distributing. More importantly, Marx highlighted the fact that modern capitalist societies require workers who recognize that their physical means of subsistence depend on this political economic system of creating wealth for others. This second characteristic of alienated labor is what made Hollywood workers such an apropos case study.[1] Movies were arguably the most powerful products the United States produced through a vast economy of laborers whose existence depended upon this product, which surpassed the value of the labor and devalued the work of the laborer. Looking back on early media production studies, we can see the ways that Leo Rosten and Hortense Powdermaker in particular theorized the concept of alienation through their empirical studies of Hollywood labor, work practices, and subjective experience.

Although shifts in the global political economy from production-based to consumer-based has rendered some of Marx's insights obsolete, it is his attempt to relate political economy to the formation of subjectivities that seems still useful to ponder today. In this chapter, I argue that we can still theorize alienation, but that it must come through empirical cases that contribute a broader understanding of work experience in light of what Luc Boltanski and Eve Chiapello call the "new spirit of capitalism," the zeitgeist that encompasses the present realities of capitalist production.[2] To illustrate, I draw upon a single event in a longer ethnography of reality television casters as a new worker category in the television industry. The event—a casting call that failed to attract any participants—reveals some of the central ways in which local production studies might theorize forms of alienation in a grounded way, and why television industry workers labor to erase all traces of these theoretically productive moments.

Social Theory in Two Early Production Studies

Leo Rosten's study of 1930s Hollywood begins with a simple restatement of division between superstructure and base, or the difference between the opulence of movies and the material conditions that produce them. Like other worker communities, Hollywood is a social, not geographic entity, but unlike them, the public aura of their symbolic product shadows the real processes of capital accumulation: "the public never sees [J.P.] Morgan making money or [Henry] Ford making cars; but it does see [actor] Robert Taylor making faces."[3] This equivalence, between money, cars, and faces, is the basis for the alienation, where thousands of workers are anonymous, "in the shadow" of a product with more value and power in the global economy than themselves.[4] Hollywood merely indexed the national split between estranged labor and its objectified forms.

While certainly not radical in his deposition, Rosten was centrally concerned with the dialectic between workers' material conditions and their subjectivities. World War II, the closure of European film markets, and the enforcement of antitrust laws laid bare a political economy that accelerated capital accumulation: "The manufacture of movies substituted the problem of selling a commodity for the problem of 'having a wonderful time.' Hollywood was forced—more or less—to shift its attention from the Arabian Nights to Dun and Broadstreet."[5] Driven by profit motives, workers now sought individualist goals that emphasized competition over solidarity and strategic alliances over organic community. The objectification of their labor extended to self-objectification, in which elites consciously realized the need to promote their own celebrity through extravagant spending and highly public conjugal relations. Elites "cease to be individuals and become business institutions," writes Rosten, who interestingly observes them as the most alienated class.[6] Paid far below business elites and less powerful than political elites, Hollywood elites seemed to have an "unconscious need for anxiety," that kept them swinging between elation and despair.[7] Unable to assess their own value except through income and status comparisons, elites worked long hours but were perennially dissatisfied and discontent.

This insight that alienation was tied to the production process over the social class of the worker continued to be a dominant theme in Hortense Powdermaker's ethnography of Hollywood in the late 1940s. Like Rosten, Powdermaker found workers motivated first by profits, especially at the top of production hierarchies, where "the game becomes the ends and is played compulsively."[8] In addition, though, she spent far more time with workers at the bottom of these hierarchies, whose externalized labor rendered them as property that she compares to feudal serfs, African American slaves, prostitutes, and indentured servants.[9] Although Marx characterizes alienation as a state of being under modern capitalism, Powdermaker's metaphors and their accompanying biographical stories of Hollywood actors, writers, and directors seem to show that profit is not the only value in a capitalist political economy. Rather, producers and executives often rejected a profitable employee in return for an imaginary ownership over the product. In this case, the studios hid net profits of films to exert greater control over their contracted producers, allowing executives to claim the product was in fact their creation.

The key to ownership in Powdermaker's text is the lack of freedom that workers trade for success in the industry. Freedom is not a break from alienation, in particular the estrangement that results from the division of labor, but seems to imply a role for workers to more openly collaborate in the labor process. When time rationalization, bureaucratic management, and commercial technologies displace the natural technologies of the self, "brains and talent."[10] Powdermaker claims that producers deceive themselves into thinking of themselves as autonomous competitors rather than individuals tied together by their potential for creative expression and hard work. Her assertion that freedom was not just desirable for many workers, but completely possible despite alienation seems to give insight into why some workers accepted exploitative conditions in exchange for a self-realization through "a human form of collaboration."[11] This obvious contradiction, alienation but self-realization through collaboration, adds a layer to the social theories of the day, showing that capitalism would be even more effective if it allowed workers to collaborate to realize each individual's organic talents.

Powdermaker and Rosten contribute empirical evidence to social theorizing of the era, most notably the piercing critique found in Max Horkheimer and Theodor Adorno's *Dialectic of Enlightenment*.[12] For them, alienation connected production and consumption, succeeding in "sacrificing whatever involved a distinction between the logic of the work and that of the social system."[13] Workers participate in an increasingly efficient industrial system of mass production and consumption, making them eventually "redundant as producers" of standardized objects and the liberal ideology of individual merit, competition, and desire.[14] Elites control these processes of material and social standardization, while also reaffirming their unflinching allegiance to the system. On these points alone, Rosten's and Powdermaker's studies extend Horkheimer and Adorno's perceptions of alienation. First, they showed how different types of producers in Hollywood experienced alienation differently. Indeed, Rosten's elites were in many ways the most alienated. Second, these authors envisioned collective modes of creative ownership over production that would allow more control over the process while embedding them deeper in a system still driven by alienated labor and profit motives. In this respect, Powdermaker the anthropologist, not the social theorist, is almost prescient in foregrounding the current era of team-based production and flexible work conditions that simultaneously liberate and harness creativity to generate profit. She predicts, "To liberate the unused resources of talent in Hollywood entails changes in the way of thinking, in the system of production which reflects the way of thinking and, finally, in the allocation of power."[15]

Compare these grounded theories of the dialectics of subjective formations and material exploitations with the relative lack of class critique today. In the new lexicon of production studies, producers frequently "negotiate" their way through "complex" social networks that all have more or less the same status and power. Producers are still anxious in studies that chart processes from the making of a documentary to the selling of a television series, but workers are also more likely to have independent agency and feel vindicated by a successful final product. In part, the political economy of the industry has changed. Film and television industries simultaneously promote teamwork and flexibility while espousing piecework and outsourcing. Creative production has been industrialized per Horkheimer and Adorno, but the production processes resemble more a bygone era of bohemian artists than the individuated factory floor. In their discussion of these material shifts, Luc Boltanski and Eve Chiapello propose that a new spirit of capitalism has stifled intellectual social critique by co-opting the language of 1960s liberation into managerial-speak.

> [S]uccess in this new spirit—autonomy, spontaneity, rhizomorphousness capacity, multitasking (in contrast to the narrow specialization in the old division of labour), conviviality, openness to others and novelty, availability, creativity, visionary institution, sensitivity to differences, listening to lived experience and receptiveness to a whole range of experiences, being attracted to informality and the search for interpersonal contacts—these are taken directly from the repertoire of May 1968.[16] But these themes, which in the texts of the May movement were combined with a radical critique of capitalism ... are often to be found in the neo-management literature autonomized, as it were—represented as objectives that are valid in their own right, and placed in the service of forces whose destruction they were intended to hasten. The critique of the division of labour, of hierarchy and supervision— that is to say, the way industrial capitalism alienates freedom—is thus detached from the critique of market alienation, of oppression by impersonal market forces.[17]

In one way, we might speculate that the new economy for film and television co-opted the values of artists in Powdermaker's era and turned them profitable, thus silencing critique from many who framed alienation in terms of factory work and assembly-line production.

In another way, though, the problem of social theorizing might also be a methodological issue. Rosten and Powdermaker, as other chapters in this volume develop more fully, had a special access to Hollywood's production personnel. Rosten worked in the industry; Powdermaker entered it on her own. In contrast, much of our work today comprises interviews on the phone or electronic correspondences, methods that open considerable distance between what subjects say about themselves and what they do. Observational methods are similarly limited. Executives give access to researchers to emphasize commercial successes and obscure failures. Corporate events are staged in spaces and at times when networks, advertisers, and trade industries celebrate themselves to gain market advantage and position themselves against competitors. Given these difficulties, the job of building social theories grounded in the local experiences of practitioners seems as much a question of finding case studies that illustrate the times and places where the unexpected occurs and the rhetoric of achievement is called into question. Such was the case of a 2007 casting call in which I was a participant-observer.

The Casting Call as a Case Study in Alienation

I wanted to go to a casting call to witness what I had been interviewing workers about for over two years at this point. I was interested in reality casters, that is, the workers who cast the people that we eventually see under the broad umbrella of reality television programs. Reality casters are a prime example of invisible labor; their work is objectified in the cast member whose value is measured in ratings and advertising rates that can never be passed back to the caster. Production companies rarely even acknowledge the work of the caster in the form of program-ending credits, which themselves have become illegible video streams alongside previews for other programs. Despite these mechanisms of alienation, casters in phone interviews were largely sanguine about their efforts, its value to the television industry, and their experience of the daily routines. When the opportunity arose for me to attend a live casting call as a participant-observer, I jumped to attend. I wanted to see how well the reality of the work matched with interviewees' self-appraisals of their work.

Like many casting calls, this one had to be organized quickly and somewhat at the last minute. The program succeeded in its extension through the television season, from the original nine episodes to thirteen. The producers were elated, but suddenly they would need four more episodes in an abbreviated time frame, from the initial three months of production now to a single month. Christmas holidays were looming and there would be few opportunities to get cast members if the production team did not act quickly. "Andrew," a casting associate for the program, felt the pressure.[18] "This is the time I get nervous," he told me. "There's always the risk that no one shows and the affiliate puts all this work into the event for nothing."

The fear that labor would be wasted is a very real risk in assessing the value of a casting call. Television network affiliates frequently help production companies organize casting calls in the hope that a local person will be selected for the cast. The local person is a commodity that boosts affiliates' advertising rates for the program and can be tied to promotional events for the station. One classic example: Fox News affiliates frequently chronicle the progress of local contestants on their network's program *American Idol*. In turn, the network program often broadcasts these local outpourings of emotion for the local contestant at planned fan parties and welcome home gatherings sponsored by the affiliates. The longer the local stays in the program, the higher the exchange value for the affiliate. The search for a local cast member is therefore a type of lottery for numerous workers who gauged their own success on the chance that their work could be objectified in the form of a contestant, character, or participant who not only appeared on the screen, but might reappear. This economy was the basis for workers' anxieties throughout the production team, broadcast networks, and their affiliates, as well as the foundation for guaranteed alienation from the product of their labors.

The anxiety was palpable around this particular call, which targeted families with small children. I arrived well ahead of the 3:00 p.m. start time to a kids' daycare facility, one in which upper-middle-class families bought memberships so that their children had a designated play space in the large urban environment in which they grew up. Andrew's team and the local television affiliate had convinced the owner of the facility that by hosting the call, they would cross-promote the daycare company. The owner, "Jeff," said he expected no less than thirty families as he cleared two spaces in the kitchen area: one table for interviews and another for those queued to interview. On the first table, Andrew had neatly arranged pens and applications. He searched for chairs and made phone calls to the television affiliate contacts. "Natalie," Jeff's employee, had laid out a spread of cookies, crackers, juice boxes, and other snacks for at least fifty attendees on the second table. She also inflated helium balloons and decorated the entire warehouse space with streamers. Jeff placed a life-size standee from the program at the front door with signs he had commissioned from the local copy shop. Nervously, he chewed out the mail service representative that had guaranteed that twenty copies of the book authored by the program's host would arrive in time. Jeff had invested several hundred dollars in accessorizing the call. He said he just wanted "to break even" to justify his investment, but he spent the afternoon talking about how much the event cost and how he hoped to generate new customers and turn a profit to justify the work. "I think we'll have at least thirty families today," Jeff said again, repeating his sanguine prediction, but perhaps less sure of himself this time.

Andrew was less optimistic on this point, guessing that perhaps five families would attend the call. He knew from experience that families were a difficult demographic if only because it required the target audience to coordinate their schedules and travel to a remote location. Further, it was the first cold snap of the winter season in the city, making an outdoor excursion even less likely. We sat down at the interview table and waited. A news cameraman for the affiliate station who arrived to record the expected crowd also waited. "If there's a fire, I'm out of here," he stated, but three hours later, we were all still there. Not a single applicant came to the casting call.

Jeff was distraught, having spent weeks on preparation and invested income on the event no one came to. The cameraman was bored, flipping through children's books in the play area. Even Andrew, who was upbeat in his interactions with me, was now disappointed, having incorrectly predicted that his efforts would bear results. Although he did not expect a crowd, he hoped that applicants would at least call into the daycare to inquire about the call. The only product produced after four people worked for five hours that day was a videotape of Jeff's three children, Andrew, and me watching an episode of the program itself on television. The cameraman delivered the tape to the affiliate newsroom for the evening's late night broadcast.

The invisible and, ultimately, unproductive labors of workers for the production company, the television affiliate, and the daycare, as well as the owner belie the obvious aspects of alienated labor involved in many, if not most, casting calls. Quite simply, a lot of time and effort goes to waste in finding "real people" that could just as easily be found next door, at the supermarket, or in the shopping mall. The exchange value of the call relates more to whether local media industries can capitalize on an on-screen participant as a brand, something that may have no relation to the efforts of those involved with casting calls. Instead, the process of the casting call and its reception by the people I observed gives some insights into how alienation makes working subjects. This particular casting call demanded coordination and collaboration between various types of workers, which, in the beginning, seemed full of potential and enthusiasm, but, ultimately, resulted in boredom and some isolation as workers faced the individual consequences of the call's failure. The clear separation of the production process from the product created anxiety, and then disappointment, when the process failed to produce the applicants. At another level, though, the business owner Jeff most embodied these emotions. He clearly felt the most at stake in attracting publicity, so much so, he commodified his own kin in a staged news clip. In contrast, Andrew, who felt pressure to deliver participants for the program, could also look to other mechanisms for gathering applicants, such as phone calls and the news clip itself, which would promote calls to the production base in Hollywood. "People will see the episode tonight and then the news story that we want local families," he said. "After the program airs, we can get 100–200 calls. So this [event] is all part of outreach." Whereas alienation made for nervous workers throughout the operation, calling attention to their lack of control over the object, the investments in each person's role still led to individuated experiences of the event, creating tensions.

Another factor that might help us to understand these tensions were the trajectories of these workers, in particular Jeff and Andrew. The former had left a career in hotel management to become a business owner. The latter was an artist by training, working as a casting director to support his primary career goal. Both talked about these alternative careers during the long wait for applicants. Andrew stressed, "I really do this to pay the bills." In contrast, Jeff said he "put everything" into the business, "My years in hospitality are the basis for what I'm trying to do here." While this might be a facile comparison, it is also possible to see how media industries manage alienation by spreading the risk of failure through organizational networks. Production studios benefit when they hire workers who can defer their insecurities either to other collaborators or to other pursuits outside of the industry. Of course, these insecurities return, as in that nagging feeling that Andrew had at the beginning of the event. Yet, the object lesson of the casting call might be how failure in the production process has the power to reveal workers' alienation to themselves, but the industry's structure also gives them the alibis for explaining it away. Again, workers experience this differently. The younger casting director still hoped his art would be the path from alienation, explaining away the failure of the day as a step towards unification with an artist community; while the older business owner narrated the success of this event as an indicator of whether his skills from the hospitality industry could help him achieve his own financial independence.

Productive Theorizing from Production Failures?

Alienation seems to be a continuing feature of modern production, whether in the refurbished industrial space of a daycare or in the post-industrial practices of the reality caster waiting for the next contract. Production studies offer the opportunity not just to confirm the ongoing presence of this social phenomenon locally, but theorize, from the ground, how it "works": making producers into productive subjects. Television programs, the result of hundreds of microprocesses from script-writing to distribution, rely on thousands of collaborative efforts, but without some form of fieldwork, it's hard to know how these collaborations manifest to make workers accept the fact that the arrangements result in uncompensated labors. While one case study cannot illuminate the range of possible experiences of alienation, it can become one of the building blocks for a theory that shows the variations among workers, based on their role in a collaborative project, their career trajectory, and their future opportunities. This is an opportunity not to repackage the insights of past production studies, but to replace it in light of a new economy of film and television production.

The casting call seemed to present alienation not just in flashes of recognition that the work was devalued, usurped, or erased, but also in the deferral to the next project. For this reason, local production studies might also focus more on failures in the production process, what did not work or go well according to industrial standards. Not only are the failures simply necessary for defining success, they can be productive in themselves as a critique of capitalism. Failures, as Judith Halberstam has noted, open the potential for re-imagining resistance as a queer space, not quite submissive but not quite revolutionary either.[19] In this sense, the casting call that failed to attract attention was precisely the moment that revealed the real work of casters: to justify the failure, create an alternative narrative of the event, and move on. Still, a resistive spark remained. Despite his enthusiasm for the job and the optimism for the future, Andrew complained that at times his job seemed "thankless" to him, "I've cast shows where I don't even get invited to the final wrap party." If alienation operates to disconnect workers from their labors, we see in Andrew's comment a recognition and a rejection of any starry-eyed admiration for the industry, perhaps sowing a seed for future resistance.

Notes

1 David McLellan, ed., "Economic and Philosophical Manuscripts (1844)," in *Karl Marx: Selected Writings*, 2nd ed. (Oxford: Oxford University Press, 2000), 89–91.
2 Luc Boltanski and Eve Chiapello, *The New Spirit of Capitalism*, trans. Gregory Elliott (London: Verso, 2005).
3 Leo Calvin Rosten, *Hollywood: The Movie Colony, the Movie Makers* (New York: Harcourt, Brace and Company, 1941), 18.
4 Ibid., 32.
5 Ibid., 28.
6 Ibid., 123.
7 Ibid., 39.
8 Hortense Powdermaker, *Hollywood the Dream Factory* (New York: Little, Brown and Company, 1950), 99.
9 Ibid., 85, 149, 215.
10 Ibid., 288.
11 Ibid., 303.
12 Max Horkheimer and Theodor W. Adorno, *The Dialectic of Enlightenment* (1947; London: Continuum, 1976).
13 Ibid., 121.
14 Ibid., 150.
15 Powdermaker, *Hollywood the Dream Factory*, 303.
16 This date refers to the radical student movements in France and beyond.
17 Boltanski and Chiapello, *The New Spirit of Capitalism*, 97.
18 All names have been changed in accordance with the guidelines for human subjects' anonymity as required by the Tulane Office of Human Research Protection. In addition, all names of identifying features of the program associated with this casting call have been obscured to the best of my abilities.
19 Judith Halberstam, "Notes on Failure" (lecture, University of Illinois, Champaign Urbana, IL, April 14, 2006).

Chapter 2

Industry-Level Studies and the Contributions of Gitlin's *Inside Prime Time*

Amanda D. Lotz

Across the industry, television underwent massive changes during the first years of the twenty-first century. Both the trade and popular press prognosticated loudly about the imminent death of this or that aspect of the medium, often reporting with unrestrained certainty of the revolution that the development of the moment (DVR, product placement, online video, etc.) would bring to the industry and by default, American culture. Such coverage nearly always excerpted the bright shiny object or development from the complicated and interconnected practices of the broader circuit of television production that variably might be affected, as if a change in a practice such as advertising would not too bring changes in production or distribution practices. The consequences of each new technology or shift in practice were inextricable from adjustments throughout the production process though, and the critical study of television required an approach that avoided the revolutionary prophesies of isolated "developments of the moment" and instead necessitated examining the interconnections among new technologies and practices. Such a situation warranted a production study of the television industry.

In the following pages, I distinguish the particular category of the "industry-level" study and examine a classic example of such research that arguably remains a standard bearer of media research: Todd Gitlin's 1983 book *Inside Prime Time*.[1] Despite the fact that Gitlin researched this book over twenty-five years ago, his study of the US television industry remains a key piece of institutional literature in terms of both his findings and his methods. I close the chapter with some comments on my own exploration of the television industry in the early twenty-first century, for which Gitlin's study proved influential in designing an approach to examine the nexus of multiple industrial changes.[2] I also address some of the challenges of reproducing industry-level studies of television and other media industries today.

Locating Industry-Level Analysis

Scope, Methods and Theories

In a chapter on studying the production of media fiction, television scholar Horace Newcomb and I suggest five "levels of analysis"—national and international political economy and policy, specific industrial contexts, particular organizations, individual productions, and individual agents—at which studies of media industries and productions might take place.[3] The distinction of various levels is taxonomic, not evaluative, meant to offer the most preliminary of organization to the broad range of objects of analysis available to those studying media institutions. The chapter offers methodological guidance to scholars interested in researching media production and identifies the range of topics available in this area that offers considerable variation in method, key theoretical assumptions, and objects of study.

Much of the existing critical[4] research on media industries and institutions focuses at the most macro level of national and international political economy and policy, which is differentiated not only by the scope of its object of analysis, but also by the methods and theories that commonly undergird its examination. Such studies have expansive scope, yet they are typically informed by data such as broad statistical measures that do little to reveal the daily functioning of media or the situation of particular media workers. This research provides some vital clues about how media industries operate. For example, much of the "conglomeration" literature can be classified in this way, and studies such as those by Bagdikian and McChesney have noted the increased scale of media conglomeration and argue this trend has resulted in decreased competition over the past few decades.[5] But these studies tell us little about how these conglomerates actually function, such as who makes decisions, how various divisions interact, or what level of centralized coordination and control might exist. They also do not address the persistence of small companies within the cultural industries, as noted by Hesmondhalgh.[6]

On the other side of industry-level studies on the scope-ordered taxonomy Newcomb and I delineate, we also find a considerable amount of scholarship. The three most narrowly focused levels of study include: "particular organizations" (studios, production companies, or networks), "individual productions" (a single film or television series), and "individual agents" (the body of work of a director, writer, or producer). Studies that address these levels differ from those of national and international political economy and policy not only in their scope of focus, but frequently also in the methods used to examine them. Studies at these levels of analysis are often informed by ethnographic methods such as participant-observation, or interviews that provide rich detail or "thick description" in anthropological parlance. At this more micro level of focus, researchers place much emphasis on understanding the complexity of practices and the varied agency of those who may work within vast media conglomerations. Studies at these levels often have not supported deterministic hypotheses proposed by theories produced at the macro level, or at least have suggested that the daily processes of production of media industries are far more complicated than the macro-level views might have the field understand.

Industry-level studies exist then in between the particularity of studies of specific studios, networks, and "productions" (i.e., a certain show or film) and the broadest vantage for examining these issues, studies of the national and international political economy and policy level. Media studies literature contains comparatively few industry-level studies, likely because of the methodological and theoretical challenges of making sense of media operation at this level. Industry-studies' object of analysis necessitates a negotiation among the methods of the more macro political economy scale and micro examination of individual organizations or productions. Carefully designed industry-level studies are able to remain grounded in empirical data and contribute to "middle range" theory useful for understanding the "complex, ambivalent and contested" nature of cultural industries.[7]

In order to establish a manageable scope, studies of specific media industries typically narrow their focus to a particular national context and a particular industry within that context. Admittedly, this is increasingly challenging given the interconnections among media industries and the important role of international or at least geocultural regions in the production and circulation of the goods they produce. For example, it is impossible to understand the US television industry without including practices related to the vital role of international sales and distribution to its economic model, while the minutia of operational norms in different countries simultaneously make it impossible to coherently study anything as broad as the global television industry.

Traditionally, studies attempting the breadth of industry analysis have been more descriptive than critical and have tended toward a view of the operation of media industries from afar—with expansive breadth but limited detail of the experiences of individual workers and their daily activities.[8] These studies rely heavily on aggregate economic data such as total production expenditures and receipts, rarely addressing either particular practices involved in day-to-day operation or the final textual product. The industry-level studies that I focus on in this chapter use theoretical and methodological tools that sacrifice some of the breadth common to studies of the national and international political economy and policy level in the pursuit of more clearly seeing smaller, meaningful operations of individual workers and their organizational routines.

It may be impossible to include all aspects of any media industry in a single study, or a single chapter of a book, but those at the industry-level do use "the industry" as their object of analysis. In contrast, in her detailed study of the production of talk shows, Grindstaff attends little if at all to the industrial forces behind the talk show that lead to norms such as its production of new episodes for every weekday, its lack of any kind of syndication to other television markets, or factors of audience composition or measurement.[9] It is not that her study is incomplete without such consideration, merely that attention to such factors distinguish studies at the level of industry from her study, which examines a set of shows of a common form. The conceptual focus of "industry-level studies" is on the dynamic connections of the whole, even though this might necessitate aggregating examinations of various components of industry operation over an array of chapters or in discrete sections. More narrow studies of particular productions might too reveal the arrangements of institutional and organizational power and agency involved in media production in great detail, but industry-level studies foreground interconnections and broad processes. For example, issues related to norms of distribution and exhibition might be mentioned in a study of an individual production, but an industry-level study would focus upon how these broader processes delimit the opportunities afforded to productions in general.

Theoretically, such industry-level studies are driven by a desire to understand the operation of media industries in a manner that emphasizes constitutive under-standings of media and society. This has led some scholars to dig past economic and structurally determinist arguments that emphasize macro-level features such as ownership, commercialism, and regulation to examine the actual functioning of various facets of media industries. Early versions of this work emphasized the organizational features, although often with little attention to how they differed from other industries.[10] Joseph Turow's approach to examining the operation of media industries provides a valuable tool for conceptualizing the interconnections within the production process.[11] Turow's work offers a framework for consider-ing the forces affecting industry behavior and cultural production beyond those that focused on broad features such as economics and the commodification of entertainment. Instead, Turow's definition of power as "the use of resources by one organization in order to gain compliance by another organization" explores the indi-vidual agency of everyone from financiers, to producers, to agents, to the catering services.[12] His power roles approach deliberately rejects proposing a hierarchy of influence, and instead makes apparent the agency of those whose activities remain obscured by macro levels of analysis.

In the last decade, renewed attention has been paid to the intersection of the cultural and economic factors central to the study of media institutions. The particularities of approach vary somewhat and names for such research include: "circuit of cultural production" (Paul du Gay et al.), "cultural economy" (Paul du Gay and Michael Pryke), "creative industries" (John Hartley), "cultural industries" (David Hesmondhalgh), "critical industrial practices" (John T. Caldwell), and "critical media industry studies" (Timothy Havens, Amanda Lotz, and Serra Tinic).[13] These approaches are not particular to industry-level study, nor are they interchangeable as variations exist in how they understand the relationship of media creation and cultural power. What unites them, however, is that each provides more sophisticated theoretical framing of the operation of media industries than has characterized previous work and each offers tools useful for the building of more robust industry-level studies.

Arguably, several important studies and theoretical frameworks for the study of media industries anticipated cultural studies' turn back to examinations of the industry in recent years. Joli Jensen lays out an "interpretive" approach to studying media industries in 1984 that derived from James Carey's theories of the constitutive nature of communication. Jensen's argument for an interpretive approach and Richard Johnson's model for the role of production in cultural studies research, published in 1986, both offer key works that have been underutilized. Their approaches allow greater advancement in culturally based studies of media industries, but cultural studies work attended more to examinations of texts and audiences during the last two decades of the twentieth century.[14] As cultural studies-identified scholars have begun to reestablish media industries as a common site of study, they've turned back to the approaches offered by Jensen, Johnson, and more recent conceptualization by D'Acci in an effort to create shared theoretical language for their projects.[15]

Understanding and Assessing *Inside Prime Time*

Well before the theoretical developments noted above, Todd Gitlin's examination of the US television industry offered a valuable application of an industry-level study. *Inside Prime Time* is the result of the seven months Gitlin spent interviewing "some 200 industry people" and observing network operations and production practices.[16] The outcome is a comprehensive look at the forces that, in a general sense, affect the creation of television series and schedules.[17] He reveals how network executives, particularly those who make programming decisions and compile internal research, selected primetime programming in the late 1970s. Gitlin details the complicated and inexact processes by which executives evaluate content with regard both to what advertisers will find acceptable and to its likelihood of achieving a profitable balance between mass and niche audiences. His interviews with producers, writers, actors, and directors detail their experiences negotiating with network executives, while he also observes procedures at the networks and speaks with these cultural workers as well. In bringing together his story of the operation of commercial network television and why dominant industrial norms lead to the texts shared by millions each evening, Gitlin occasionally contextualizes institutional practices that extend beyond the purview of the network (such as ratings gathering). *Inside Prime Time* is primarily an examination of the role of the network in television production. While the US television industry is obviously much broader than the networks—including local stations and the complex variables that factor into national and international syndication—the network was an appropriate focus for an industry-level examination of television at this time. By focusing on the network, Gitlin exposes the intersection of many industrial operations—advertising, audience research, program development—consistent with the comprehensiveness of industry-level research.

In introducing the book, Gitlin acknowledges that he first set out to understand the relationship of primetime series' commercial success and the prevailing social trends of the culture. He seeks to explain how the same commercial media system could shift from producing and popularizing culturally and politically relevant shows such as *All in the Family* and *M*A*S*H* to the comparatively escapist fare of *Charlie's Angels* and *Dallas* in the matter of just a few years.[18] Gitlin observed that although scholars and critics might regard shows such as *All in the Family* to be exceptional creative texts in terms of their ideological underpinnings, the industrial practices that brought about these shows were not exceptional. It was not the case, as some might presume, that the industry had intentionally pursued series infused with liberal politics and sustained cultural criticism and then shifted its goals to more mindless narratives. Gitlin found that creative production did not feature such explicit or deliberate ideological construction, so his guiding research questions consequently evolved into ones more focused on generally understanding "who put the images on the small screen and for what reasons."[19] In the end, the book still reveals how the complexity of forces and practices in that era—namely economic factors much more than those plainly political—led the television industry to tend toward a narrow range of content with a consistent ideology. Perhaps ironically then, it is regardless of *his* intentions that *Inside Prime Time* can be read to have meaning and significance far greater than its anecdotally rich recounting of the process of making network television in the 1970s.

Gitlin's in-depth descriptions and examinations of important, yet previously obscured and unconsidered, components of production span the proposal of show ideas to networks, the long negotiations of specifics of form, to the forces that ultimately lead to cancellation. Unlike the broad data that might have supported his study, he relies upon, as he notes, Clifford Geertz's ethnographic "thick description" of the myriad processes, practices, and players involved in a series finding its way to viewers' screens. Gitlin captures the unpredictability and variance of processes including audience research and measurement, scheduling, and agent representation that more recently have been theorized by Miege and Hesmondhalgh as components of the "complex, ambivalent, and contested" operation of media industries.[20] His perspective defies explanations of media industry functioning as an inevitably consistent and coherent outcome of ownership structures, commercial mandates, or regulatory norms. Gitlin does not suggest how this case of US television in the early 1980s might be applicable to understanding the operation of other cultural industries or those in other national or historical contexts; instead the value of *Inside Prime Time* comes from its methodology of field-based industrial analysis. His fieldwork offers a model for examining industrial practices—particularly those of entertainment television.

Inside Prime Time appeared just three years after *The Whole World is Watching*, Gitlin's revised dissertation that provided an incisive analysis of the news media's portrayal of the sixties social movements. Whereas in the earlier project, Gitlin explores the dynamics of hegemony between media industries, in the later project, Gitlin scarcely mentions hegemony or other critical concepts despite delivering a compelling look at the industry's practices. Those familiar with Gitlin's previous work might have expected a more systematic argument regarding how established and ingrained practices of program acquisition or the conventional wisdom of what advertisers and audiences prefer limit textual output. Subsequent researchers have replicated Gitlin's methods and theorized how the stories the industry tells itself about what will succeed, how things are, or must be lead to the perpetuation of a distinctive symbolic universe with particular ideological and creative boundaries that serve as a key site of cultural power.[21] For example, drawing from research based on interviews and observation, Havens, in what he terms "industry lore," and Caldwell, in what he distinguishes as "trade story-telling," theorize how conventional practices reveal the hegemony of certain industrial norms and, in turn, contribute to the hegemony of textual content. But Gitlin avoids characterizing the processes he details in these terms within the pages of *Inside Prime Time*. In many ways his 1979 article "Prime Time Ideology: The Hegemonic Process in Television Entertainment" is necessary co-reading.[22] In the article, he provides a critically rigorous assessment of television's hegemonic functions, yet still focuses curiously more on the form of content than in outlining how the practices, routines, and conventions of network operations circumscribe that content.

There is little evidence that indicates that Gitlin set out to write a book that would provide an important model of industry-level media study that still can be read as an essential piece of literature about television some twenty-five years later. Indeed, Gitlin's anecdote-heavy accounts, sparing use of footnotes, avoidance of anything approaching "theory," and use of a writing style befitting the trade division that published the book could suggest he did not intend it to provide a major academic contribution. In fact, these matters of style and composition were key criticisms leveled by many academic reviewers who expressed disappointment with the trade style he used and his omission of direct references or a formal bibliography.[23]

Gitlin's approach might be explained by the fact that his object of analysis was uncommon for literature about television at this time. Muriel G. Cantor's *The Hollywood TV Producer: His Work and His Audience*, which she researched in the late 1960s and first published in 1972, stood as one of the few sociological studies of contemporary television production.[24] At the same time Gitlin was wandering through network executive suites, Horace Newcomb and Robert Alley were interviewing top producers for their book *The Producer's Medium* and brought a curiosity about television's creative process that differed from Cantor's more social science-driven search for systematic explanations.[25] Similarly, acclaimed television producers Richard Levinson and William Link had just published their own monograph that revealed the producer's view of industry processes.[26] Unlike existing research on the US television industry, Gitlin's early 1980s study looked more broadly at the larger industrial practices, routines, and imperatives in which producers exist, but play a constrained role.

Further, it should be noted that television studies was just beginning to estab-lish itself as Gitlin wrote, and any serious engagement with television—be it with texts, audiences, or institutions—was still uncommon in any academic space. This was the era of Jerry Mander's *Four Arguments for the Elimination of Television*, a title that indicates the predominant disdain for television in many academic quarters, and suggests the complicated dynamics of Gitlin's serious assessment of the enter-tainment television industry at that time.[27] Although contemporary researchers might now take for granted that television is a meaningful and important site of analysis, this was not a presumption that Gitlin would have made. Some of the academic criticism Gitlin received then may have arisen from his following his critical indictment of a "valid" cultural form (news) with a book more explanatory, and some might say celebratory, than critical of a still debased cultural form (fiction or "entertainment").

The other main line of television industry literature contemporary to Gitlin's research bears much in common with *Inside Prime Time*. Until Gitlin's book, the most extensive examination of the practices of the industry as a whole was published by *Variety* critic Les Brown in his 1971 book *Televi$ion: The Business Behind the Box*.[28] Like other monographs written by media journalists such as Sally Bedell, Ken Auletta, and Bill Carter that have followed, Brown's book detailed the nuances and intricacies of television's industrial operations.[29] Top journalists on the television beat commonly have sustained access to industry workers that most academics only dream of, and their accounts are consequently often filled with information gained on or off the record in interviews with the medium's key decision makers. The detail of these books adds complexity to academics' often simplistic understanding of crucial economic processes, such as how advertising is purchased or how and why an advertiser might explicitly exert influence on the creative process. However, the journalists' accounts typically lack—in varying degrees—any critical framework for understanding the meaning of the machinations of the industry in terms of broader sociocultural concerns that are the goal of academic accounts. To be sure, the work of Brown and Auletta in particular, is smart, well informed, and conceives of television as playing an important role in culture, even if they don't trot out the theoretical citations one would find in academic scholarship. And despite the limited use of footnotes and other academic conventions that make *Inside Prime Time* appear comparable to Brown's and Auletta's work, Gitlin's academic training and activist vantage point do seep into his work and offer a more critical angle than those writing more exclusively for a trade audience.

An important contribution of Gitlin's work, especially given the field's predominant attention to producers before and during his research, was to make plain how many other significant sites, roles, and routines exist that scholars must attend to in seeking to elucidate the process of cultural production. Indeed, television producers, like film directors, are exceptionally important to understanding the creative process, as television is commonly described as a "producer's medium" with creative authority afforded to the producer. Yet, by expanding his focus to the industry-level, Gitlin's considerable attention to networks and the many roles that supersede the producer reveals opportunities and constraints that producers negotiate that the producers may not be aware of or of which they don't readily acknowledge. Gitlin provides a frame through which we as scholars of media might better understand the practices and structures that affect cultural creation by contextualizing the role of producers. Gitlin's work is notable as well for his vivid explanations of the manifold processes involved in television production and the manner in which he makes these practices accessible to the lay reader.[30] The value of such industry studies comes from its demystification of the extensive layers of managers and decision makers, the complexity of ratings, scheduling, and program testing, and the nuances of managing creative workers and predicting the behavior of fickle audiences.

Industry-Level Studies in the Era of Niche Media

In the twenty-five years since Gitlin completed his research, however, the institutional organization and competitive environment of the US television industry has changed considerably and significantly reduced the centrality of the broadcast networks. In fact, Gitlin unwittingly captured the end of an era. The days of the three-network past have become a hundredfold multichannel present of narrowly targeted channels. Television distribution is no longer constrained by a bottleneck of three networks or limited spectrum space, but flows through wires, airwaves, and over satellite links to televisions, computers, and even mobile phones. Developments in technology and distribution have in turn brought changes to the process of making and financing television. Advertisers have sought new (and returned to old) strategies for reaching audiences, and viewers now pay for their content in increasingly varied ways. Also fading are the days of audiences watching at appointed times. Gitlin completed his study before the mass adoption of VCRs adjusted viewing habits—transformations that have been further and more significantly altered by DVRs, online streaming, and digital downloading. The very bounds of "television" now grow more uncertain by the day as audiences increasingly view content long understood as television on a diverse array of screen devices and pay for that content through varied models, all of which create new constraints and possibilities for the industry's creative workers.

In designing a study of the US television industry after the network era, I attempted to reexamine much of the terrain covered by Gitlin and negotiated the challenge of seeking to expand critical understanding of some of the industrial aspects he omitted, such as the process for buying television advertising. At the same time, I also hoped to revisit components that had adjusted since the early 1980s, particularly audience measurement technologies.[31] As a result, I focus on the many practices that circumscribe the norms and possibilities for the content of US television programming that exist outside his focus on the confines of the network, while maintaining features of his methodology.

In addition to tranformations in the television industry, the status of television as an academic object has evolved considerably since *Inside Prime Time*. This allowed my focus as a television scholar to detailed knowledge of the history, norms of practice, and texts of the medium. Part of my training included constant reading of trade press to maintain familiarity with the nuances of industrial practice, and as such, this type of research figured far more centrally in my work than it did for Gitlin, who explored non-news media for the first time in the research for *Inside Prime Time*. I read trade publications such as *Television Week* and *Broadcasting and Cable* for years before establishing my own theories of industry operations and identifying key industry players, issues, and events. These trade publications also functioned as a data source—primarily in the form of quotations from top industry executives who I might not reasonably expect to interview. When possible I sought interviews with industry workers, but my book *The Television Will Be Revolutionized* is more heavily informed by participant-observation of industry events and conferences over four to five years, as well as four weeks of observing the buying and planning of advertising for television. I did not have the opportunity to spend six months in Los Angeles, as Gitlin did, yet the rapid pace of change during my own research period made a longer span of fieldwork valuable for illuminating the shifting perceptions of industry decision makers.

Attending industry conferences and events also provided considerable information and perspective that marks the broadening of production study from the site of a particular organization or production to the industry-level. Such expansion of the conceptual boundaries of "production" is supported by methodological calls by Caldwell and theoretical models such as the circuit of cultural production.[32] Meetings and trade shows provided the opportunity to hear top-level executives discuss the evolution of their businesses, access to the industry's narrative of change, and a fleeting sense of where the practitioners with decision-making capabilities thought television was headed. Attending these conferences across varied sectors of the industry (consumer electronics, cable, syndication, advertising) was also helpful for identifying attitudes toward changing practices throughout myriad processes required in the production and circulation of television. Gaps in understandings of the precise procedures involved in the buying of advertising led me to attend more to economic aspects of television production that are still based in New York, necessitating that I spend a number of weeks as an observer of both the upfront buying process and the day-to-day operations of media buyers and planners.[33]

The broadcast television networks and their workers figured much less centrally in my study. The networks' role as standalone giants was substantially altered by the processes of conglomeration that occurred in the intervening years and left the networks as components of massive corporations. This significant adjustment in industry structure decreased the importance of any one network as the site for analysis, and the general practices of program development and audience testing continue to perform the same roles Gitlin described. Grounded studies of conglomerate operation and the consequences of ownership structure remain lacking and perhaps warrant analysis comparable to, yet obviously distinct from, industry study. Moreover, the continuity of twenty-first-century networks' operations indicate their greatest weakness as new post-network era technologies and distribution practices developed largely in spite of their efforts to maintain the status quo. Networks were not leading the way into the new era, rather television was being redefined by technologies, distribution possibilities, advertising practices, and audience behavior.

Some of the challenges I faced in revisiting the television industry at the beginning of the millennium confront almost all scholars studying the contemporary US media landscape. Substantial adjustments in core industrial practices have changed many aspects of the global television environment, while broader shifts from mass to niche foci require reconsideration of the scope and assumptions of all studies of media industry operations. Although "mass" use plays a foundational role in nearly all theoretical approaches to media study, few media now gather the heterogeneous audiences assumed by such theories. Niche audience targeting has become the standard of operation in magazines, film, music, and television in a manner that makes it difficult to speak meaningfully about these as coherent industries. This requires reassessment of strategies for industry-level study because it has become decreasingly possible to make broad claims about "the magazine industry" and requires instead assessment of more niche units such as the cable news industry, the women's magazine industry, or Hollywood blockbuster films. These industrial subareas remain connected to broader structures, but as media continue to operate with niche-based strategies that lead to specific industrial norms, researchers must continue to reconsider the scope of studies required to make valid and consequential claims.

Conclusion

Industry-level analyses comprise only a small part of the production literature, and conducting such studies remains challenging given the complicated negotiations researchers must make in determining scope, level of detail, and methodology. Georgina Born's rich study of the BBC provides another excellent example, although it is possible only as a result of an uncommon level of access that might only be found in public service media.[34] Two excellent studies of the British magazine industry, focusing on a particular moment of change in both women's and men's magazines respectively, offer fine examples of how this work might be pursued in other media industries. Anna Gough-Yates's explores the forces that gave rise to shifts in the address of women's magazines by expertly combining sociohistorical, industrial, and textual analysis.[35] Similarly, Ben Crewe brings these features together to assess the rise of and changes in men's magazines in the 1990s.[36]

As should be obvious, industry-level studies of television offer scope and context that complement the insights gained from both the more macro national and international political economy level and the more focused study of individual productions. *Inside Prime Time* offers a valuable model in its detail, accessibility, and grounded analysis. Approaching such research in the contemporary context now requires attention to the opportunities and limitations derived from the industrial transitions that are sweeping many media industries. Often, the adaptation of practices encouraged, if not required, by digitalization and globalization reveals the arbitrariness of industry lore and other hegemonic practices governing cultural production. Creative industries change then because new conditions support new textual output and because shifts in industrial practices create new hegemonies that govern production practices. Rich understandings of media operations require studies at all these levels from the macro to the micro and with a mixture of methodologies including aggregate data analysis and the ethnographic. Indeed, negotiating the balance among the vast array of research sites available with industry-level scope and the detail afforded through qualitative methods can be challenging. However, valuable and manageable amounts of information can be gained by focusing on the practices that intersect various components of media industries and by relying on the work done by previous scholarship to describe key areas of industry operation.

Notes

1 Todd Gitlin, *Inside Prime Time* (New York: Pantheon Books, 1983).
2 Amanda D. Lotz, *The Television Will Be Revolutionized* (New York: New York University Press, 2007).
3 Horace Newcomb and Amanda D. Lotz, "The Production of Media Fiction," in *A Handbook of Media and Communication Research*, ed. Klaus Bruhn Jensen (New York: Routledge, 2002).

To be sure, Newcomb is responsible for the intellectual heavy lifting here, and the classification of levels is his.

4 My discussion of industry studies here focuses on scholarship that engages in *critical* study of media industries. This excludes work that is primarily descriptive or administrative in nature, but does encompass a body of varied research by scholars who mostly locate their intellectual base in either political economy or cultural studies. (For example, Alison Alexander, James Owers, Rodney A. Carveth, C. Ann Hollifield, and Albert N. Greco, eds., *Media Economics: Theory and Practice* (Mahweh, NJ: Lawrence Erlbaum, 2004); Douglas Gomery and Benjamin M. Compaine, *Who Owns the Media?: Competition and Concentration in the Mass Media Industry* (Hillsdale, NJ: Lawrence Erlbaum, 2000).) Enumerating the finer theoretical points between these camps or analysis about how power operates or celebrating the operations and output of the industry, is not my intention for this chapter. Rather, I wish to engage with work that questions the hegemonic processes involved in cultural production, in other words, "critical" scholarship.

5 Ben Bagdikian, *The New Media Monopoly* (Boston: Beacon Press, 2004); Robert W. McChesney, *The Problem of the Media: U.S. Communication Politics in the 21st Century* (New York: Monthly Review Press, 2004).

6 David Hesmondhalgh, *The Cultural Industries*, 2nd ed. (London: Sage, 2007), 174.

7 Robert Merton, *Social Theory and Social Structure* (New York: Free Press, 1968); Hesmondhalgh, *The Cultural Industries*, 3.

8 See, for example, Alexander et al., *Media Economics*; Gomery and Compaine, *Who Owns*.

9 Laura Grindstaff, *The Money Shot: Trash, Class, and the Making of TV Talk Shows* (Chicago: University of Chicago Press, 2002).

10 Richard A. Peterson, "Five Constraints on the Production of Culture: Law, Technology, Market, Organizational Structure and Occupational Careers," *Journal of Popular Culture* 16, no. 2 (1982): 143–152.

11 Joseph Turow, *Media Systems in Society: Understanding Industries, Strategies, and Power* (New York: A.B. Longman, 1992).

12 Turow, *Media Systems*, 24.

13 Paul du Gay, Stuart Hall, Linda Janes, Hugh Mackay, and Keith Negus, *Doing Cultural Studies: The Story of the Sony Walkman* (London: Sage, 1997); Paul du Gay and Michael Pryke, "Cultural Economy: An Introduction," in *Cultural Economy: Cultural Analysis and Commercial Life*, eds. Paul du Gay and Michael Pryke (London: Sage, 2002); John Hartley, ed., *Creative Industries* (Malden, MA: Blackwell, 2005); David Hesmondhalgh, "Politics, Theory and Method in Media Industries Research," in *Media Industries: History, Theory, and Methods*, eds. Jennifer Holt and Alisa Perren (Malden, MA: Blackwell, 2009), 245–255; John Caldwell, *Production Culture: Industrial Reflexivity and Critical Practice in Film and Television* (Durham: Duke University Press, 2008); Timothy Havens, Amanda D. Lotz, and Serra Tinic, "Critical Media Industry Studies: A Research Approach," (forthcoming).

14 Joli Jensen, "An Interpretive Approach to Culture Production," in *Interpreting Television: Current Perspectives*, eds. William Rowland and Bruce Watkins (Beverly Hills: Sage, 1984); Richard Johnson, "What is Cultural Studies Anyway?" *Social Text* 16 (1986): 38–80.

15 See Havens, Lotz, and Tinic, "Critical Media Industry Studies"; Julie D'Acci, "Cultural Studies, Television Studies, and the Crisis in the Humanities," in *Television after TV: Essays on a Medium in Transition*, eds. Lynn Spigel and Jan Olsson (Durham: Duke University Press, 2004).

16 Gitlin, *Inside Prime Time*, 13.
17 Gitlin does provide a more expansive look at two shows, *American Dream* and *Hill Street Blues*. Although the attention particularly to *Hill Street Blues* features great detail, its focus remains on the interaction between the show's creative staff and the network, rather than focusing in on a production study at the level of a particular show.
18 His assumption that *All in the Family* was more culturally relevant than *Dallas* goes uninterrogated.
19 Gitlin, *Inside Prime Time*, 13.
20 Hesmondhalgh, *The Cultural Industries*; Bernard Miege, *The Capitalization of Cultural Production* (New York: International General, 1989).
21 Timothy Havens, "Universal Childhood: The Global Trade in Children's Television and Changing Ideals of Childhood," *Global Media Journal* 6, no. 10 (2007), available at http://lass.calumet.purdue.edu/cca/gmj/sp07/gmj-sp07-havens.htm (accessed 7 February, 2007).
22 Todd Gitlin, "Prime Time Ideology: The Hegemonic Process in Television Entertainment," *Social Problems* 26, no. 3 (1979): 251–266.
23 See reviews by Muriel G. Cantor, "Review: The Perils of Prime-Time Politics," *Contemporary Sociology* 13, no. 4 (1984): 417–419; Elihu Katz, "Review: *Inside Prime Time*," *The American Journal of Sociology* 90, no. 6 (1985): 1371–1374; Donald Lazere, "TV Hegemony," *Journal of Communication* 34, no. 2 (1984): 170–172; Bernard Roshco, "Inside Prime Time," *Social Forces* 64, no. 3 (1983): 827–828.
24 Muriel G. Cantor, *The Hollywood TV Producer: His Work and His Audience* (New York: Basic Books, 1972).
25 Horace Newcomb and Robert S. Alley, *The Producer's Medium: Conversations with Creators of American TV* (New York: Oxford University Press, 1983).
26 Richard Levinson and William Link, … *Stay Tuned: An Inside Look at the Making of Prime-Time Television* (New York: St. Martin's Press, 1981).
27 Jerry Mander, *Four Arguments for the Elimination of Television* (New York: Harper, 1978).
28 Les Brown, *Televi$ion: The Business Behind the Box* (New York: Harcourt Brace Jovanovich, 1971).
29 Sally Bedell, *Up the Tube: Prime Time TV and the Silverman Years* (New York: The Viking Press, 1981); Ken Auletta, *Three Blind Mice: How the TV Networks Lost Their Way* (New York: Random House, 1991); Bill Carter, *Desperate Networks* (New York: Doubleday, 2006).
30 He shares this in common with Brown, as well.
31 See Lotz, *The Television*.
32 Caldwell, *Production Culture*; du Gay et al., *Doing Cultural Studies*; John Thornton Caldwell, "Cultural Studies of Media Production: Critical Industrial Practices," in *Questions of Method in Cultural Studies*, eds. Mimi White and James Schwoch (Malden, MA: Blackwell, 2006).
33 These research experiences were facilitated through the National Association of Television Program Executives (NATPE) Faculty Development Grant program and the Advertising Education Foundation (AEF) Visiting Professor Program.
34 Georgina Born, *Uncertain Vision: Birt, Dyke and the Reinvention of the BBC* (London: Vintage, 2005).
35 Anna Gough-Yates, *Understanding Women's Magazines* (London: Routledge, 2002).
36 Ben Crewe, *Representing Men: Cultural Production and Producers in the Men's Magazine Market* (New York: Berg, 2003).

Chapter 3

Leo C. Rosten's Hollywood

Power, Status, and the Primacy of Economic and Social Networks in Cultural Production

John L. Sullivan

Myths about Hollywood have excited the public imagination since the early twentieth century. The popular media and the movie studios' own marketing have continually portrayed motion picture production as magical and fantastic, heralding the individual achievement of a few creative professionals.[1] This celebration continues despite the realities of industrialized division of labor and creative outsourcing which are prominent features of today's media production environment.[2] Motion picture production has also become increasingly one of a number of media production enterprises that are managed by large, global conglomerates.[3] The 2007–2008 strike by members of the Writers Guild of America (WGA), for instance, exposed for public view the growing disconnect between those who make their livings as cultural producers in Los Angeles and the middle managers in giant media conglomerates who oversee their creative efforts.[4]

Contemporary scholars who train their collective eye on the processes of production in Hollywood still have relatively few exemplars to guide them in their analysis. While anthropologist Hortense Powdermaker's[5] study of Southern California's movie-making community is often cited as a foundational work by scholars of cultural production, the first person to cut through popular myths about Hollywood films by systematically uncovering the personalities, organizations, and social dynamic behind them was Leo C. Rosten.[6] In *Hollywood: The Movie Colony, the Movie Makers*, Rosten applied many of the same techniques that he had honed in his earlier study of Washington news correspondents[7] by amassing a wealth of empirical data including interviews, questionnaires delivered to production personnel, government statistics, market data, and casual observations of media elites.

Although the business of producing, distributing, and marketing motion pictures has undergone substantial changes since Rosten infiltrated Hollywood's high society, his 1941 treatise on the people behind the movies remains a theoretical and methodological touchstone for academics conducting media production studies today. This chapter briefly charts the aims of Rosten's research into the "movie colony" of the late 1930s and suggests that, while the networking of creative labor and globalization have transformed the movie business since then, Rosten's approach to the study of motion picture production still provides useful guidance for contemporary scholars seeking to explore the connections between economics and culture in Hollywood.

Contextualizing Rosten's Approach to Studying Hollywood

Before outlining some of Rosten's key claims and their relevance to today's media production scholars, some context regarding Rosten himself and the Hollywood he encountered is necessary. A Polish immigrant to the United States at the age of three, Rosten grew up in Chicago, graduating from the University of Chicago with a bachelor's degree and then a doctorate in political science in 1937.[8] As a student of Harold Lasswell's, Rosten emerged from his doctorate education firmly rooted in Chicago School traditions of empirical, positivistic sociology, sharing Lasswell's fascination with the mass persuasive power of the media, particularly motion pictures. Before he undertook the task of placing movie producers under the social scientific microscope, however, Rosten was first drawn to Hollywood with a desire to become a screenwriter himself. He recalled in his memoir that

> I always nursed a secret fantasy that one day I would get to Hollywood to become part of the empyrean of films ... I did not dream that I would arrive in Hollywood by accident (it was cheaper to buy an excursion-special to Los Angeles, from Washington, than to Phoenix, Arizona, where I was headed on a mission of mercy), or that I would start a short-lived career as a screenwriter soon after passing my exams for a higher degree in political science.[9]

Rosten worked as a screenwriter in 1937 and 1938 for the small studio Major Pictures, though he never saw any of his stories reach the screen. In fact, the company soon went bankrupt, forcing Rosten to reevaluate his choice of career. One of the fortunate consequences of his brief stint as a screenwriter was his ability to gain access to Hollywood's creative culture as an insider:

> I was disemployed, but scarcely discouraged; working in a studio, sweating out story lines, hanging around sound stages, talking shop with the odd wizards of the cutting rooms, observing the wiles of producers and resisting the blandishments of starlets—all these were to prove priceless for another purpose. They gave me entree to the dinner tables and swimming pools of the movie colony—as a professional, not a gawker.[10]

Like some scholars who study media production, Rosten began as a professional insider who found himself intellectually fascinated by the social milieu of Hollywood and its impact on the production of motion pictures. He obtained a grant from the Carnegie Foundation (and later more funds from the Rockefeller Foundation) for a two-year study of Hollywood in late 1938, hired "several sociologists and a statistician," and began what he called the "Motion Picture Research Project".[11]

Rosten began his work on Hollywood at a time of widespread public and scholarly interest in motion pictures and their effects on society. The Payne Fund Studies,[12] still the largest scholarly effort ever undertaken to understand the effects of motion pictures, was published in 1933, followed by Margaret Thorp's[13] 1939 treatise on the effects of Hollywood on audiences and American culture, which was published while Rosten was in the midst of the "Motion Picture Research Project." Along with a focus on the social consequences of movie content, Rosten's work also reflected a growing chorus of concern about economic concentration in the motion picture industry. For much of the decade the Big Five vertically integrated studios—MGM, Paramount, Warner Brothers, 20th Century Fox, and RKO—enjoyed a golden age of profitability and control over every aspect of the business. Anticompetitive practices such as blind-selling and block-booking minimized the economic risks to the studios and stifled competition from smaller firms and studios.[14] Yet over the course of his research project, Rosten witnessed an industry increasingly in crisis as it found itself in the crosshairs of Franklin D. Roosevelt's Justice Department. In 1938, the government filed suit against the industry, claiming that the studios had violated the Sherman Antitrust Act. A host of federal and state attorneys general filed similar lawsuits against the studios in the ensuing two-year period. In 1940, the Big Five successfully negotiated a Consent Decree with the government which averted further legal proceedings while protecting the ability of the studios to force some films on exhibitors.[15] These skirmishes with the government, along with declining foreign box office receipts due to hostilities in Europe, signaled the beginning of a decline in the golden age of studio-dominated Hollywood. It was this unfolding transition that formed the context for Rosten's observations on the "movie colony."

Given the centrality of the motion pictures to Americans' everyday lives, particularly during the depths of the Great Depression, and the close connection between Rosten's project and the documentary impulse which guided many scholars and activists to closely examine "in situ" lived experiences during the Depression era,[16] it is difficult to imagine why Rosten's analysis is not more widely remembered by today's media production scholars.[17] Indeed, the reception of the book at the time in the *New York Herald Tribune*[18] and the *New York Times Book Review* was wholly positive, with the *Times* declaring that "Mr. Rosten delivers what is really the first intrinsic social estimate of the oddest community in America and the most screw-whacky business in the world."[19] There are at least two possible explanations for Rosten's relative obscurity today. First, despite its rigorous sociological grounding, the book itself is rather breezily written—Rosten's analysis unfolds in quasi-journalistic prose, with industry statistics cited only briefly as support for his more general observations about Hollywood. As one academic reviewer put it, "this volume is not the kind of a report that social scientists usually make. It is rather a journalistic description of the movie colony and its work."[20] In this respect, Rosten's engaging style (which was no doubt intended for a general audience) stands in stark contrast to Powdermaker's more sober, scholarly assessment of Hollywood movie production. Rather than meticulously documenting his interactions with movie producers, Rosten uses these interactions in their totality to offer a more generalized meditation on the movies and the culture of celebrity which surrounds Hollywood filmmakers.

Rosten's *Hollywood* book was also an accidental victim of history. As he recounts in his memoirs, after receiving advanced copies of the positive reviews in both the *Herald Tribune* and the *Times* (which were to appear in print in their Sunday book editions on the same day),

> I took my breakfast, that lovely Sunday morning, preening with pride and telling myself that the years of drudgery were really worthwhile: the grueling gobs of statistical analysis, the inescapable disappointments and frustrations, even the rumors with which my name had been blackened … The telephone interrupted my blissful reverie, and a friend's voice, oddly thick, asked: "Have you been listening to the radio? I just caught the goddamnedest news bulletin. This announcer says the Japs have bombed Pearl Harbor."[21]

Indeed, in a cruel twist of fate, national reviews of Rosten's book were published on December 7, 1941, just as news of the surprise attack on Pearl Harbor crackled over the radio airwaves, plunging the country immediately into war. Although perhaps forgotten by a public focused on news from the Pacific, the positive reviews of the *Hollywood* book did not escape the notice of one of President Roosevelt's advisors, who contacted Rosten the very next day about working for Archibald MacLeish at the Office of Facts and Figures in Washington, DC. Rosten's extensive knowledge of the intricacies of Hollywood's social networks made him a valuable liaison between the movie industry and the US government's growing efforts to employ motion pictures as domestic propaganda. Rosten later became Deputy Director of the Office of War Information and coordinated the government's efforts to synchronize Hollywood's storylines with Washington's war priorities.[22] Although the war deprived Rosten's book of critical public and scholarly attention, it nevertheless opened a door to Rosten's continued involvement with the industry during the wartime years.

What can modern media production scholars take away, then, from this study of Hollywood in the late 1930s? As a primer on the social and economic environment of contemporary Hollywood, the utility of Rosten's book is quite limited. It goes without saying that the US motion picture industry has changed dramatically since Rosten completed his research. In this chapter, I propose a series of tangible benefits to reconsidering Rosten's work today. First, Rosten's critical epistemology is an instructive starting point for analysis. For Rosten, the potential power of film to shape culture necessitated a careful look behind the scenes to the individuals who produced media entertainment. Second, his sociological approach to understanding Hollywood—taking into account not simply the occupational roles of media producers but also the social and relational dynamics of Hollywood's social scene—establishes an important precedent for today's media production scholars. Third, while Rosten did not necessarily approach the study of Hollywood from a political economic perspective, both the Hollywood book and an earlier outline of cultural production research published in 1939[23] point to key structuring elements of the industry including management–labor relations, limiting pressures from the government and outside interest groups, and contradictions between creativity and commerce which impacted the daily lives of the individuals he studied. As I argue in the conclusion, these connections between the political economy of media production and the sociology of media producers are critical to contemporary analyses of cultural production.

A Critical Epistemology for Cultural Production Analysis

Rosten's analysis begins with a strong purpose, which is to train a critical eye on the production of motion pictures because of its powerful influence on attitudes and behaviors for millions of people. He asks, in essence: Why should academics focus on the production of something as ephemeral and inconsequential as the movies? The argument he follows is one which hews closely to the pervading belief about movies at the time, specifically (1) that they were the subject of too much "foolish adulation" and (2) that their messages were a source of potentially powerful influence on the viewing audience.

Rosten's first notion that Americans spent too much of their time idolizing Hollywood films and the actors who starred in them is a claim which has it roots firmly in the high culture/low culture debates that occupied much academic and popular thinking about mass media in the 1930s and 1940s. In an aesthetically conservative vein, reminiscent of Adorno's Culture Industry critique,[24] Rosten marveled over the public's capacity to flock to the movie idols of the day, and was particularly intrigued and perturbed by the many forms of celebrity worship he witnessed. He writes that

> The sheer magnitude of this adoration invites awe. Each day millions of men, women, and children sit in the windowless temples of the screen to commune with their vicarious friends and lovers, to ride with Autry, love with Garbo, fight with Gable.[25]

Additionally, he argued that the public was misled by the rags-to-riches stories that dominated the tabloids and the silver screen. Unlike other industries, Rosten argued, those who were successful in Hollywood were perceived to be there because of their luck rather than because of some talent or tenacity (even though in his survey of the industry roughly half of all movie producers had worked in Hollywood for fifteen or more years). At this point, it's safe to say that the high/low culture debate has been decisively settled. It is now widely realized by scholars that popular or "low" cultural messages offer at least as much insight, if not more, into the social and cultural fabric of society.

The second chief motivation for Rosten's study of Hollywood moviemakers, however, arose from his concern—no doubt encouraged by his mentor Harold Lasswell—that motion pictures had a profound impact on individual viewers and society as a whole. As he notes in his final chapter entitled "The long arm of Hollywood,"

> No matter what the intentions of the movie makers may be, no matter how unconscious they may be of the effects of their product, no matter how reluctant Hollywood may be to manipulate the subtle and persuasive power at its disposal, the movies exert an influence which is vast and profound.[26]

Rosten outlines a number of indictments of motion picture content, including pervasive racial stereotypes (noting that "Hollywood's racial typologies are forever dismaying"), intoxicating images of stylized but unrealistic romanticism, and unbridled consumerism. Although he is careful to avoid the claim that Hollywood films actively perpetuate these stereotypes and "banalities" on a helpless public, Rosten does note, however, that "Hollywood, through the movies, *reinforces* our typologies on an enormous scale and with overpowering repetitiveness."[27] Rosten's concern for the influence of media on individuals' outlooks through countless repetition pre-dates some of the key tenets of George Gerbner's media theories in the mid-1970s. Gerbner himself constructed a holistic theory of communication study, claiming that the analysis of media content (which he called "message systems") should be combined with the study of media production ("institutional process") such that the long-term effects of these messages ("cultivation") could be assessed.[28] It is noteworthy that Rosten himself approached the study of media production from a concern about the effects of motion picture content, suggesting that the economic conditions of production can play a decisive role in the perpetuation of damaging social stereotypes.

These central claims form the backbone of Rosten's inquiry into motion picture production. In essence, the starting point for an analysis of cultural production here is his notion that media messages are important catalysts in shaping and maintaining aspects of social structure. Insofar as those structures reinforce inequalities or stereotypes, the system which produces them should be thoroughly understood in order to propose and effect change. This is a powerful rationale for today's media production scholars to consider, although it is certainly not the only one which can justify sustained inquiry into media production practices. Understanding the relationships of power and the corporatization of cultural production to meld it into a capitalist system is also a powerful rationale, even if it did not drive Rosten's analysis of Hollywood film production.

Hollywood as a Social System

One of the central insights of Rosten's text is that "Hollywood" is not just a geographic location where motion picture production takes place. Hollywood is also a dynamic social system, replete with status relationships, hierarchies, unrest and conflict, and unique individual personalities. Rosten argues that, when subjected to systematic inquiry, the social system of Hollywood works much like other social systems. In fact, there is nothing particularly noteworthy about motion picture workers save for the fact that they are the focus of much popular fascination:

> Hollywood can be placed under the microscope of social science like a slide on which we see, in sharper and isolated detail, the organic processes of the larger social body … When seen as a social complex, when viewed with insight, when studied with patience and analyzed with detachment, Hollywood loses many of its bizarries.[29]

Rosten's central influence in building this argument was the groundbreaking work of Robert Staughton Lynd and Helen Merrell Lynd,[30] who undertook the largest ever sociological study of an entire community (Muncie, Indiana, which they dubbed "Middletown" to protect the anonymity of their subjects) in the late 1920s and again during the depths of the Great Depression. Like the Lynds' study of "Middletown," Rosten was committed to placing a positivistic, objective eye on the vagaries of Hollywood's social and professional life. As he would explain later in his memoirs, "I wanted to analyze the community that makes movies for the world the way an anthropologist might study the Maori."[31]

Rosten's overall approach to studying Hollywood, though not necessarily anthro-pological in nature as he later indicated,[32] is certainly phenomenological in his focus on the social interactions among Hollywood elites both on and off the studio lot. Rosten wrestles with the characteristics of those who make their liv-ing in Hollywood, including their sociodemographic makeup, social habits, and observable behavior patterns. Though he intersperses these "hard" data with numer-ous anecdotes and observations about the moviemakers, Rosten relies almost exclusively throughout the book on numerical data gathered from government sources such as Treasury Department documents and Securities and Exchange Commission (SEC) filings and on surveys he administered to over 800 directors, actors, screenwriters, and producers. The data about Hollywood reveal a fasci-nating macrosocial picture that is often missing from modern-day observational accounts of media production routines. For instance, Rosten discovered that Hol-lywood of the late 1930s was "young" ("6.2 percent of the movie colony are under 40 years of age; over a third are between 30 and 40") and not nearly as well paid as the public may have imagined, with only a handful of producers, writ-ers, directors, and actors making large annual salaries. Hollywood emerges from this statistical portrait as a mecca for eager young creatives seeking to make their fortunes, though it ultimately only satisfies a small percentage of these grandiose dreamers.

Rosten divides the social structure of Hollywood into three concentric circles, with the largest circle encompassing "all of the thirty thousand movie work-ers and movie makers," the middle capturing "the movie colony" (producers, actors, directors, and writers, for example), and the center research for "the movie elite, some two hundred and fifty persons who, to an arbitrary but use-ful index, earn $75,000 or more a year."[33] Rosten's exclusive focus on the movie colony—particularly his emphasis on its most inner circle and their social dynam-ics as constituted outside of the boundaries of the workplace—is perhaps one of the most fascinating aspects of the book. In Rosten's estimation, the well-heeled in Hollywood form a kind of nervous elite, constantly seeking validation for their financially privileged status from others in this higher socioeconomic echelon. Rosten observes that "Hollywood's elite has no respect for itself. Here is a skill-rich group which feels inferior, which accepts with embarrassment the derision of others."[34] This nervousness in Hollywood is also due to the chronic uncertainty of the economic environment there. Rosten writes: "The volatility of fortune in Hollywood subjects its personalities to a severe and persistent strain."[35] Despite this undercurrent of unease, however, Rosten discovered that elites in Hollywood ignored many of the economic realities of the business during their seemingly ubiquitous after-hours cocktail parties and social gatherings, choosing to focus on the creative or aesthetic aspects of their work, thereby giving the social environment of Hollywood a "feverish, self-fascinated quality."[36] Before Mills'[37] groundbreaking book on social elites, Rosten recognized that power and influence is often concentrated in a small number of people who dictate the terms not just of business, but of social interaction within Hollywood, including parties, award shows, and other informal social gatherings. Rosten's work essentially linked both spatial and social geography, anticipating a number of important contemporary production studies of Hollywood that pay particular attention to the "spatial systems of production, work, and social life."[38]

Was Rosten a Political Economist?

As noted earlier, Rosten was clearly interested in approaching motion picture production in Hollywood as a social force in culture. However, there is ample evidence in the book to suggest that Rosten was cognizant of the economic structures which shaped the production process. In the preface, in fact, Rosten pointed to other areas that he believed were equally critical to an understanding of the dynamics of Hollywood, but which had to be "reserved for a later volume." These areas covered topics that occupy the nexus of political economic analyses of cultural production today: "(a) the economics of movie making, picture costs, markets, profits, financial practices; (b) the Motion Picture Producers and Distributors Association [the Hays Office]; (c) the production code and censorship; (d) Hollywood's guilds and labor problems."[39] In a separate article published prior to the completion of the book, Rosten lays out a careful rationale and research plan for his Motion Picture Research Project. This earlier manuscript provides an even clearer picture of Rosten's conviction that underlying economic realities of capitalist cultural production should be part and parcel of an analysis of Hollywood, including "competition and monopoly practices," "government interference" (policies and regulation), "collective bargaining in Hollywood" (labor–management relations and conflict), and "labor organization in the industry."[40] Unfortunately for today's media production scholars, however, wartime exigencies, Rosten's work for the government, and his later success as a fictional author apparently precluded him from returning to complete the second volume of his Hollywood book. Still, there are a number of clues to Rosten's political economic perspective throughout the book that warrant mention here.

For example, Rosten utilizes SEC filings to compare the motion picture industry with other industries in the US in 1937, examining its volume of business, net profits, and executive remuneration. What he finds is rather startling: Rosten's research places Hollywood fourteenth out of eighteen industries in terms of volume of business (behind oil refining, steel, and meat packing, for instance), and eleventh out of eighteen in terms of total assets. Despite these figures, he finds that executive pay in Hollywood both as a percentage of net profits and total volume of sales is second highest, meaning that much more of the profits from the industry go to executive salaries. This economic context provides compelling background detail for some of the conflicts between producers and creative workers.

Rosten's focus on social and economic power leads to another important insight for contemporary scholars about the contradictory nature of cultural production. As Hesmondhalgh[41] and Ryan[42] have observed, unlike other industries, workers in cultural industries enjoy a great deal more autonomy over their labor, since the originality or uniqueness of their productions is crucial to market success. The trouble for creative corporations, however, is that artistic production is inherently *irrational* from an economic standpoint, because creativity cannot be routinized to produce unique cultural products on a regular basis. In his opening chapter describing the general outline of the "movie colony," Rosten astutely acknowledges this contradiction between art and commerce, noting that while mass production is the key to Hollywood's profitability, the originality of each film is critical to audience appeal:

> Hollywood must continue to satisfy and aim at an audience, in the United States alone, of more than 50,000,000 people a week. (Or it should reduce its costs beyond recognition, which would mean revolutionizing the star system and the production system, and abandoning the ferocious competition for talent and stories—at which point the Department of Justice might step in). An audience of this gigantic size means that, unlike book publishers or magazine editors or play producers, Hollywood must appeal to mentalities ranging from six to sixty, from stevedores to seminary students, from barmaids to dowagers ... *Hollywood is geared to a mass market, yet it cannot employ the* methods *of mass production. Each picture is a different picture and presents unique demands.*[43]

This conflict between the concerns of creativity on the one hand and commerce on the other is well documented throughout the book. Perhaps the most compelling example of this emerges in his discussion of screenwriters; which is not surprising given Rosten's previous vocation as a struggling screenwriter. Based upon his interviews, he uncovers a general loathing with which screenwriters greet the demands of both management and the market, remarking that:

> Most writers in the movie colony echo the words of Dalton Trumbo: "The system under which writers work [in Hollywood] would sap the vitality of a Shakespeare. They are intelligent enough to know that they are writing trash but they are not intelligent enough to do anything about it." But it is not

a question of intelligence; it is a question of power, economics, reality, and personality structure.[44]

Rather than view this tension between creativity and commercial imperatives as an inherent contradiction in cultural production, however (as Ryan and other Marxist scholars of cultural production have done), Rosten roots these tensions firmly in the social and economic relationships among the members of the movie colony. He writes:

> The movie executives, for the most part, and the movie boards of directors are in New York; the management is in Hollywood. Management gets big money for itself and big money for the talents it employs. This raises production costs, which prevents profits from rising. Movie profits are drained off and channeled into the hands of the movie elite—the producers, the executives, the ranking talent. Because of the scarcity of first-rank movie talent and management, their power to command great salaries is unchallengeable. No movie company has solved this dilemma.[45]

Here Rosten connects a structural feature of cultural production—the uneasy coexistence of creative labor and corporate management—to the pervasive sense of nervousness and tension felt within the social environment of Hollywood. Further, because creative labor is more "scarce" than abstract labor, Rosten notes that Hollywood's talent increases the value of its labor (and therefore its power vis-à-vis producers) which begins to cut into the profitability of their works for the studios. Rosten's outline of Hollywood in 1941 is still prescient today, as tensions continue between the motion picture producers and the Hollywood talent revolving around the scarcity of creative labor and the resulting value of that labor in the market.

Bringing Rosten's Hollywood into the Twenty-first Century

Though Rosten's book captures but one snapshot in the history of US motion picture production, there are a number of important insights about media production that can be found in this groundbreaking work. First, his instructive sociological approach is one of the book's great contributions. Rosten details how there are different social strata in Hollywood, as there are in other communities and organizations, and that the web of social relationships plays a powerful role in structuring the working community of Hollywood. This is no less true today than it was in 1939. In the chapters on the production activities of actors, directors, and especially writers, Rosten's observations and survey responses uncover numerous tensions between the creative "talent" and management. These tensions are for the most part a visceral response by creative workers to the many constraints which shape motion picture production.[46]

The Hollywood of the twenty-first century presents numerous challenges to scholars who wish to utilize Rosten's study as a road map to understanding the social dynamic behind industrialized movie production. For one, the concept of "Hollywood" as an economic and social zone of media production has changed rather dramatically, particularly given the rise of runaway production and global-ized outsourcing of some forms of cultural labor. While motion picture studios are still located in Hollywood, production has been increasingly globalized to take advantage of low-cost, non-unionized labor in other parts of the world.[47] Additionally, the major studios in Hollywood have become much more than simply motion picture production firms—they now serve as the content-generating nexus of much larger international multimedia conglomerates. Finally, advances in tech-nology unimaginable in Rosten's era, such as digital production and exhibition, online distribution, and the decreasing cost of video production equipment for consumers, have challenged and expanded the very definition of a media producer.

Given these challenges, however, there are some central insights in Rosten's tome that can guide scholars today. First, his notion that cultural production is firmly situated within social and economic networks should be a key starting point for con-temporary analyses of media.[48] Though there will be the inevitable temptation for scholars to presuppose that new technologies of digital production and distribution via computer networks are key catalysts for change in Hollywood, Rosten's analysis points to the ways in which these new technologies are embedded in existing social structures. Hollywood's cooperation with—or co-optation of—computer man-ufacturers and software engineers to prevent the digital reproduction of motion pictures is one example of the ways in which supposed technologies of consumer freedom are constrained by existing legal and economic structures. Second, the ongoing struggle between the creative and commercial impulses of motion pic-ture production that Rosten uncovered in 1941 are still relevant to today's media production environment. In fact, media workers' strategies for negotiating their daily struggles with the realities of industrialized cultural production are a key focal point for ongoing research on media production practices. Although Rosten never completed the second volume of his Hollywood research, contemporary scholars of media production are carrying on the torch by connecting cultural practices to their social and economic contexts.

Notes

1 Robert Alan Brookey and Robert Westerfelhaus, "The Digital Auteur: Branding Identity on the *Monsters, Inc.* DVD," *Western Journal of Communication* 69, no. 2 (2005): 109–128;

John T. Caldwell, "Critical Industrial Practice: Branding, Repurposing, and the Migratory Patterns of Industrial Texts," *Television & New Media* 7, no. 2 (2006): 99–134; John L. Sullivan, "Marketing Creative Labor: Hollywood 'Making of' Documentary Features," in *Knowledge Workers in the Information Society*, eds. Katherine McKercher and Vincent Mosco (Lanham, MD: Lexington Books, 2007), 69–83.

2 Toby Miller et al., *Global Hollywood 2*, rev. ed. (London: BFI, 2005); Janet Wasko, *How Hollywood Works* (London: Sage, 2003).

3 See David Waterman, *Hollywood's Road to Riches* (Cambridge, MA: Harvard University Press, 2005).

4 Peter Bart, "Writers Face Faceless Enemy," *Variety*, December 21, 2007, http://www.variety.com/article/VR1117978127.html?categoryid=2821&cs=1&nid=4056.

5 Hortense Powdermaker, *Hollywood the Dream Factory: An Anthropologist Looks at the Moviemakers* (Boston: Little, Brown, 1950).

6 Leo Calvin Rosten, *Hollywood: The Movie Colony, the Movie Makers* (New York: Harcourt, Brace and Company, 1941).

7 Leo Calvin Rosten, *The Washington Correspondents* (New York: Harcourt, Brace, 1937).

8 Margalit Fox, "Leo Rosten, a Writer Who Helped Yiddish Make Its Way Into English, Is Dead at 88," *The New York Times*, February 20, 1997.

9 Leo Calvin Rosten, *The Many Worlds of Leo Rosten; Stories, Humor, Social Commentary, Travelogues, Satire, Memoirs, Profiles, and Sundry Entertainments Never Before Published; with a Special Introduction, Background Notes, Revelations and Confessions, All Hand-written and Themselves Worth the Price of Admission*, 1st ed. (New York: Harper & Row, 1964), 118.

10 Ibid. See also Sherry Ortner's chapter in this volume.

11 Ibid.

12 W. W. Charters and Motion Picture Research Council, *Motion Pictures and Youth, a Summary*, Motion pictures and youth; the Payne fund studies (New York: The Macmillan Company, 1933); for a complete summary, see Garth Jowett, I. C. Jarvie, and Kathryn H. Fuller, *Children and the Movies: Media Influence and the Payne Fund Controversy*, Cambridge Studies in the History of Mass Communications (New York: Cambridge University Press, 1996).

13 Margaret Farrand Thorp, *America at the Movies* (New Haven: Yale University Press, 1939).

14 Thomas Schatz, *Boom and Bust: The American Cinema in the 1940s*, History of the American Cinema (New York: Charles Scribner's Sons, 1997), 16.

15 Ibid., 20.

16 Such as James Agee and Walker Evans, *Let Us Now Praise Famous Men* (Boston: Houghton Mifflin Company, 1941); Federal Writers' Project, *These Are Our Lives* (Chapel Hill, NC: University of North Carolina Press, 1939).

17 A number of current and classic cultural production texts do not even reference Rosten or his Hollywood book. These include: Miller et al., *Global Hollywood 2*; David Hesmondhalgh, *The Cultural Industries*, 2nd ed. (Los Angeles, CA: Sage, 2007); Todd Gitlin, *Inside Prime Time* (New York: Pantheon Books, 1983); Barry Dornfeld, *Producing Public Television, Producing Public Culture* (Princeton, NJ: Princeton University Press, 1998); Wasko, *How Hollywood Works*; Allen John Scott, *On Hollywood: The Place, the Industry* (Princeton, NJ: Princeton University Press, 2005). Rosten is given prominent mention, however, in the most recent book by John T. Caldwell: *Production Culture: Industrial Reflexivity and Critical Practice in Film and Television* (Durham, NC: Duke University Press, 2008).

18 Ben Ray Redman, "Folks who Make our Movies," *New York Herald Tribune Books*, December 7, 1941, Sunday edition.

19 Bosley Crowther, "The World that Is Hollywood: A Comprehensive Survey of the Industry's Slightly Ersatz Community," *The New York Times Book Review*, December 7, 1941, sec. 6.

20 Mark May, "Review of ROSTEN, LEO C. Hollywood: The Movie Colony; The Movie Makers," *The ANNALS of the American Academy of Political and Social Science* 221, no. 1 (May 1, 1942): 224.

21 Rosten, *The Many Worlds of Leo Rosten*, 119.

22 See Garth Jowett, *Film: The Democratic Art*, 1st ed. (Boston: Little, Brown & Co., 1976).

23 Leo C. Rosten, "A 'Middletown' Study of Hollywood," *The Public Opinion Quarterly* 3, no. 2 (April 1939): 314–320.

24 Max Horkheimer and Theodor W. Adorno, *Dialectic of Enlightenment* (New York: Herder and Herder, 1972).

25 Rosten, *Hollywood*, 11–12.

26 Ibid., 357.

27 Ibid., 360.

28 George Gerbner, "Communication and Social Environment," *Scientific American* 227, no. 3 (1972): 153–160.

29 Rosten, *Hollywood*, 5–6.

30 Robert Staughton Lynd, *Middletown, a Study in Contemporary American Culture* (New York: Harcourt, Brace and Company, 1929); Robert Staughton Lynd, *Middletown in Transition; a Study in Cultural Conflicts* (New York: Harcourt, Brace and Company, 1937).

31 Rosten, *The Many Worlds of Leo Rosten*, 118.

32 It is entirely possible that Rosten was referencing Hortense Powdermaker's 1950 Hollywood book in his memoirs, though without naming her explicitly. Given the strong sociological focus of Rosten's book, it is unlikely that he would have aligned his approach with anthropology during the time he was conducting the research. Although this is speculative, the increased attention given to Powdermaker's book by scholars relative to his own book may have prompted Rosten to suggest in his memoirs that he had conducted a detailed anthropological study of Hollywood a decade prior to Powdermaker's study.

33 Rosten, *Hollywood*, 33.

34 Ibid., 70.

35 Ibid., 42.

36 Ibid., 36.

37 C. Wright Mills, *The Power Elite* (New York: Oxford University Press, 1956).

38 Scott, *On Hollywood*, 7; See also Caldwell, *Production Culture*.

39 Rosten, *Hollywood*, vii.

40 Rosten, "A 'Middletown' Study of Hollywood," 19–20.

41 Hesmondhalgh, *The Cultural Industries*.

42 Bill Ryan, *Making Capital from Culture: The Corporate Form of Capitalist Cultural Production* (Berlin: Walter de Gruyter, 1992).

43 Rosten, *Hollywood*, 27–28; emphasis added.

44 Ibid., 309.

45 Ibid., 86.

46 This notion of economic, legal, and social constraints on production which filter down into everyday interactions of cultural workers anticipates many aspects of

Peterson's later "production of culture" approach within sociology; Richard A. Peterson, "The Production of Culture: A Prolegomenon," in *The Production of Culture*, ed. Richard A. Peterson (Beverly Hills, CA: Sage Publications, 1976), 7–22.
47 Miller et al., *Global Hollywood 2*.
48 Indeed, this is the analytical jumping off point for Caldwell's recent book on cultural production in Hollywood; Caldwell, *Production Culture*.

Chapter 4

Privilege and Distinction in Production Worlds

Copyright, Collective Bargaining, and Working Conditions in Media Making

Matt Stahl

Any division of cultural industry labor—whether local, national, or global—is defined not just by an allocation of tasks and responsibilities but also by the varying working conditions within that system. "Working conditions" does not refer here simply to the degree of comfort or satisfaction one experiences at film and television work (is it too cold or too hot, can I go to the bathroom when I choose, are the rules and expectations clear, are my co-workers and supervisors kind or cruel, do I exercise my creative capacities in my work, and so on). The term also refers to political and economic aspects of work including remuneration, control of the work process, ownership of the products of labor, the rights and obligations of employers and workers, and workers' access to health and pension benefits. Thus there are two broad, interrelated but analytically distinguishable sets of concerns—*subjective* and *structural*—involved in studying media production labor: the social-psychological experience of work on the one hand, and its political-economic conditions and organization on the other.

Copyright and collective bargaining play central roles in shaping the subjective and structural working conditions in worlds of capitalist media production—or "cultural industries"[1]—in the ways that they allocate privileges and produce and sustain forms of stratification. Privileges such as proprietary rights for authors and employer obligations to unionized workers play a major role in determining media workers' abilities to generate and maintain income, accumulate wealth, enjoy adequate health care, and plan for a secure retirement, in addition to enhancing their abilities to freely express and actualize themselves at work.[2] But how are such privileges allocated? Why do cultural industry workers—from scene painters and sound engineers to film directors and rock stars—experience such divergent working conditions?

At first glance, privileges and distinctions in media production can seem to follow naturally from differences in the kinds of tasks media workers do and the kinds of skills they bear. Indeed, the language used by industry professionals and observers in the press reinforces commonsensical distinctions between "creative" and "technical" labor. Against this common sense, this chapter suggests that arrangements of privilege and distinction in production worlds are the cumulative results of struggle between industry groups. These results, codified in law and/or custom, become normalized over time, to the point that they seem to be "reflections" of "inherent" differences between categories of workers, rather than *basic elements* of those differences.

The first section of the chapter focuses on how copyright separates—in fact, creates—authors and non-authors, conferring proprietary rights on authors and denying such rights to non-authors. But authorship is not a simple function of creativity: copyright's doctrine of "work for hire" allocates authorship and ownership of intellectual property produced in the workplace to employers, alienating employee media workers and also enabling the dispossession of most freelancers. The second section focuses on unionized employees who have won "quasi-proprietary" rights against the logic of work for hire through their willingness to strike. But there are stratifications even among these workers; this section also discusses the "line" that divides "creative" from "technical" employee labor and supports the differential allocation of privileges to those who fall on either side of it. The last section presents further distinctions: between workers who belong to unions and guilds and those who don't, and between workers in Hollywood (and the liberal-democratic world more generally) and those in countries characterized by more repressive employment regimes.

Copyright and Work for Hire

Copyright law distinguishes between those who can claim authorship of their work and those who cannot. This distinction is meaningful because being able to claim authorship, even in part, of a work of intellectual property means being privileged to enjoy, at least in part, the proprietary powers associated with copyright. Authorship claims are important because they guarantee certain legal property rights. At a most basic level, these boil down to the right to exclude others from the unauthorized use of the property in question; at a practical level, authors are entitled to royalty income from the marketing of their property. But legal authorship is not a straightforward concept. While the commonsense meaning of "author" suggests simple original creation, the legal designation is not essentially linked to creativity or originality. This is demonstrated in the operation of copyright's doctrine of *work for hire*, which intervenes into the cultural workplace and divides authors from non-authors, primarily on the basis of the employment relationship and secondarily on the basis of the kind of intellectual property that is being produced.

The doctrine of work for hire in the US emerged after the Civil War in conjunction with the growth of commercialized intellectual property and entertainment industries.[3] Work for hire decrees that when copyright-eligible products are produced by *employees* (and in certain cases by freelancers), the *employer* is the author (and hence the holder of the copyright for the duration of the copyright term). Work for hire thus creates authors out of employers who may not be creative in any conventionally recognizable way, in fact who may not even be people but firms. Cultural industry companies hire creative workers and contract with creative freelancers to work on collaborative projects like films, magazines, or recordings. However, companies' freedom to market products and appropriate profits depends on their ability to exclude numerous creative workers from the magic circle of authorship. Work for hire makes this separation and property alienation possible. By defining employers as authors, work for hire guarantees companies exclusive proprietary rights, free of the claims of workers who, without work for hire, would be "joint authors"—equal sharers of copyright's protections.

The US Copyright Act of 1909 codified work for hire and obliterated the rights that creator employees had previously enjoyed to the products of their labor.[4] Ever since then, employers have been empowered to appropriate the products of creative or intellectual labor the same way they do the products of other forms of labor. On this basis, freelancers (or "independent contractors") would seem to enjoy some advantages, but for most of the twentieth century courts lumped freelancers together with employees and simply alienated them all. Legal scholar Marci Hamilton shows that in the early (mid-1960s) stages of drafting what would become the 1976 Copyright Act, members of Congress wanted to change this situation and ensure that freelancers would have authorship of the works they produce on special commission, outside of the normal employment relation.[5] Since freelancers were not employees, the framers of the law reasoned, they shouldn't be subject to work for hire. The film and publishing industries got wind of this pending change and lobbied strenuously to prevent it—such a change would have disrupted their modes of production and income streams. As a result, the 1976 Copyright Act specifies nine categories of cultural work—including films, television shows, magazines, and encyclopedias—that, when contributed to or made on "special commission" (i.e., by freelancers rather than employees), can be considered work for hire, *as if* they were produced by employees.

It is because of this second "prong" of work for hire that film companies can make extensive use of creative freelancers without worrying about those creative workers having authorship rights. The "raw marketplace power" of corporate producers of films, magazines, and other such cultural products—in combination with competition among an oversupply of workers for relatively scarce jobs—forces most freelancers to give up demands for authorship and accept work-for-hire status in order to earn a living.[6] When viewed through the legal lens of work for hire—rather than, say, through aesthetics and critical theory in the humanities—authorship is a function not of creativity or responsibility or originality but of the ability to use capital to employ or contract with creative workers.

Inalienable Rights for Authors

Authors enjoy a remarkable privilege not shared by other workers. The 1976 Copyright Act vests a proprietary right in authors to terminate the "transfers" of their creations to cultural industry companies. In sectors such as book publishing and recording, many creators work as legal authors who license their creations to corporations in the business of marketing them. Such licenses, or "transfers," convey most rights to the corporation and allow the corporation to prohibit others (including the authors themselves) from any "unauthorized" uses of the property. For example, most recording contracts stipulate that the recording artist may not market the recording in question herself or offer it to another record company. However, the 1976 Act declares that copyrights held by *natural* (i.e., individual, not corporate) authors may be reclaimed by those authors thirty-five years after transfer, "even if the author has contracted not to do it."[7] Any creative worker who can defend the claim of authorship is endowed by copyright law with this right; it is *inalienable* because it cannot be transferred through contract or gift.

Cultural industry firms tend to prefer the outright appropriation of creative works (through work for hire) to the licensing of them, and they work hard to restrict many classes of creators from becoming authors, particularly through lobbying and legislation. The testimony of illustrators and graphic artists before a Congressional committee exploring a pair of bills that would have limited the effects of work for hire on freelancers helps clarify the stakes of these battles for cultural industry workers. Legal scholar Johanna Fisher Stewart recounts the testimony of Robin Brickman, a freelance illustrator, who told Congress that as a freelancer who produces illustrations eligible for work-for-hire designation under prong two,

> I have to pay for my studio, utilities, art supplies and equipment. I do not get group health insurance, paid vacation, sick leave or unemployment insurance. *I feel trapped* ... The minimal pay I get for work for hire means that I have to take any job I can get.[8]

These early 1980s bills failed to pass; companies emerged victorious from this confrontation and work for hire was further naturalized and normalized through another Congressional stamp of approval.

Freelancers like Brickman remain extremely vulnerable. However, for unionized employees, collective bargaining cuts against and compensates work for hire's alienating power. For those workers who are able to join unions and guilds, collective bargaining creates "quasi-proprietary" rights, and promises significant degrees of social protection and security (e.g., health care, retirement benefits) to protected employees. As with authorship, these privileges too are the product of confrontations and contests, and do not reflect "inherent" differences in workers or work processes.

Collective Bargaining and Residual Rights

Cultural industry workers who belong to unions and guilds enjoy a range of ownership-like privileges regarding the properties they have worked on. These privileges derive largely from their capacity collectively to withhold their labor from employers by striking, and take the form of royalty-like "participation" in income streams.[9] However, even among these employee creators, the uneven allocation of quasi-proprietary "residual" rights creates hierarchies of privilege that correlate to differences in working conditions. The most important hierarchical division of cultural industry workers is known in Hollywood as "the line" between "creative" and "technical" labor.

"The Line"

Like those between "author" and "non-author," distinctions between "creative" and "technical" workers, and the different privileges that attach to those designations, appear durable and natural even though they too are the result of historical struggle. They are sedimented in the institutions, organizational forms, and worker self-understandings found in centers of US cultural production and routinely referred to in trade journals, industry reference and "how-to" guides, as well as by workers themselves when they talk about their jobs and their industry.[10] In entertainment industry parlance, these two categories are known as "above the line" and "below the line." "The 'line' to which these employment classifications refer," write industrial relations researchers Alan Paul and Archie Kleingartner, "is found in [motion picture, television, and other cultural industry] project budgets. Creative work is accounted for above the line; below-the-line expenses include craft and technical labor, materials and supplies, and so on."[11]

Paul and Kleingartner analyze the "three-tier" compensation system characteristic of Hollywood above-the-line or "talent" guilds. The three tiers are (1) low minimum scale payments, which encourage employers to try out new workers; (2) personal service contracts, which allow established stars to contract over the minimum scale payments virtually without limits; and (3) residuals, which are extra-salary payments for the reuse of produced material that contribute to guild members' economic and social stability, particularly at the lower rungs of the entertainment industries' career ladders. My focus here is on the last of these three.

"The principle of payment for repeat use," write Paul and Kleingartner, "goes back at least to 1941, when the American Federation of Radio Artists' Transcription Code required that performers be paid their original compensation each time a program they had recorded was replayed."[12] This payment was demanded by creative workers on the logic that each time a recorded performance was replayed, there "was less employment for new product."[13] When a property is "reused"—when, for example, a film is shown on television or a series is rerun—above-the-line guild members receive *individual* residuals in the form of direct payments. Below-the-line union members, on the other hand, have gained *collective* residuals. These are figured based on a contractually defined percentage of industry revenues, and take the form of company contributions to union health and pension funds.

Above the Line

Residuals are important to above-the-line workers in guilds like the Writers Guild of America (WGA), the Screen Actors Guild (SAG), the American Federation of Musicians (AFM) because they act as "deferred minimum compensation,"[14] helping them to remain financially afloat in periods of scant work. Residual payments, stretching out over the life of the commercial, television show, song, or other qualifying production, thus make it easier for neophytes to enter the industry—a little work, even at minimum scale, goes a long way if it gets reused.[15] Payment on work produced under residual regimes "continues as long as the product continues to be sold."[16]

The residual system has become linked to a subjective sense of authorship and ownership, even though, as employees, talent guild members are legally alienated through work for hire. As an officer of the AFM told me, "the creativity level with musicians is high enough that even the playing of somebody else's material, the interpretation of it, is considered an intellectual property," that is, a work of authorship. According to this industry veteran, residual agreements between guilds and companies are "based on the fact that nobody, really, can totally *buy* someone else's intellectual property, [that] there's always a thread leading back to that original person."[17] This (mis)understanding reflects a subjective interpretation of *structural* dimensions of cultural industry work at this highly skilled level. Back-up musicians' idea that their contributions to recorded songs are their individual "intellectual propert[ies]" that "nobody, really, can totally *buy*" suggests the experience of authorship even where there is no legal authorship.

Television and film writers also exhibit an authorial self-understanding, expressed through rhetorics of creativity, responsibility, and sometimes even of authorial ownership. Like studio musicians, writers affiliated with the WGA are alienated through work for hire. However, writers have won back some of the rights that copyright law reserves for employers through collective action. These are called "separated rights" because they have been separated from the "bundle of rights" vested in authors (or employers) by copyright. They include the right to a first rewrite of material in production, the right to perform revisions after major elements of the material have been changed by producers or other writers, rights to be credited in certain ways, and the right to reacquire a script that has gone unproduced for a specified amount of time.[18] Separated rights limit the alienation of writers and support a strong sense of authorship.

Writers' sense of authorship was evident during the 2007–2008 WGA strike. The strike primarily concerned companies' uncompensated use on the Internet of material written by WGA members. The companies had been making entire television episodes and feature films available on the Internet, with advertising, without making reuse payments to the writers. Network and studio executives, represented by the Association of Motion Picture and Television Producers (AMPTP), argued that this was "promotional" use that did not constitute programming and therefore did not trigger reuse payments. The WGA argued the contrary position from many angles, and made extensive use of rhetorics of creativity, responsibility, and property.

Under the aegis of "United Hollywood" writers and their supporters publicized the strike and their concerns through the production and Internet dissemination of short videos of one to ten minutes.[19] Many were reports from the picket line, featuring writers and their families, SAG actors, politicians, union officers and fans; others were comedic and/or educational; some pored over the labor history of the WGA; all argued that the AMPTP was cheating writers out of reuse income to which they were entitled. The WGA members and their supporters made explicit statements about the creativity and responsibility of writers in many of the picket-line videos. A writer for *The Daily Show* remarked that the strike "is about whether writers should get paid when media companies make money using *their work* online."[20] David Lindelof, writer for the television show *Lost*, argued that the writers seek "a small residual in exchange for *our creations* as people stream them and download them."[21]

Profits and profit sharing were also topics of explicit comment. Jason Alexander, formerly of *Seinfeld*, was clear: "This is all about profits, this is not about salaries … It's about profit participation, and it's about high time that this guild in particular start to see some profits from what they do."[22] LA city council member Bill Rosendahl told an outdoor crowd that "We're having a great time in the industry right now. Profits are up. Those profits need to be shared with the *people who create the product*."[23] Terry George, writer of the film *Hotel Rwanda*, made explicit the resemblance of residual rights to author rights. He told writers, supporters, and press at a Hollywood rally that "our work is the basis of their profit and that we should participate in it. This is about royalties, it's about copyright, and it's about residuals."[24] In other words, the strike (and the Internet) provided a platform for writers to articulate their sense of themselves as *natural* authors unfairly denied rights attaching to *legal* authorship. The 2007–2008 WGA strike lasted several months and resulted in Internet rules that favor writers: companies must now pay residuals on non-promotional material used on the Internet (the new contract is very specific in its definitions of what is and is not promotional).[25]

Above-the-line residuals link separated rights, conceptions of authorship, and employer obligations and result in individual, royalty-like payments collected from companies and disbursed to members by the guilds. Below-the-line workers also benefit from residuals payments but they do so collectively, through enhancements to benefits rather than direct payments.

Below the Line

Below-the-line residuals are calculated based on the annual revenues of entertainment industry companies and are made by companies directly to union health and pension funds under the umbrella of the International Alliance of Theatrical and Stage Employees (IATSE). Workers qualify for these benefits by meeting criteria such as working a certain number of hours in a year. Therefore, while below-the-line residuals play an important role in economic stability and social mobility, they do not play such an important role in keeping open the lower rungs of the occupational ladder or in recognizing and reinforcing a sense of authorship in the way that above-the-line residuals do. Moreover, the below-the-line status of many demonstrably creative workers—such as animation storyboard artists—denies them official recognition of their creative work.[26]

Animation storyboard artists provide an example of the patent creativity of much below-the-line work; they are crucial to the development of characters and stories, particularly in animated films (although this is sometimes also the case in animation for television). These below-the-line "technical" workers contribute a great deal of new material as they develop animated films and television shows.[27] As one storyboard artist told me,

> We're doing more than storyboarding, we're sort of getting to know the characters and sometimes we'll add dialogue in, so then it starts getting into the gray area, like with [a major animated film], and a lot of the artists, the storyboard artists, came up with the gags that made people laugh, but at the same point then the writers are being paid a lot of money and it's their name, so people think that the writers wrote all these gags and funny stuff.[28]

As *employed* creative workers they are alienated through work for hire, and as *below-the-line* employees they are denied storytelling credit and individual residuals. In part to compensate for animation artists' exclusion from authorship and above-the-line privileges, and to keep these highly creative workers coming back every day to their sometimes sixty- to eighty-hours-per-week jobs, major animation studios offer unusual amenities. One major Burbank studio offers a free commissary and free massages all day. But despite their routine dispossession and designation as "technical" rather than "creative," what seems to underpin artists' "consent" (to use the language of labor sociology[29]) is the opportunity to use their artistic and storytelling skills in meaningful ways in their professional work, to fulfill their sense of themselves as "authors."

The storyboard artists I interviewed said that neither the long hours nor their supervisors' tantrums were the most unpleasant aspects of their jobs. Worse than that were the occasions when they were required simply to act as drawing machines with no freedom to exercise their creative abilities. Respondents used the term "wrist" to describe the heightened degrees of alienation they experienced when they were asked *not* to create new material. One artist told me that her supervisors were

> not looking for your creative input, they just want you to draw what they tell you to draw. They don't give you much freedom to come up with ideas. [It's] almost where they know exactly what they want, and [they don't] want you to mess with it, so you just draw it. That's what a wrist is, it's not the wrist with the brain, it's just the wrist.[30]

When storyboard artists are supported in making investments in the story and characters, they are generally more happy to provide "non-proprietary" authorial work.[31] Conversely, when their contributions are overlooked or shot down, some storyboard artists take it quite hard:

> It's tough because if you're an artist, then you've always been able to draw and it's been very much a part of who you are and your identity and what you're good at and very intertwined with your whole emotional self. So when you're doing it for a living and you're getting criticized, it's not just criticizing your work, it's criticizing *you, you're* the failure and it's very tough on you, you get depressed about it and it can put you in a very down mood.[32]

When directors and producers require storyboard artists to subjugate their authorial sensibilities and become mere transcribers, or subject them to sometimes withering criticism, these creative workers struggle with their commitments to their employers, and sometimes with their choice of profession.

Where above-the-line workers are explicitly designated "creative" and entitled to reuse payments that reinforce their sense of authorship, their below-the-line "technical" colleagues do not have these privileges. However, through organizing and collective bargaining, below-the-line workers have secured significant social and economic security—healthcare, the possibility of a comfortable retirement, and the ability to enjoy these benefits no matter which (signatory) employer they work for at any given time—that are generally not available to workers who are not members of unions.

Further Distinctions between Strata of Media Workers

Two additional categories of animation workers provide examples of further distinctions between cultural industry workers: those who work in non-union US studios, and those who work in "offshore" studios such as those in North and South Korea, the People's Republic of China, and India.

Some major non-union studios also devote significant resources to maintaining consent and keeping their workers returning to ambiguous, high-pressure work environments every day. But where *collective* bargaining agreements protect the security of work and benefits on the basis of unionized workers' power collectively to withhold their labor, workers at non-union studios only get the security and benefits for which they are *individually* powerful enough to bargain. One freelance animation designer told me about a co-worker

> [w]ho was really down for a couple weeks there because his art reviews weren't going well. He was drawing characters and the producer and the art director didn't like them, and he was thinking "fuck, this can't go on this much longer and you know, me continue to work here." I mean, he can get away with a couple weeks getting them wrong, but you know, eventually, if he keeps doing things that the producer doesn't like, he's going to be put onto another film or let go.[33]

This respondent points out the stark vulnerability of non-union workers to arbitrary treatment based on whether or not a worker can please his or her superiors. His co-worker experienced anxiety about the security of his job based on his dependence on the art director's subjective evaluation of his drawings. If the art director decides the drawings aren't to his or her liking, the artist could be shifted to another project or simply laid off. Under the Animators Guild contract, on the other hand, if an artist is not producing work that supervisors like, then employers are constrained from laying off workers. In most circumstances, employers are required to put the artist onto another project, even if that means investing in retraining. An employer who is not a signatory to the Animators Guild contract has no obligation to their employed artists beyond what those artists can individually command; only rarely can individuals command terms similar to those of union contracts.

Still less privileged are those cultural industry workers residing in Mainland China or South or North Korea. The US and Europe have been outsourcing animation production work to Asia since the 1960s; the trend really took off in the late 1970s, and has played an increasingly important role in animation production for the US and global markets ever since.[34] The reason is simple: US and European studios find cheap, skilled, and obedient labor in abundance. According to the owner of Film Roman, the largest independent television animation studio in the US and producer of *The Simpsons*, "[i]f we had to do animation here, it would cost a million dollars instead of $100,000 to $150,000 to produce a half hour, and nobody could afford to do it except for Disney."[35] Animation personnel at one studio that John Lent studied go to work seven days a week (with paid overtime), but "their only time off is a short vacation at Lunar New Year." Conditions are very different from those in the US and Europe: "[b]ecause of the scarcity of job opportunities and, in some cases, anti-union or anti-strike legislation, Asian animation workers usually do not strike or cause upheavals and stoppages."[36] In many cases, animation workers are paid quite well relative to their neighbors working in other sectors, yet, according to Zou Quin, an animator who had worked for both a Chinese state animation house as well as a private offshore studio, "it is brainless work. The workers are exploited. When they asked the boss for more money, he said okay, but you have to work harder. They stopped requesting pay increases."[37]

Guy Delisle is an animation professional who has documented his experiences as a supervisor in both Mainland China and North Korea in two (literally) graphic works, *Shenzhen* and *Pyongyang*.[38] These works offer testimony regarding the situations of the Asian animation personnel and the North American and European supervisors who carry out the dictates of globalized cultural production. In North Korea, Delisle is closely monitored by a government translator/handler with whom he reports having some telling interactions (see below).[39]

In this interaction, the repressive state apparatus—that makes it possible for US and European cultural industry companies to take advantage of extremely low labor costs in politically unfree countries like North Korea—becomes eerily visible to Delisle.

Conclusion

In this chapter I suggested that both *structural* and *subjective* aspects of working conditions be taken into account in studies of production. I argued that the differential allocation of privileges and the correlating distinctions that play important roles in determining working conditions are not based on measurable differences of creativity or responsibility, but that they result from specific confrontations in the realms of legislation, the courts, and collective bargaining. I presented modes

Figure 4.1 "Where is this super animator?" (Created by Guy Delisle, courtesy of *Drawn and Quarterly*, 2008).

of cultural industry worker stratification in order not only to show how privilege and distinction operate in production worlds, but also to draw attention to the constructedness of the definitions (of "author" and "non-author," of "creative" and "technical") that provide their justification. Starting with authorship, I suggested that these distinctions do not *reflect* observable, noncontroversial differences in creativity, but that they actually serve to *produce* and/or *sustain* particular (im)balances of power. Ending with "offshored" cultural labor in politically unfree societies, I hope to have convinced the reader of the relevance of these modes of stratification for understanding commercially organized cultural production.

Critical scholars rarely tie studies of media creativity back to the sorts of determining structural and legal precedents outlined in this chapter and thus tend rarely to question the legitimacy of existing institutions such as authorship, work for hire, or the above-the-line/below-the-line distinction, and individualized, global "free" labor. The media researcher's refusal to accept existing institutions as "desirable" or "natural" or even "fixed" simply because they exist, and his or her willingness to dig into the structures of privilege and distinction in the worlds in which culture is produced—in other words, into legislative, judicial, and labor relations contests over issues of property and power—fosters the development of a critical perspective. Such a perspective requires that we recognize that struggles over power and property are ongoing, unresolved, and perhaps not ultimately susceptible to final resolution; it holds that established institutions and relations need not be accepted as legitimate or fixed, and that they can be changed.

Notes

1 David Hesmondhalgh, *The Cultural Industries*, 2nd ed. (London: Sage, 2007).
2 I generally use the term "privileges" where it is often customary to use "rights" in order to highlight the difference between authorial or bargained-for rights and universalist democratic rights.
3 Catherine Fisk, "Authors at Work: The Origins of the Work-For-Hire Doctrine," *Yale Journal of Law and the Humanities* 15, no. 1 (2003): 32–70.
4 Ibid., 11–32.
5 Marci Hamilton, "Commissioned Works as Works Made for Hire under the 1976 Copyright Act: Misinterpretation and Injustice," *University of Pennsylvania Law Review* 135 (1987): 1291–1293.
6 Johanna Fisher Stewart, "The Freelancer's Trap: Work for Hire Under the Copyright Act of 1976," *West Virginia Law Review* 86 (1984): 1306.
7 Geoff Hull, *The Recording Industry*, 2nd ed. (New York: Routledge, 2004), 39.
8 Stewart, "The Freelancer's Trap," 1306 (emphasis added).
9 Alan Paul and Archie Kleingartner, "Flexible Production and the Transformation of Industrial Relations in the Motion Picture and Television Industry," *Industrial and Labor Relations Review* 47, no. 4 (1994): 669–670.
10 On below-the-line working conditions in the film industry, see *Who Needs Sleep?* DVD, directed by Haskell Wexler (The Institute for Cinema Studies, 2008).
11 Alan Paul and Archie Kleingartner, "The Transformation of Industrial Relations in the Motion Picture and Television Industries: The Talent Sector," in *Under the Stars: Essays on Labor Relations in Arts and Entertainment*, eds. Lois Gray and Ronald Seeber (Ithaca: ILR Press, 1996), 161, n. 3. Paul and Kleingartner do not question the industry's distinctions between "creative" and "technical."
12 Paul and Kleingartner, "Flexible Production," 669.
13 Writers Guild of America, West, "Residuals Survival Guide," July 10, 2004, http://wga.org/.
14 Paul and Kleingartner, "Flexible Production," 672.
15 Ibid., 671.
16 Ibid., 669.
17 Matthew Stahl, "Non-Proprietary Authorship and the Uses of Autonomy: Artistic Labor in American Film Animation, 1900–2004," *Labor: Studies in Working-Class History of the Americas* 2, no. 4 (2005): 98.

18 Writers Guild of America, West, "Creative Rights for Writers of Theatrical and Long-Form Television Motion Pictures," and "Understanding Separated Rights," September 3, 2008, http://www.wga.org.

19 Examples can be found on the website YouTube (http://youtube.com) under the sites for videos made by "wgaamerica" and "wgadottorg."

20 TDSwriters, *Not The Daily Show, With Some Writer* (Writers Guild of America, 2007) 4 min., 24 sec.; from http://www.youtube.com (accessed September 2, 2008).

21 Wgaamerica, *Lost & Desperate* (Writers Guild of America, 2007) 1 min., 35 sec.; from http://www.youtube.com (accessed September 2, 2008).

22 Wgaamerica, *Which Side Are You On?* (Writers Guild of America, 2007) 7 min., 45 sec.; from http://www.youtube.com (accessed September 2, 2008).

23 Wgaamerica, *California Officials Picket CBS* (Writers Guild of America, 2007) 5 min.; from http://www.youtube.com (accessed September 2, 2008).

24 Wgaamerica, *International Solidarity Day—Terry George* (Writers Guild of America, 2007) 2 min., 38 sec.; from http://www.youtube.com (accessed September 2, 2008).

25 On the emergence and contemporary concerns of above- and below-the-line guilds and unions, see Douglas Gomery, *The Hollywood Studio System: A History* (London: BFI Publishing, 2005), 185–197, 299–308. Important details from the new WGA contract can be found on the guild's website: http://www.wga.org/subpage_member.aspx?id=2204.

26 For a discussion of animation workers' failure to take advantage of an organizing opportunity that could have brought them individual, above-the-line residuals, see Tom Sito, *Drawing the Line: The Untold Story of the Animation Unions from Bosko to Bart Simpson* (Lexington, KY: University Press of Kentucky, 2006), 240–244.

27 Stahl, "Non-Proprietary Authorship," 99–102.

28 Ibid., 100.

29 On consent in the workplace see Michael Burawoy's discussion of the "securing and obscuring of surplus value," *Manufacturing Consent: Changes in the Labor Process under Monopoly Capitalism* (Chicago: University of Chicago Press, 1979), 25–30.

30 Stahl, "Non-Proprietary Authorship," 101.

31 Ibid., 99.

32 Ibid., 102.

33 Freelance animation visualization artist, interview with the author, October 15, 2004.

34 John Lent, "Overseas Animation Production in Asia," in *Animation in Asia and the Pacific*, ed. John Lent (Bloomington: Indiana University Press, 2001), 239–245.

35 Ibid., 240.

36 Ibid., op. cit.

37 Ibid., 243.

38 Guy Delisle, *Pyongyang* (Montreal: Drawn and Quarterly, 2005); Guy Delisle, *Shenzhen* (Montreal: Drawn and Quarterly, 2006).

39 Delisle, *Pyongyang*, 91.

Part II

Producers: Selves and Others

Figure 5.1 Entourage Press Line. Photo by John Caldwell, 2007.

Chapter 5

Self-Serve Celebrity

The Production of Ordinariness and the Ordinariness of Production in Reality Television

Laura Grindstaff

In the late 1990s I spent several years doing participant-observation on two nationally televised daytime talk shows; besides working as a production assistant behind the scenes, I conducted more than eighty interviews with both producers and the "ordinary" people who appeared on the shows as guests. I was interested in the process by which people who are not professional experts or celebrities are brought into televisual discourse: what strategies are deployed to "produce" them, why they participate, and what the terms of their participation reveal about relations of inequality—particularly class inequality—in the United States.[1] Currently I am researching a new project on reality television, the centerpiece of which is the MTV series *Sorority Life*. MTV filmed its debut season of the show at UC Davis, where I teach. Consequently, I have been able to interview a dozen of the young women involved in the filming, including those who played starring roles, with an eye to some of the same concerns about representation and inequality addressed in my earlier work.

   What I offer here is an exploration of these two case studies as a way to reflect on what it means to produce "ordinariness" in a television context. By "context" I mean not just the fact that shows are broadcast and viewed on television but also that television itself exists in a multimedia, multimediated environment in which the participation of "real people" is increasingly common. Although the trend toward reality TV arguably has more to do with the political economy of the media industries—including neoliberal labor policies—than with anything else,[2] it nevertheless presents new opportunities for getting on screen, and new challenges for producing television. The reality trend also has implications for how scholars think about media visibility and celebrity for specific social groups. For the talk shows I studied, which I named *Randy* and *Diana*, ordinariness was constructed primarily as a class-based concept: the "best" guests were not only forthcoming about the personal details of their lives, but also willing to "play" themselves with a maximum of emotional and physical expressiveness in ways that reinforced prevailing class-based cultural stereotypes. On *Sorority Life* the gendered dimensions of ordinariness take center stage, with producers and participants co-constructing narratives of white femininity revolving around issues of heteronormative attractiveness and sexual display. In exploring why "ordinary" people desire television exposure, I complicate what celebrity means in the reality-TV context and challenge its characterization by critics as a mere "politics of the self,"[3] the ultimate expression of self-absorption.

Taken together, then, these two case studies provide a lens through which to examine the social and cultural dynamics of reality programming—particularly as understood from the perspective of "ordinary" character-participants, the group most neglected by scholars of the genre. While academic studies of reality TV have multiplied along with the number of shows themselves, the vast majority examine the political-economic forces behind the genre, the politics of representation as they play out on individual shows, or select fan activity as accessed online. By contrast, my scholarship is informed by a tradition of research in sociology often labeled "the production of culture school." The analytic thrust of this tradition is a focus on "how the symbolic elements of culture are shaped by the systems within which they are created, distributed, evaluated, taught, and preserved."[4]

The particular strands of production-of-culture research that have been especially useful to me as an ethnographer are those that explore, in an interpretive but empirically grounded manner, the nature of the reality constructed and disseminated by media institutions as well as the specific processes by which this construction takes place.[5] Drawing on first-hand engagement with different genres of reality television, I take seriously the anthropological injunction that "culture is good to think with," asking who has access to mass-media stardom, who/what shapes media production practices, and how these practices promote certain versions of reality over others. I am interested both in the representations of "ordinariness" produced for audiences and in the ordinariness of the production process itself. The former has less to do with averageness or typicality than with finding individuals who fulfill particular genre demands, demands shaped by the same cultural stereotypes of gender, race, class, etc. governing much traditional dramatic programming; the latter relates to the everyday life skills of emotion-management that production staff bring to their jobs. I introduce the notion of "self-service television" to capture the ways in which these two dimensions intersect: producers engage in emotion-work in order to orchestrate potentially dramatic situations—i.e., they erect the physical and emotional scaffolding out of which "good" performances emerge—so that so-called ordinary people can deliver "good" drama to audiences. Hopefully one outcome of this analysis is to encourage greater self-reflexivity about what it means to be both a producer and an "ordinary" person in the era of reality programming.

Producing Ordinary People

As John Caldwell so richly documents, the very concept of production is complex in the postnetwork industrial moment because of technological developments coupled with increasingly unstable business and labor relations.[6] The rise and proliferation of daytime talk shows (*Geraldo*, *Maury Povich*, *Sally Jessy Raphael*, *Ricki Lake*, *Jenny Jones*, *Jerry Springer*, etc.) in the 1990s occurred at the cusp of the "old" and "new" eras of television, as the dominance of the original networks crumbled under federal deregulation policies and increasing competition from cable and satellite companies. Although talk shows aired on basic cable stations and followed a more or less traditional production format (with above-the-line creative staff and below-the-line technical staff working in more or less traditional roles in large studios), they also presaged the reality-programming trend of the next century by relying on "real" people as talent and incorporating emergent notions of audience interactivity via live studio audiences, phone-in response lines, and web-based fan sites. At the height of the talk-show boom in the late 1990s, the period in which I conducted my research, there were twenty different talk shows on the air and competition for ratings was fierce. Gone were the "nice" days of *Donahue*, in which well-heeled, middle-class guests debated whether white families should adopt black children; instead, audiences watched "trashy" guests deliver the "money shot" on episodes with such titles as "Mom, Stop Prostituting Me!" or "Loser, Butt Out of My Life!"[7] *Randy*, the second of the two shows on which I worked, was reputed to be the most outrageous; not coincidentally, it eclipsed even *Oprah* in the ratings in the coveted 18–35 demographic.[8]

Reality programming is to the first decade of the twenty-first century what talk shows were to the 1990s. As many scholars have observed, the term "reality TV" is something of an oxymoron; the wide range of programming that can be subsumed under the label—quiz shows, game docs, audition and dating shows, docusoaps, emergency rescue shows, etc.—are "real" only insofar as they eschew professional actors and traditional scripts.[9] Representing a loose compilation of related genres rather than a single set of conventions, reality TV has gained a strong foothold in the contemporary media landscape both in the US and abroad. According to Mark Andrejevic, reality shows are particularly well suited to global media production because they combine local casts and viewer participation with customizable transnational formulas at a fraction of the cost of traditional dramatic programming. Indeed, the unpaid labor of participants on reality shows allows producers, investors, and networks to profit enormously from lowered production costs.[10] During the first season of *American Idol* in the US, more people voted to select a winner than voted in the 2000 presidential election, while the same year the season finale of *Survivor* attracted more viewers than any other program except the Superbowl.[11] Although not as popular as *Survivor*, the original *Sorority Life* series attracted roughly two million viewers per episode.[12] Modeled after MTV's *The Real World*, the formula was straightforward: put a group of six "ordinary" women together in a house and follow along as they pledge an "ordinary" sorority, mixing observational footage with interviews.

Today, there are dozens of reality-based formats on network and cable TV, and there are even reality TV "schools" whose training programs promise to give would-be participants a competitive edge in the pursuit of media celebrity (see http:// www.newyorkrealitytvschool.com). As with daytime talk shows, interactivity is an important component, with online viewers and fans replacing the more traditional concept of studio audience. A survey commissioned by *American Demographics* reports that 25 percent of those who watch reality shows read or post messages on affiliated websites, and that among viewers who identify themselves as "avid fans" of reality TV, 75 percent do so.[13] The US version of *Big Brother*, in fact, was more popular online via live web-feeds than on "regular" television.[14]

The question then arises, who/what is a "producer" in the face of increasing media interactivity/surveillance and shifting modes of corporate control? Given the persuasive arguments of Michel de Certeau, Henry Jenkins, and others that consumption is part of, not separate from, production, the question is hardly new. But it gains purchase and complexity in the contemporary media environment. Certainly the talk-show guests I interviewed or the young women who starred in *Sorority Life* could be considered "producers" of a sort, since it is their personal lives—their actions, interactions, and experiences—that generate the drama broadcast on television. Potential "producers" also include members of a studio audience who ask questions of a guest, or viewers at home who vote contestants off a program. And what of the culture-jamming exploits of the *Big Brother* fans documented by Pamela Wilson? By managing to communicate directly with the contestants inside the official production site, these fans succeeded in influencing the narrative trajectory of the show.[15]

At the same time, heightened interactivity does not erase the asymmetry between production and consumption established during the pre-reality era. While some scholars view interactivity as a form of empowerment, it's important to remember that much online activity can be (and is) subject to surveillance and formal regulation. Moreover, the participation of viewers and audiences represents an additional source of unpaid labor from which television networks benefit. Most important for this chapter, to consider everyone a potential producer is to minimize both the power and responsibility traditional production staff exercise in the reality arena. In reality genres as in traditional dramatic programming, certain staff behind the scenes sport the designated title "producer" (or associate or assistant producer); they are tasked with specific types of work and bear particular responsibilities.

In the talk-show context, this title applies specifically to the creative personnel responsible for finding and assembling guests, crafting a coherent story out of the guests' real-life experiences, and getting the guests to perform their story with maximum emotional and physical expressiveness. Producers and associate producers typically work together in pairs, the former having greater authorial control (and taking the fall should things go wrong). Officially, both are positioned "above-the-line" in industry parlance, but the gross distinction "above" (creative) and "below" (technical) obscures the important hierarchies and distinctions operating *within* as well as between categories. The talk-show producers I observed and worked under were well aware that daytime talk—with the obvious exception of *Oprah*—was not the most prestigious of television genres. Most were young and, especially at the associate producer level, relatively inexperienced; some acquired their jobs straight out of school, typically with BAs in communications or journalism. The older (over 30) employees usually had news or documentary experience, and some had production experience at other shows within the genre. At *Randy*, a few producers were former tabloid magazine reporters. Women outnumbered men by roughly two to one, and white producers outnumbered producers of color by roughly the same ratio. Virtually everybody was looking for something "better" and most saw their current positions as stepping-stones to more lucrative, prestigious careers in, preferably, primetime dramatic programming. However, I saw little evidence of such career mobility for these folks during the years I researched *The Money Shot*. Thus there are multiple types of producers—high-status Hollywood men of the sort interviewed by Caldwell or spoofed on hit shows like *Entourage* or *Curb Your Enthusiasm*—and there are producers—people who find themselves on their knees begging a gas station attendant to reconsider his decision to withdraw from the show moments before taping is scheduled to begin.

I have less direct knowledge of the producers for the MTV series *Sorority Life*, since my data for this second case comes primarily from the character-participants themselves. What I do know, though, is that above-the-line producers figured less prominently in the day-to-day lives of the participants during the course of filming the series than did the camera and sound operators—below-the-line workers who nevertheless took on some of the same functions as the above-the-line producers I worked alongside in the talk-show arena. In the observational mode of reality TV, those recording action on the fly rather than those constructing storylines from behind the scenes form the ever-present backdrop against which participants play their roles. In this context, camera operators as well as the regular production staff work in a producer-like way to construct the structural conditions for encouraging or discouraging particular types of performances. By extension, the camera itself becomes a subjective element with a productive function—a "tool that means," to borrow a phrase from Caldwell.[16]

In what sense is production "ordinary"? Producers themselves, not surprisingly, tend to characterize their work as anything *but* ordinary. Those in the talk-show business emphasize the chaotic, improvisational nature of the production process and the gutsy, even heroic qualities necessary to succeed—the result of the fact that talk-show guests are not (or not supposed to be) professional actors, so a good performance is never guaranteed. Just as below-the-line technical staff in Holly-wood tell war stories to make (positive) sense of their work worlds in the face of technological change and economic uncertainty,[17] talk-show producers, too, craft narratives suggesting that, despite the low status of the genre and its decep-tively simple format, getting real people to deliver the money shot on television is not as easy as it might seem. As Caldwell notes, such production discourses are themselves cultural performances that strengthen ties among workers as well as justify/legitimate the work to others.[18]

Talk-show producers are certainly correct that a tension between scriptedness and spontaneity structures their activities behind the scenes—as it does, to varying degrees, the activities of virtually all creative staff employed in reality-based media. "Real" people are targeted, ostensibly, for their lack of specialized media training; moreover, their cues for behavior—for crafting characters and storylines—are typically embedded in situations (and in other characters) rather than encoded in formal scripts, and this looseness creates considerable uncertainty for producers. In the case of talk shows, uncertainty is exacerbated by the particular ways ordinariness is defined and the types of people chosen to personify it.

Guests are "ordinary" not only because they lack professional expert or celebrity credentials, but also because they are experiencing some problem or crisis—which is why they respond to on-air plugs soliciting their participation and why producers find their stories compelling. In the media as in the culture at large, "realness" or "ordinariness" signifies misfortune or disadvantage more readily than prosperity or privilege; statistical averageness or typicality has little to do with it.[19] Paradoxically, this construction of ordinariness helps maximize both the probability of emotional expressiveness and the unpredictability associated with it—a situation further complicated by the emphasis on surprise encounters and confrontations on talk shows, which requires producers to minimize pretaping interaction with unsuspecting guests (to avoid giving away the surprise) but prevents them from developing a sense of the guest as a performer. How, then, to guarantee good (that is, dramatic) television using ordinary people? The normative route for both talk shows and reality programs has been to cultivate conflict situations, but this, too, creates production problems if participants quit or become too unruly to manage.

And yet the specific techniques and strategies that producers draw upon to produce the sort of ordinariness prized by reality television *are* quite ordinary in the sense that they rely on the everyday life skills of emotion management. The concept of emotion management, or emotion work, has been theorized most thoroughly by sociologist Arlie Hochschild.[20] She argues that emotional expressions can be understood as mediums of exchange and that people work on their emotions in light of taken-for-granted assumptions about what it is appropriate to feel (and convey) in a given situation. "Emotion work" thus refers to the act of trying to change in degree or quality an emotion or feeling according to latent social guidelines. When feelings are commodified and exchanged as an aspect of labor power in the workplace, *emotion work* becomes *emotional labor*.

Not surprisingly, emotion work traditionally has been better understood and more often used by dependent women of the middle classes as one of the offerings they trade for male economic support. As for others of low status, emotion work has had high "secondary gains" for women outside as well as inside the home (consider female-dominated occupations such as nursing, social work, waitressing, or caregiving). Studies show that, generally speaking, women tend to be more adaptive and cooperative than men and when women resist these behaviors they risk being labeled "unfeminine." This is not to say men are immune to emotion work; however, among the middle classes, they are more likely to manage feeling in order to persuade, enforce rules, or secure compliance while women manage feeling in the service of, in Hochschild's words, "making nice."[21] Of course, when their jobs do require men to make nice, men may find themselves performing emotional labor in "feminine" ways. Indeed, in the postindustrial low-wage service economy, gender, class, or race categories are less the issue than the persistence of status hierarchies in which workers of all sorts—albeit not independently of these categories—make a special resource out of feeling.

In the talk-show arena, where most producers are middle-class white women, there are clues to the emotion work embedded in the production process in the metaphors they employ to describe their work. There are two general types. What I call *orchestration metaphors* refer to the overall process of pulling a show together (producing a talk-show is like planning a wedding, throwing a big dinner party, cooking a complicated meal with many ingredients, or, in the case of *Randy*, running a three-ring circus) while *interaction metaphors* refer to various aspects of finding and working with guests. Depending on the talk-show and specific episodes being produced, interaction metaphors can evoke intimacy/domesticity (initial contact with guests as a "blind date" and subsequent contact as "courting" or "babysitting") or they can evoke control and aggressivity (producers "go hunting" or "dumpster diving" for guests, deliver "locker-room pep talks" to keep them committed, and act as "lion tamer" or "referee" during performances). The overarching metaphor I use in *The Money Shot* obviously comes from film pornography: producers "fluff" guests so the guests can "show wood" to audiences. The resulting money shot can be soft-core or hard-core, depending on the show.

The emotional labor intimated by these metaphors is extensive, and hardly optional; it's fundamental to the construction and success of reality-based genres. Talk-show producers must establish a personal connection with guests, learn about guests' (troubled) lives, listen to their heartaches and complaints, and persuade, persuade, persuade—persuade guests to participate, stay committed to participating, and follow through with an expressive performance, all under the pressure of deadlines and the relentless pace of the production process. Not surprisingly, burnout is common. Producers spoke of their work variously as exhausting, exhilarating, frustrating, and heart-wrenching; they had to constantly monitor and manage their own feelings and emotional displays in order to manage the feelings and emotional displays of others. Sometimes the feelings were "genuine," involving what Hochschild calls "deep acting," and sometimes they were consciously put on, the result of "surface acting." Either way, their emotional labor positioned production staff as "ordinary" workers using the "ordinary" life skills of emotion management, despite the extra-ordinariness of what they produced.

As for *Sorority Life* and other "docusoap" reality shows, one could argue that participants here, too, bare their "private parts" in public, just according to a different logic of performance. And while participants did not speak of being "hunted" or "fluffed" specifically, their accounts of how producers (and other production staff) secured their participation and shaped their performances point to some strikingly similar forms of emotional labor—the main difference being that this labor is dispersed across different categories of workers rather than limited to those bearing the title "producer" per se.

The production of *Sorority Life* involved mobile camera crews documenting every action of the young women who lived in the Pledge House, as well as key participants in the sisterhood of the featured sorority. Filming took place over the course of a ten-week academic term, during which time the sorority held several rush events, fourteen young women were chosen to pledge the sorority (only six of whom lived under surveillance in the House), and the pledge process itself unfolded. Hundreds of hours of footage were shot to compile thirteen half-hour episodes. The sorority, "Sigma," was a small, Jewish-themed organization attractive to MTV largely because it was not affiliated with the National Panhellenic Conference (PNC) and thus not bound by PNC's prohibitions on media exposure. (Consistent with MTV's preferred construction of "ordinary" sorority life, the matter of its Jewishness was never addressed in the series, except during the first episode when several rushees admitted to knowing nothing about Judaism. The sisters I spoke to also downplayed the religious dimension, for the sorority was not exclusive and typically handed out bids to all women wanting to pledge regardless of religious affiliation.) The sisterhood, initially divided over whether to be filmed, ultimately voted to do the show because they were proud of their small organization and wanted to give it the visibility they felt it deserved.

Not surprisingly, when the show aired, it was not a heartwarming representation of communal harmony. Overall, the series showcased a great deal of drinking and partying (two of the pledges celebrated their 21st birthdays on the show), and considerable bickering, including one bar scene in which a pledge accuses a sorority sister of acting "slutty" and gets slapped in the face. Scenes of the sisters and pledges getting along together were relatively rare, as were scenes of the women studying, doing community service, or performing philanthropic sorority activities—despite the fact that, during the course of the filming, all of these activities occurred. The show was entirely consistent with the "girls gone wild" image of American sororities that the members of Sigma told me they so badly wanted to avoid. Certain pledges, having no similar attachment to the organization, naturally cared less than the sisters about monitoring their own behavior. Moreover, five of the six pledges who lived in the House—chosen for this privilege by the show's executive producer rather than the sorority, after the sorority had accepted their bids—were clearly targeted for their "camera-friendly" qualities. All were young and attractive college students; five of the six were white (three blond, two brunette). The one woman of color, a Latina student, was physically larger than the rest and entered the Pledge House at the last minute, as a replacement for a girl who withdrew.

Like the talk-show guests I studied, the pledges and sisters had varied motivations for participating (more on this later) and therefore required somewhat different kinds and levels of emotional labor from production staff. Getting Sigma to sign on for the project, for example, was a hard sell. Like any good talk-show producer working on a family of reluctant guests, the executive producer of *Sorority Life* targeted those who favored participation and who were influential within the group. (According to the sisters I interviewed, he sympathized with their concerns about television exposure and with their desire to challenge negative stereotypes of Greek life; he claimed to be a former fraternity brother himself.) Ultimately, of course, it was for the women to decide, and in the end the supporters won out on the belief that they could, if they were careful, control their own representation. Two of the pledges were similarly hesitant, committed to the sorority but not to the idea of twenty-four-hour surveillance. They required persistent "courting" on the part of producers, including frequent visits, lengthy personal conversations, and reminders of the material goods awaiting them: laptops, cell phones, clothing, cosmetics, and free housing for the term in the Ikea-inspired Pledge House, complete with outdoor swimming pool. As it turned out, during the course of filming, the pledges also took trips to Lake Tahoe and Las Vegas, at least partially funded by the production company.

Any suggestion here of heterosexual dating is not coincidental. Talking with the pledges about their experience of the production process, I was struck by its aura of sexual/romantic intimacy. Because of the show's premise, there was no central casting call or audition process—participants had to be chosen from the existing sorority and from the pool of young women who chose to rush it. Accordingly, producers, both male and female, scoured local bars and restaurants looking for "hotties" to whom they could promote the upcoming rush events. At these events, which served as de facto audition sessions, producers identified certain women as especially promising and subsequently pursued them with phone calls, encouraging them to continue rushing the sorority. Ultimately, however, the pool of potential pledges emerging from the rush process was small because the sorority was small and relatively unknown; as a consequence, the power relations of an MTV casting were reversed, with producers having to entice participants rather than the other way around.[22]

Once in the house, the six pledges saw little of the executive producer; it was the mobile camera crews who figured most prominently in the day-to-day filming of the show. There were four crews, each consisting of a camera operator, a sound person, a producer/director, and sometimes a production assistant. With one exception, the below-the-line technical posts (camera and sound) were occupied by men while the producer roles were not gender-specific. The result was a traditional dynamic in which the pledges were positioned as the female subjects/objects of a largely male gaze. The cameras were their shadows, watching them as they talked, ate, took a nap, applied lipstick, or read a book, as they shopped for groceries or school supplies, as they carried out their sorority obligations, and, especially, as they danced and drank at local clubs. All the women said they grew accustomed to the cameras with time but never forgot they were there. None could carry on a normal romantic relationship and yet, in the words of one pledge, "we were constantly surrounded by all these hunky [camera]men."

Although the pledges were forbidden to acknowledge the camera crews during filming, they got unequivocal emotional cues from different crew members about their performances in the form of yawning, frowning, or looking bored, or, conversely, smiling or looking interested or sympathetic. According to one pledge, "I always had in the back of my mind, 'okay, don't be boring' ... I felt some unseen pressure to be not boring ... it's insane having cameras around you all the time." This same pledge felt that, in retrospect, her excessive partying was largely an escape from the pressures of being watched, because alcohol helped her care less about the cameras (and, secondarily, her behavior). Obviously this was good for producers, too, which is why, according to my interviewees, they never failed to pick up the tab. To follow through on the dating metaphor, producers in this scenario are taking on the familiar (male) role of plying the girl with drinks so she'll relax and "put out."

There is much more to say about the ordinariness of the production process, but I will simply reiterate that the emotional labor discussed here, while not unique to talk shows or reality shows, is nevertheless an outcome of working with "real" people rather than professional celebrities. Incorporating ordinary people into entertainment television places enormous pressure on producers to simultaneously cultivate individual *performers* and to create/control the *performative context*—that is, to erect the conditions of possibility for maximizing emotional expressiveness. In the case of talk shows and reality shows, this emotional scaffolding is built on familiar cultural scripts (white trash guests, girls-gone-wild sorority pledges) which in turn allow guests to "serve themselves" to their performances. In other words, because the performances of reality participants are largely "ready-made" by the structural conditions of their participation, which in turn draw upon familiar cultural clichés, they can "serve themselves" to their roles without the benefit of extensive training, scripts, rehearsals, or extensive negotiations with directors. Emotion work is essential to this sort of self-service television because the building blocks of expressiveness, despite being "premade," are nonetheless porous and their enactment sometimes unstable. Participants might resist the script and the conditions that subtend them—as when a guest or participant refuses to emote on camera—reminding us that, as much as producers prepare the set, it is real people—not professional actors—who must carry the scene.

Self-Serve Celebrity

As much as producers like to complain about the unpredictability of working with ordinary people, the business is generally less risky than they suggest because ordinary people typically know the rules of the game; the scripts they follow are familiar cultural terrain. Ironically, the "authenticity" of a character or storyline does not preclude the performance of cultural clichés; in fact, as Brian Moeran has noted, "mediated authenticity" seems to call for them.[23] This is both because of the time and space constraints that affect all media, and, as we have seen, because easily recognized templates are easy for ordinary people to enact without explicit scripting or rehearsal; as noted, such templates facilitate self-service acting. To quote Alison Hearn, "much like donning Mickey Mouse ears at Disneyland, becoming a part of the immersive television experience involves adopting a persona consonant with its dictates."[24] Given the importance of interactivity to reality-based genres, recognizable personas—the jock, the vixen, the girl next door—can hail audiences as well.[25]

Why should we care about the "ordinary" production of "ordinary" people? What of import is being produced? This chapter is not an essay on the cultural significance of reality-based media per se, but if the dimensions of emotional labor outlined here are a cause and consequence of the increasing visibility of ordinariness across the media landscape, it's worth considering the "work" being done by this visibility.

It is tempting to consider the proliferation of opportunities for media exposure for ordinary people to be an essentially democratizing force. To be sure, the more dispersed possibilities for production and distribution in the new-media era do seem to hold out the promise of a mediated public sphere less monopolized than before by traditional voices and interests. In the words of Graeme Turner, "the celebrity offered to contestants through reality TV, contestants defined for us by their ordinariness, would certainly seem to constitute a more democratic phenomenon than a celebrity based on social, economic, religious, or cultural hierarchies."[26]

At the same time, he warns, broader demographic representation does not imply a democratic politics necessarily. It matters how one defines "democratic." Although some reality programming is reported to have more social diversity than fictional programming,[27] still, compared to the overall population, the majority of the participants are young, attractive, white, straight, middle class, and able-bodied. And given the population as a whole, their actual numbers are quite small. There is also the larger political-economic context to consider, which determines the specific contours of the media landscape and circumscribes its points of access. The proliferation and expansion of industrial modes of representation might just as easily suggest, to quote Turner again, "a process of increased commodification rather than enhanced political enfranchisement."[28]

Further, it matters what one does in the so-called new mediated public sphere. Bickering with your in-laws or humiliating your ex-spouse is not the same as arguing the merits of welfare reform. Of course, there is room for both discourses on television, but the issue is *who* gets associated with *what*. While virtually everyone gains media visibility by submitting to the implicit rules and dictates of the industry, not all conditions of entry are equal: the more invisible people are within mainstream media—by virtue of their political actions or convictions, physical attractiveness, educational credentials, occupation, age, class status, sexuality, race, or gender—the higher the price of admission is likely to be. Hierarchy doesn't disappear just because ordinary people are now invited to play the game. Television is not and never has been a forum for expressing the interests and urgencies of ordinary people as such since the very conditions that subtend their entry into the discourse always transform them into something else—and this "something else" typically reinscribes preexisting inequalities.

Given the persistence of inequality, it is important to ask what draws ordinary people to participate in the various discourses of television, and to distinguish between media exposure and media celebrity. My backstage production experience with talk shows taught me that the motivations of ordinary people for media exposure vary widely, and that only sometimes is the desire for celebrity part of the mix. When people have an ax to grind, a cause to champion, or a life-changing experience to share, wanting to impart information or have one's feelings/experiences publicly validated may outweigh considerations of stardom or fame. In such cases, the "communicative" as opposed to the "ritual" function of media tends to hold sway.[29] Of course, different sets of desires can operate simultaneously since one's efforts to, say, champion a cause might well be enhanced by achieving celebrity status. This is not to say talk-show guests are indifferent to media celebrity, only that the lure of celebrity is conceptually impure, often enmeshed with other motivations and concerns. As important is the desire to feel important and special, regardless of any media-related outcome. Particularly for the poor and working-class guests on the talk shows I studied, being flown across the country, chauffeured around in a limousine, put up in a four-star hotel, and placed at the center of intensive production efforts was reward enough. Here, the desire to be part of the machinery of television is less communicative than ritualistic, less a matter of stardom or fame per se than of existential validation in ways normally off-limits to them. This strikes me as an entirely ordinary concern, the extra-ordinariness of their performances notwithstanding.

With observational/surveillance forms of television, participation appears to be more squarely motivated by financial and/or celebrity considerations. There may be prize money involved (as in the case of gamedocs like *Survivor* or *Big Brother*), opportunities for product endorsements or lecture circuits, and even ongoing media exposure and recording contracts (as in the case of some *American Idol* participants). These outcomes are rare, of course, particularly on a relatively low-budget reality show like *Sorority Life*. More common is the expectation of celebrity with a small "c," the experience of becoming recognizable for a limited time by starring in series that millions of others will see. Even here, though, what celebrity actually means to participants can vary.

For example, the existing members of Sigma who were featured on the show wanted badly to counter the stereotypes of sorority girls in general, and Jewish sorority girls in particular, as clannish, exclusive, and self-interested; they wanted to show the world that their organization was open-minded and committed to community service. One of the six pledges had a similar sense of collective obligation, in this case to the Mexican-American community. She wanted to participate (and lobbied hard to be the sixth pledge when the original choice fell through) because she wanted to increase the visibility of Latinas on national television and represent them with dignity. She was well aware of the risks that visibility posed because of the media's penchant for stereotypical portrayals; moreover, her racial/ethnic otherness was compounded by her larger physical size. Forthright by nature, she was nevertheless determined to avoid perpetuating, in her words, the "loudmouth Latina" stereotype, which explains her careful behavior on the show, interpreted by online fans as "boring."

The other pledges (only two of whom claimed any Jewish heritage) tended to be less self-monitoring. They may have been concerned about their personal image and how it would be perceived by others (notably their families and friends), but they were not representing an organization, nor did they have to worry about representing their culture or race; being white and middle class, their behavior would reflect on them as individuals, not as members of a group.[30] All four appeared to be motivated to participate primarily by a sense of personal excitement and adventure, by the chance to take part in a unique, once-in-a-lifetime event. Having grown up on *The Real World* and being familiar with a wide range of reality shows, they were comfortable with the idea of being on camera, and, as with many young people of their generation who watch television, they were well trained in the codes of self-disclosure. More important, they recognized that media exposure was an escape from, not an affirmation of, their ordinariness, that, as much as reality television might appear to democratize celebrity, its achievement was still a marker of distinction. Yet only two of the four pledges claimed to have half-serious hopes for using their television debut as a springboard for achieving "real" (that is, ongoing) media stardom.

While I can't generalize from these cases, they point to the ways in which gender, class, and ethnic difference matter to the desire for media celebrity. They challenge universalistic, psychological explanations that conflate the desire for exposure with the desire for celebrity and they challenge even those social explanations of celebrity that rely on concepts of longevity, sociability, etc.[31] Perhaps this is because most theorizing about celebrity has been based on an analysis of media texts as opposed to an analysis of the activities, practices, and talk of those who produce these texts, from both behind and in front of the camera.

Some have argued that reality programming is the ultimate expression of a culture obsessed with the minute details of the self, with individual experience as the source of all legitimate knowledge. Reality programs are what Sam Brenton and Reuben Cohen call "pocket worlds"—playgrounds for selves "immersed in the retrenched, apolitical apparatus of self-hood." They argue that watching ordinary people on reality shows is much easier than watching real selves in the real world because "the loud, first-person inflection of the genre" is consistent with the psycho-therapizing of western culture and because individual selves are stripped of "tedious socioeconomic realities."[32] While I am sympathetic to this charge, it's also important to recognize its gendered implications, for women are often linked, in the media and in everyday lived reality, both to discourses of personal experience and "private" life, and to discourses of objectification by a putatively male gaze—a pair of discourses that a show like *Sorority Life* successfully combines. Ultimately, in my view, the problem with this sort of critique is that it places the burden of social analysis on the characters and storylines, rather than on the how and why of their production.

Andrejevic has argued, and I concur, that reality television is less important for the "real" stories it tells about characters and more important for the stories it tells about the production process itself;[33] Richard Dyer says something similar when he writes, "what is interesting about [stars] is not the character they have constructed ... but rather the business of constructing/performing/being a ... 'character.'"[34] If, as Nick Couldry suggests, the media are more and more turning the representation of the ordinary into a media ritual,[35] and if, as Graeme Turner observes, the concept of celebrity plays an increasingly significant role in shaping how we construct our cultural identities,[36] it would seem to me a pressing concern to explore the strategies and practices of those on the frontlines of this transformation.

Notes

1 Laura Grindstaff, *The Money Shot: Trash, Class, and the Making of TV Talk Shows* (Chicago: University of Chicago Press, 2002).

2 Chad Raphael, "Political Economy of Reali-TV," *Jump Cut* 41 (1997): 102–109.

3 Sam Brenton and Reuben Cohen, *Shooting People: Adventures in Reality TV* (London and New York: Verso, 2003).

4 Richard Peterson and N. Anand, "The Production of Culture Perspective," *Annual Review of Sociology* 30 (August 2004): 311–334.

5 See, for example, Gay Tuchman, *Making News: A Study in the Construction of Reality* (New York: Free Press, 1978); Todd Gitlin, *Inside Prime Time* (New York: Pantheon, 1983); Joshua Gamson, *Freaks Talk Back: Tabloid Talk Shows and Sexual Nonconformity* (Chicago: University of Chicago Press, 1998).

6 John Caldwell, *Production Culture: Industrial Reflexivity and Critical Practice in Film and Television* (Durham, NC: Duke University Press, 2008).

7 Grindstaff, *The Money Shot*.

8 The conflation between ordinariness and outrageousness on a show like *Randy* illustrates clearly that the concept of "ordinary person" in reality programming reflects production discourses rather than demographics per se. Within reality genres, paradoxically, the more outrageous the guest/participant—the more raucous, expressive, and volatile—the more "ordinary" they are said to be. This is because "ordinary" exists in binary relation to "elite" or "professional," with the two categories representing opposing dimensions of emotional expressiveness. While ordinary people are expected (and groomed) to "let it all hang out," experts and professionals on television are understood to be more restrained and dignified participants. For a fuller explication of this dynamic, see Grindstaff, *The Money Shot*.

9 See James Friedman, ed., *Reality Squared: Televisual Discourse on the Real* (New Brunswick, NJ: Rutgers University Press, 2002); Brenton and Cohen, *Shooting People*; Susan Murray and Laurie Ouellette, *Reality TV: Remaking Television Culture* (New York: New York University Press, 2004); Mark Andrejevic, *Reality TV: The Work of Being Watched* (New York: Roman and Littlefield Publishers, 2004); Annette Hill, *Reality TV: Audiences and Factual Television* (London and New York: Routledge, 2005).

10 See Andrejevic, *Reality TV*; Alison Hearn, "'John, a 20-Year-Old Boston Native with a Great Sense of Humor': On the Spectacularization of the 'Self' and Incorporation of Identity in the Age of Reality Television," in *The Celebrity Culture Reader*, ed. P. David Marshall (New York and London: Routledge, 2006), 618–633.

11 Paige Albiniak, "Ideal, Not Idle Summer for Fox," *Broadcasting & Cable*, September 9, 2002, 22.

12 Spencer Morgan, "Viewers Rush to MTV's 'Sorority,'" *New York Daily News*, August 8, 2002, entertainment section.

13 Andrejevic, *Reality TV*.

14 Pamela Wilson, "Jamming Big Brother: Webcasting, Audience Intervention, and Narrative Activism," in *Reality TV: Remaking Television Culture*, eds. Susan Murray and Laurie Ouellette (New York: New York University Press, 2004), 323–343.

15 Wilson, "Jamming Big Brother."

16 Caldwell, *Production Culture*, 195.

17 See Caldwell, *Production Culture*.

18 Ibid.

19 The reliance on pathos and conflict is characteristic of traditional Aristotelean drama as well; it is not unique to talk shows, reality TV, or media narratives more generally.

20 Arlie Russell Hochschild, *The Managed Heart: Commercialization of Human Feeling* (Chicago: University of Chicago Press, 1983). See also Arlie Hochschild, *The Commercialization of Intimate Life* (Berkeley and Los Angeles: University of California Press, 2003); Stephanie Shields, *Speaking from the Heart: Gender and the Social Meaning of Emotion* (Cambridge, UK: Cambridge University Press, 2002).

21 Hochschild, *The Managed Heart*. See also Shields, *Speaking from the Heart*.

22 For an insightful account of reality-TV casting, see Vicki Mayer, "Guys Gone Wild? Soft-Core Video Professionalism and New Realities in Television Production," *Cinema Journal* 47, no. 2 (2008): 97–116.

23 Brian Moeran, "Tricks of the Trade: The Performance and Interpretation of Authenticity," *Journal of Management Studies* 42, no. 5 (2005): 901–922

24 Hearn, "John, a 20-Year-Old Boston Native," 21

25 See Hill, *Reality TV*.

26 Graeme Turner, "Celebrity, the Tabloid, and the Democratic Public Sphere," in *The Celebrity Culture Reader*, ed. P. David Marshall (New York and London: Routledge, 2002), 495.

27 See Murray and Ouellette, *Reality TV*.

28 Turner, "Celebrity, the Tabloid, and the Democratic Public Sphere," 499.

29 I am drawing here, of course, on James Carey's classic distinction. See James Carey, *Communication as Culture* (New York: Unwin Hyman, 1989).

30 For a broader discussion of this racialized phenomenon, see Ella Shohat and Robert Stam, *Unthinking Eurocentrism: Multiculturalism and the Media* (New York and London: Routlege, 1994).

31 For a summary of these theories, see David Giles, "The Quest for Fame," in *The Celebrity Culture Reader*, ed. P. David Marshall (New York and London: Routledge, 2002), 470–486.

32 Brenton and Cohen, *Shooting People*, 52, 53.

33 Andrejevic, *Reality TV*.

34 Richard Dyer, *Stars* (London: British Film Institute, 1979), 24.

35 Nick Couldry, *Media Rituals: A Critical Approach* (London: Routledge, 2003).

36 Turner, "Celebrity, the Tabloid, and the Democratic Public Sphere."

Chapter 6

Gender Below-the-Line
Defining Feminist Production Studies

Miranda J. Banks

For film and television practitioners in Hollywood, the gender gap becomes a question not only of who is hired, but what work they are asked to do. In order to engage with questions about gender equality (or inequality) in screen production, in my research, I explore theories of professional identity through the lens of labor studies and production economics. Quantitative assessments of the gender gap in film and television production often make broad claims based on overall percentages of women working within the industry.[1] Gender disparity is a critical issue in Hollywood, but in order to understand the nature of the professional landscape, it is crucial to look not just at the overall numbers, but to examine the gendering of individual professions within the industry. In other words, my interest is not solely in the gender of workers (the biological sex of individuals within certain professions), but in the gendering of work (in terms of how a particular profession might be socially constructed though gender). Here, I highlight practitioners' own perceptions of their work while framing it within a cultural history of the economic and professional hierarchies inherent in screen production.

Production studies of media are predicated on the assumption that knowledge of the cultural and industrial modes of production will not just inform, but alter one's reading not only of the media text, but of the media. This theoretical tenet underlies the methodology, and therefore the organizing structure of production studies scholarship. When these types of media scholarship are then folded into feminist production studies, projects become increasingly nuanced. This type of work provides an intervention to traditional feminist media analyses by incorporating a theorization of the material conditions of gendered labor within the context of a specific industry history. While a number of television production studies researchers take as their content female-oriented series or networks, their methodologies tend to privilege the work of creative auteurs and executives. In my own scholarship, I have found the voices of female practitioners working below the line have much to offer in their own theorizations of media production practices. Their experiential knowledge provided a corrective testing of my own academic assessments. I see feminist production studies as works which define through example what is truly at stake not just in the process of production but in the study of production as well. Feminist production studies offer a method to interrogate power and cultural capital, femininity and feminism in production communities frequently overlooked in media industry research.

This kind of feminist production study has been done before, most notably in the work of Julie D'Acci and Elana Levine. Both scholars apply Richard Johnson's circuit of culture model, which examines the cross-flow of institutional hierarchies, production flows, and audience analysis within a particular work.[2] Yet the two scholars take the circuit of culture in two different feminist directions: D'Acci expands on the contested meanings of feminism while Levine offers a feminist methodology that encompasses the reflexivity of a researcher who is also a fan. Julie D'Acci's work on *Honey West* (1965–1966) and her book-length study *Defining Women*, which combine an archival-based industrial history with feminist textual analysis, locate these television texts within the specific social history of the women's movement in order to better define the industrial struggles the creators and their networks faced, as well as the significance of the program's reception.[3] D'Acci uses a case study of this long-running series to explore how the show was a battleground for a negotiation of the terms of "feminism." In the representation of two powerful heroines, power hierarchies played themselves out behind the scenes while the creators, studio, and network tried to find, construct, and speak to the female audience for a "women's program" that existed within the predominantly male genre of the police procedural.

Though D'Acci's book fills a significant gap in the history of media production labor, her analysis of the process of production focuses almost entirely on above-the-line professionals, especially the series' stars and their writer-producers Barbara Avedon and Barbara Corday. There is good reason for this—*Cagney & Lacey* (1981–1988) stands out as a series in the US not just because it was the first dramatic series with two female protagonists, but also because it broke ground with two female creators and executive producers at its helm. Focusing on the experiences of these above-the-line workers thus makes logical sense. While there have always been female practitioners in Hollywood, rarely has there been a production with so many women in these decision-making and -breaking positions.[4]

In "Toward a Paradigm for Media Production Research," Elana Levine applies Johnson's approach to the production of *General Hospital* (1963–), a daytime soap opera.[5] In her role as researcher, Levine tracks circulation of meanings within the production environment, arguing that television production is shaped equally by cultural notions of realism and economic determinants, such as time constraints. Unlike D'Acci, Levine spends some time talking about the work of a variety of practitioners on the set—and how their labor is distinguished—and delineated—by gender hierarchies. Levine writes:

> The limits of commercial culture are more complicated than simple profit motivation or the exploitation of workers. They can affect studio size and body size, the scope of the on-screen world and the scope of femininity. An understanding of such factors not only informs the interpretation of texts, but helps us to comprehend the priorities of capitalism, the imperatives of the television medium, and the reasons behind the products the medium offers. De-naturalizing the television world in these ways is the first step to not only knowing that world, but understanding the particular ways its power is shaped and its money and meanings are circulated.[6]

This field-based analysis of the lived experience of practitioners complicates the more text-based research of media scholars who have focused on the narrative worlds of media genres. This behind-the-scenes scholarship details how tensions behind the scenes are reflected—and even mirrored—in the finished, televised text. Both Levine and D'Acci use singular female-centered television series to track issues of the politics and economics of gender, both on and off the screen.

The distinction between "above-the-line" and "below-the-line" labor is crucial to understanding the nature of production, and in turn, to seeing different possibilities for intervention by feminist production studies scholars. "Above-the-line" and "below-the-line" are industry terms that distinguish between creative and craft professions in production. The distinction is derived from a particular worker's position in relation to a bold horizontal line on a standard production budget sheet between creative and technical costs, establishing a hierarchy that stratifies levels of creative and craft labor. Above-the-line guilds include practitioners who are paid to create cultural products within a media industry. The kind of labor that they do is evaluated, both by the industry and by society, in terms of its imagination, artistry, and inventiveness. According to David Hesmondhalgh, those who work above the line are responsible for generating symbolic meanings, but this reification of "the symbolic," and of those in the foreground, speaks to larger hierarchies of cultural value explored in my own research.[7] The work of writers, directors, producers, and celebrity actors is considered, and is compensated, above the line. In terms of payment, practitioners working above the line can negotiate with production studios for residuals, a cut of the distribution and syndication rights. As such, budgets for above-the-line workers vary dramatically. Below-the-line practitioners are considered—again, industrially and socially—as craftspeople or technicians, people who work with their hands. These practitioners hold distinct trade knowledge, much of which they have learned through apprenticeships or on the job. This group would include cinematographers, editors, production designers, costume designers, gaffers, camera loaders, body doubles, etc. Typically, below-the-line costs in production budgets are standardized by union contract wage scales.

While quantitative studies by scholars, unions, or activist organizations have fruitfully tracked the percentages of women working in above-the-line fields they fail to take into account that many below-the-line occupations have been dominated by women. In my own research, I have focused on particular professions within the industry where labor has been decidedly gendered, namely on stuntwomen (who work within a male-dominated profession) and costume designers (who are, in vast majority, female). This was a twist on D'Acci's investigation of the groundbreaking women of the *Cagney & Lacey* series. Whereas Avedon and Corday—and in turn, their characters Cagney and Lacey, had to negotiate terms like "*woman, women,* and *femininity,*"[8] looking at gendered occupations, how would female workers articulate their labor and professional experience? Like Levine, I talked to practitioners about their daily lives. While Levine's research focused on a particular program, I was interested in examining a particular profession, exploring how women's work is defined, valued, and articulated within the industry. What I found in my research talking to female and male costume designers was that theirs is a gendered profession: within the context of production, costume design is devalued in relation to professions of, arguably, comparable import that are majority male. In my conversations with these professionals, I tried to listen to the language they used to describe their work and their lived experiences within the industry. What emerged was a heteroglossic history of practitioners, past and present, in which the meanings of women's work, of femininity, and sometimes even feminism, were ventriloquized through a number of people, including myself.

Here I explore costume design as gendered labor through the voices of film and television designers who talked to me about their role in creating characters, in supporting actors, and in distinguishing their work from related fields, namely that of costumer or fashion designer. In the US, this craft is not medium specific. Professionals increasingly criss-cross between media, just like studios and media corporations now do.[9]

The Work of Costume Design

In order to understand the nature of their work, I will point to a few of the issues that costume designers themselves see as daily pleasures and the difficulties they face: building character through costume, working with actors—and their egos—and distinguishing their work from that of fashion. The costume designer is the person responsible for designing, creating, and overseeing the wardrobe of all of the actors on a set. Sometimes these clothes are created from scratch, other times they are purchased at retail stores and then modified to fit a character's needs.[10] In order to create all of the costumes necessary for a production, designers will work with a team of employees, overseen by a costume supervisor. The day-to-day work of the costume designer requires skill, discipline, humility, creativity, attention to detail, and speed—all on a budget.

The central dilemma—and paradox—for costume designers is that their job is to visualize a character through a costume that should go unnoticed by the audience because it looks organic to the personality of the character. The invisibility of costume designers' labor on the screen, however, frequently means that they are marginalized on the set and in the press. For costume designers, it has not been a coincidence that their field, traditionally dominated by women, has also been underappreciated, undercompensated, and, with imprudent disregard, labeled as "women's work." Even the costume designer's tools—cloth and the needle—are those traditionally ascribed to women's domestic labor. The gendering of the profession has defined the nature of the craft in other ways as well.

A costume designer's work is created for a two-dimensional world, in that it does not matter what a costume feels like or is made of, but rather about how the costume reads on the screen. Costume designer, and former Costume Designers Guild president, Deborah Nadoolman Landis describes the central goals of her trade as twofold: first, to support the narrative by creating memorable characters, and second to create costumes that balance the image within the frame.[11] This is a team project. Costume designers work directly with the producer, director, and actor before cutting the first pattern. They design the "foreground" of the screen—namely the actors: they create clothing for every character that helps define the director's or producer's vision, and that supports the cinematographer's composition by subtly guiding the audience's attention within the frame.[12] If a costume is not right, and a viewer notices this, this extra-textual recognition pulls viewers out of the narrative, reminding them of the industrial production of the image. As Ngila Dickson, costume designer of *Lord of the Rings* (2001–2003), explains, "You never want a jarring moment for the [audience]."[13] This is precisely what is meant when costume designers discuss how their work should disappear within the image.

Costumes serve other functions as well, according to designers. They can focus a viewer's attention on a particular character, helping the viewer judge the character before he or she even speaks. Costumes can tell a story; character and personality are externalized in costumes.[14] The use of particular types of clothing affects how an actor moves in space: his or her posture, balance, and gait. Television series productions require an entire wardrobe full of clothing, shoes, and accessories for each major character from which the designer can pull out single outfits over the course of each season.

A significant aspect of a costume designer's labor is understanding how to work with an actor's individual body, thereby finessing physical and emotional labor within the same work. The first people an actor sees every morning on a set are the hair, make-up, and costume crews, all of whom are in charge of manipulating an actor's body to transform him or her into a character. For this reason alone, the relationship between the actor and these key craftspeople must be amicable, requiring a level of trust from the actor and skillfulness on the part of the costume designer. Television writer and producer, Mark Frost explains the significance of the relationship between actor and costume designer:

> The costume designer has to be a kind of geisha to the actor. They have to make the actor feel safe and protected and enhanced by what they're wearing. They have to be able to deal with people who are making themselves very vulnerable for a living, and who have a lot of emotional needs and concerns.[15]

Being sensitive to an actor's particular physical strengths and weaknesses has always been essential to this emotional work. The designer often makes actors' bodies more proportional, taller, shorter, camouflages their physical flaws, or emphasizes their strengths in order to flatter their figures on screen.[16] Costume designers use tricks of the trade to help minimize the weight that the camera will put on an actor, everything from sewing pockets together to removing belt loops to reinforcing a bodice to create slimmer curves and clean lines.[17] Costume designers also introduce new looks slowly to apprehensive actors, building up the sense of trust that the designer truly knows the most flattering clothing for an actor. This is why costumes frequently improve over the course of a television series as actors and designers learn to trust each other.

Designers said that once that trust was established, many stars wanted to continue their relationships with them. During the studio era, many costume designers' names became attached to particular starlets, making themselves, and their costumes, famous, as well. In interviews, many costume designers describe their work as being part-designer, part-costume historian, and part-psychologist. Costume designer for films such as *Taxi Driver* (1976) and *Annie Hall* (1977), Ruth Morley understands that her job depends so much on her talks with actors that she laments not knowing more about human behavior. "I wish I'd studied psychology more— I had classical training. I do a lot of sketching, a lot of talking. I bring the actor in and really count on spending a lot of time with them. I try not to force color if someone really hates it. I try not to be unreasonable."[18] Costume designer Nolan Miller, a long-time collaborator with Aaron Spelling, has said many times that he sees his craft as 90 percent psychology and 10 percent creativity.[19] Nicole Gorsuch, costume designer for television shows as varied as *Jericho* (2006–2008) and *Home Improvement* (1991–1999), explained that ultimately, no costume will look right if an actor feels uncomfortable in it:

> It's never your full image, as a costume designer. It's a combination of what everybody wants. It's like you are a diplomat, trying to get what the producers

want, what the actors want, and what the director wants. You're just trying to make everyone happy and mesh it all together and fit it into the budget, and ultimately make the actors feel comfortable.[20]

This necessity for diplomacy that is central to their labor defines costume designers' work as both a manual craft and emotional labor. Their constant workaday negotiations mirror the above-the-line activities of producers and agents. And like that of above-the-line negotiations with talent, this relationship is not always easy or, for that matter, amicable. Oftentimes costume designers find that actors, especially those who have little experience on sets, fail to understand the art and craft of costume design and make extravagant requests.[21] Costume designers say that this is only further complicated when young actors now arrive on sets with their personal stylists. While by definition, stylists' work entails managing, locating, and customizing a particular look for their client to wear (every day, for a photo shoot, for an event), most stylists know little to nothing about costume design or fabrication.[22] Stylists are attuned to fashion, to fashion designers, and to their clients but, as many costume designers would argue, they do not understand the work of costume designers, nor do they have the experience, the history, or the knowledge of the craft of costuming to be helpful to their clients on the set. Stylists like Rachel Zoe have become part of the Hollywood A-list, as have the fashion designers whose clothes are paraded on the pages of fashion and entertainment magazines as well as television shows like *Entertainment Tonight* (1981–) and *Access Hollywood* (1996–), but considering all the names that are dropped to the press and paparazzi, rare among them are those of the costume designers.

The Lure of Fashion Design

Costume designers, struggling to stay within budget, rarely have enough time or money to create costumes from scratch. More likely, costumes come from a variety of sources; some are bought, others are rented, and some are designed and crafted as original pieces. Designers say the demands on them to work faster for less money, while appeasing producers who are interested in using fashion designers' clothing, is far more prevalent than in their earlier years.[23] As a result, costume designers often take advantage of fashion designers' offers for access to their collections to supplement an actor's wardrobe.[24]

There are clear advantages to the increased access costume designers have now to fashion designers' clothes. Fashion designers create and craft original clothing and accessories seasonally to be sold to individual clients or, more often, to consumers through specialty boutiques or department stores. Clothes that come to a production from a fashion designer are usually well made and assist the costume designer in portraying a character. Often these clothes are readily available to costume designers, and they are either free or sold to the production at drastically cut prices.[25] However, a fashion designer is usually only interested in dressing the main actors in a cast. Costume designer for *Will & Grace* (1998–2006), Lori Eskowitz-Carter explained during the run of the series, "The bigger the show, the more free stuff you get—it's just the bottom line. The higher-end designers obviously want to dress my cast right now because it's a hit show with an attractive cast."[26] This leads, though, to a gross misperception that costume designers are simply shoppers.[27] Rather, the modern costume designers struggle everyday to maintain their artistic and creative goals within a commercial-run production. If a fashion designer's clothes are used as costumes, they are, without fail, the first to take credit for the costumes. This is yet another example of the erasure of the costume designer's labor: and the gross misunderstanding of the differences between costume and fashion.

The costume designers I have interviewed in my research argued that the common misunderstanding of the differences between fashion and costume is critical to their invisibility in the production process and in the press. Fashion and, through it, fashion designer court the attention of the press; whereas costume designers see their role as serving the character and the script, not their own personas. While the work of the costume designer is veiled in the process of production, a fashion designer's intention is to highlight the uniqueness of his or her work, and bring attention to the label. At the most basic level, costume is about character and fashion is about clothing. A costume is designed to be photographed, on display in a two-dimensional world, to look like something the character would wear. While it may be made from cloth, it is not simply clothing. It is used to facilitate the narrative and give shape and form to a character. In contrast, fashion is a consumable good. It is crafted to be noticed in its own right; fashion is designed for the three-dimensional world. In one case, clothing is used to define a character, in the other a character is used to define the clothing.

To say that costume and fashion are antithetical does not, in turn, imply that style has no role in the creation of a costume. Quite the opposite is true. Dress articulates character, and if the character is a young woman living in a city, attention to style and fashion would be a part of the character's persona. A costume is never intended to be fashionable or glamorous in its own right, unless, of course, this is the nature of a particularly fashionable character. But fashion and costume are not the same. Every piece of prefabricated clothing used in a film or television series must go through a process of transformation in order to become a costume. Inevitably clothes are altered—dyed, customized, tailored, or aged—to fit the needs of a character and the scene.[28] Thus, the work of the costume designer, even when using contemporary fashions, is regularly under-recognized for the larger purpose of selling a film or television series, the character, or the image of the actor. But rarely does anyone take notice, especially off the set, of who was responsible for crafting the image in needle and cloth.

Via costume, Hollywood has provided viewers with a way to understand characters. At different times, film costumes have inspired fashion trends, but it is not the costume designers' job to consider this in the production process. Instead, they must be true to the script, and their skills at developing the foreground of a character, in essence, erase their labor.

Looking toward Future Feminist Labors?

It is only when we pull apart at the seams of costume design that we, as scholars and viewers of media, can begin to see the intricacy of the artistry, and the hidden—and gendered—labor involved in its production. Misunderstandings about costume design—in particular its misinterpretations as shopping or fashion—are embedded in gendered readings of this skilled labor. When creative work "design" is described as everyday leisure "shopping," the professionalism and skill of these workers is undermined. Conflating the work of design with fashion seems to imply that clothes, whether in one's closet, on the runway, or on the set, have the same purpose and meaning. Again, fashion connotes dressing for ornamentation or style, and while a program like *Project Runway* (2005–2008) has given audiences a much better idea of the intensive labor involved in the production of fashion, fashion is seen as above costume design. On a number of occasions, the judges' harshest critiques come when they call a design "costumey." This privileging of fashion over costume makes a qualitative, hierarchical assessment—thereby defining "costume" as overwhelming, obvious, and tacky—decidedly not the work of skilled hands of a craftsman or artist.

Gender plays into the collaborative nature of film and media production—not just in what is produced but in how. In subtle ways, much of the work women do in Hollywood is—both through language and through economics—treated as "women's work." Through agencies and organizations, women within the industry are trying to redefine their work as artistry and crafts worthy of professional respect—and commensurate pay. There are a great number of women working in Hollywood today. Hollywood history shows that women have always played pivotal roles in production. A critical reappraisal of the data on gender breakdowns within industry professions tells a far more compelling tale about the economics of production. And without understanding, even just a bit, about the collaborative nature of production and the methods and traditions of compensation, we would be lost in understanding the shifting nature of the text. The numbers game offers little understanding of the lived professional landscape.

Feminist production studies pull from varied disciplines in order to grapple with questions of gender within historical, industrial, institutional, and aesthetic frameworks. This type of scholarship demands an understanding of the interconnectedness of these different registers and their interrelations: grounding a reading of production within a distinct sociohistorical and economic context to examine a text, a profession, a character—even an individual—as a cultural and anthropological artifact. Exploring these disparate points of convergence in production at each of these registers provides a heuristic, integrated vision of media. In many ways, what D'Acci and Levine argue for is that for media scholars, the studies of production, industry, and text are always integrally intertwined. The scholar cannot truly understand one without at least a base knowledge of how hierarchies of power in production, distribution, and reception affect the process and the product.

A more nuanced assessment and analysis of the conditions and economics of gendered production labor provides a glimpse into the complex gender dynamics at play within this creative industry. These choices of who is working behind the scenes and how they are compensated for their work are essential to the production of the final product, translating to what we see on screen. Occasionally, these workers come out of the woodwork, such as when the Writers Guild of America hit the picket lines from November 2007 to February 2008. When the writers went on the streets, the gender and racial disparity within the profession of screenwriting was laid bare on the picket line: the majority of picketers were male, and almost all were Caucasian. While this kind of underground history of gendered labor within Hollywood itself may not make a great script, it could be part of a larger, both scholarly and industrial, feminist project to bring awareness, and change, to the practices of making media.

While at first the notion of a feminist production study may seem only a viable method of analysis within the realm of production communities that have a majority of women, it is precisely the gender biases in production that need to be explored and uncovered. Embedded industrial theorizations of production culture must be harvested from practitioners and analyzed by scholars at every point in the production process. In this case study, I have focused on a profession dominated by women in order to explore why this production community has been defined as "women's work." But the gendering of professions in film and media production is visible throughout the industry. Elsewhere, I have explored the work of stuntwomen—and how they negotiate their careers—and their ideas about women's work—within a profession that has traditionally been deemed quite macho—or masculine. For women struggling to gain recognition within the industry, and for feminist scholars interested in gender and representation, studies that track the gendering of the production landscape offer insight and a nuanced interpretation of the lived media landscape.

We who study Hollywood often write from positions of cultural distance and privilege. We see the final product, and we may know a bit about the key players in the production. As work like D'Acci's and Levine's shows, there is a whole other drama being played out behind the scenes. And tensions often surround questions of such complicated and ever-changing terms as femininity and feminism, not only on the set and screen, but also in the classroom. Just as production practices change, or notions of gender equality shift, so must scholars' methodologies for interpreting them change as well. With the extensions of film and television's boxes and screens, defining professional positions and establishing compensation rates across media platforms become central not only to how the industry conceives of itself and its future, but also how it hopes to make profits.

Notes

1 For example, Martha Lauzen's annual *Celluloid Ceiling* reports. See Martha Lauzen, *The Celluloid Ceiling: Behind the Scenes Employment of Women in the Top 250 Films*, Department of Communication, San Diego State University, CA, 2002–2007.

2 Richard Johnson, "What is Cultural Studies Anyway?" *Social Text* 16 (1986–1987): 38–80.

3 Julie D'Acci, *Defining Women: Television and the Case of Cagney & Lacey* (Chapel Hill, NC: University of North Carolina Press, 1994); Julie D'Acci, "Nobody's Woman? Honey West and the New Sexuality," in *The Revolution Wasn't Televised: Sixties Television and Social Conflict*, eds. Lynn Spigel and Michael Curtain (New York: Routledge, 1997), 72–93.

4 Even Sherry Lansing, who would later become the first woman to run a major motion picture studio, was involved with the development and green-lighting of the project. D'Acci, *Defining Women*, 19.

5 Elana Levine, "Toward a Paradigm for Media Production Research: Behind the Scenes at *General Hospital*," *Critical Studies in Media Communication* 18 (2001): 66–82.

6 Ibid., 70.

7 David Hesmondhalgh, *The Cultural Industries* (London and Thousand Oaks, CA: Sage, 2002), 22, 70–73; Miranda J. Banks, "Bodies of Work: Rituals of Production and the Erasure of Film/TV Production Labor", PhD diss., University of California, Los Angeles, 2006.

8 D'Acci, *Defining Women*, 8. See Chapter 4, "Negotiating Feminism," 142–167.

9 Over the course of these two industries' histories, often the business models of one have been borrowed and adapted to the other. During its early formation, television was far more closely aligned with the radio industry than with the film industry. In fact, for the first thirty years, the major corporations in the television industry all had their start in radio. But now, with corporate conglomeration and the media mergers of the last twenty years in particular, the ties between radio, television, and film have been established within new paradigms.

10 Gina McIntyre, "Style Factor: Designing Hollywood Is Divided over Just What Role High Fashion Should Play On-Screen," *The Hollywood Reporter*, May 7–13, 2002, 18.

11 Deborah Nadoolman Landis, interview with the author, May 24, 2005.

12 Ibid.

13 Shalini Dore, "Designing Women," *Variety*, February 19, 2002.

14 This can go back to the most basic representations of character. For example, think of the hero in the white hat and the villain in the black hat in early Westerns.

15 Todd Coleman, "But Can She Do 1949?: Who Gets the Work" *The Hollywood Reporter*, January 27, 1992, S-27.

16 "Screen Sorcery Gives the Girls Needed Curves: Many a Glamorous Figure Appears Above Criticism Through Designers' Art," *New York Tribune*, May 25, 1941.

17 Leonora Langly, "The Man Who Shapes Stars: An Exclusive Interview with Couturier Nolan Miller," *The Hollywood Reporter*, November 1, 1985, S-9.

18 Mary Lisa Gavenas, "Cut from the Same Cloth: Five Designers Talk Shop," *The Hollywood Reporter*, December 9, 1988, S-24.

19 Nolan Miller, interview with the author, March 28, 2003. Also, Langly, "The Man Who Shapes Stars."

20 Nicole Gorsuch, interview with the author, May 3, 2004.

21 Randee Dawn, "Hem and Haw: The Costume Designers Guild Wants Everyone to Know that It Does More than Just Women's Work," *The Hollywood Reporter*, February 18, 2005, 25–26; Simi Horwitz, "Stitches in Time: Welcome to the World of the Wardrobe Supervisor," *Back Stage West*, December 9, 2004.

22 Karla Stevens, interview with the author, October 30, 2005; Gorsuch, interview.

23 For example, Ngila Dickson was given a ten-day turnaround schedule to create up to a hundred costumes for each episode of *Xena: Warrior Princess* (1995–2001). Not only did she do this, but Dickson did such an outstanding job that she was given the Best Contribution to Design Award for New Zealand Television in both 1996 and 1997. She has since gone on to be nominated multiple times for and once awarded the Oscar for costume design in film. Mimi Avins, "The Battle of the Epics," *The Los Angeles Times*, February 29, 2004, E12.

24 Valli Herman-Cohen, "Masters of Anonymity," *Los Angeles Times Magazine*, August 19, 2001, 42.

25 In order to create ease of access to fashions from their store in 2001, Barney's New York added a studio-services department that sells or rents their stock to studios. In Herman-Cohen, "Masters of Anonymity."

26 McIntyre, "Style Factor."

27 Nadoolman Landis expresses her frustration about this misperception: "Contemporary costume design, whether in film or in television, is a cinema art form continually undervalued and misunderstood. The notion that contemporary costumes are 'shopped' by designers, reaching the screen unaltered, with fashion designers' labels intact, is an oft-repeated urban legend with no substance. We are often asked the innocent question, 'Where did you get it?' The answer is, we designed it." From Deborah Nadoolman Landis, *Screencraft: Costume Design* (Burlington, MA: Focal Press, 2003), 9.

28 Costume designer, Jeffrey Kurland says: "I can honestly tell you, though, that I have never bought a piece of clothing in a store that I have actually put on a persona and put directly on-screen. It's always recut, redone to that person for that character." In Jan Lindstrom, "Temperamental Mates: Despite Common Goals, Designers, Supervisors Often at Odds," *Variety*, November 21, 1997, 32.

Chapter 7

It's Not TV, It's Brand Management TV

The Collective Author(s) of the *Lost* Franchise

Denise Mann

> The show is the mother ship, but I think with all the new emerging technology, what we've discovered is that the world of "Lost" is not ... circumscribed by the actual show itself ...[1]
>
>

Lost executive producer/showrunner Carlton Cuse

In the midst of a post-millennial era of crisis and change—technological, industrial, and cultural—the networks are placing a new set of extraordinary demands on members of the TV production community. In particular, show creators and their writing teams are being expected to create high-concept, high-profile, multi-platform "TV blockbusters"—also known as "transmedia franchises"—that successfully mobilize a host of ancillary revenue streams, engender merchandising opportunities, and spawn a multitude of spin-offs, including digital content and promotions for the web. In this new, post-network TV workplace environment, *Lost* head writer-producers (aka showrunners) Carlton Cuse and Damon Lindelof see their expanded role as synonymous with that of the brand managers who oversee major, nonentertainment brands like Coca-Cola and Ford Motor.[2] Adopting the methodology and focus of production studies, I argue in this chapter that the changed workplace environment and industrial circumstances associated with network television production in the age of the Internet have greatly altered the practices of collective "authorship" even though industry discourses publically adhere to obsolete paradigms—namely, the designation of the singular voice of the "auteur"—when discussing the creation of so-called "quality" TV programs like *Lost*.[3] Whereas media scholar and provocateur Henry Jenkins optimistically describes transmedia franchises in *Convergence Culture* as exciting and dynamic new creative frontiers and opportunities to engage in peer participation entertainment, this chapter considers the negative cultural impact on production culture of having heightened demands placed on television writer-producers who, albeit well paid for their efforts, have been handed greater responsibility for steering massive, global, corporate TV empires like *Lost*.[4] After briefly surveying production studies from the 1980s to the present and highlighting the challenges facing scholars conducting production studies today, I turn to a case study of the making of *Lost* (2004–) to demonstrate the ways in which showrunners Lindelof and Cuse have taken a leadership role in helping brand the show and the network. A number of factors complicated this effort including: changing audience patterns, new digital technologies, and the recent Writers Guild of America (WGA) strike. While many showrunners (including Lindelof and Cuse) welcome the creative and financial opportunities associated with transmedia franchises, the fact remains that the success of their show has created an implicit pressure among other writer-producers to replicate this type of branded entertainment.[5] As one Hollywood insider notes,

> You now need what we call the six-pack of executive producers; and it's not because there's no one person who can do it. It's because these shows are so big that it's humanly impossible for one person to executive produce the show. So you have shows that have middle management, just like corporations have middle management. That's a function of how big the shows are today.

Today's blockbuster-style television production circumstances contrast with the past when a single "showrunner" ran everything including both the writing room *and* the actual production. While Lindelof and Cuse together *are* today's equivalent of "that guy," they remain headquartered in Los Angeles and focused on running the writers' room, overseeing all aspects of postproduction (i.e., editing, music, etc.), *and* to the extent possible, overseeing the promotional 2.0 content and other platforms that relate directly to the show's story or characters. Remarking on the new trend in managing today's large-scale television productions, one insider attributes the change from a single TV showrunner to a "six-pack of executive producers" to the fact that networks are demanding drama series that have "a big scale and theatrical [film] quality."[6] Increasingly, the networks believe that the high-production values in most TV dramas today are what are drawing viewers to television. Some insiders argue that *Lost* may have contributed to the high cost of producing television today by sparing no expense when it came to making the pilot; the production crew was forced to spend exorbitant amounts in order to meet unrealistic deadlines, including engaging in the herculean task of dismantling, transporting, and reassembling an entire plane on location in Hawaii.[7] Given the cost associated with these few, big-budget shows, it becomes incumbent upon the network to fill the rest of their "slate" with large numbers of inexpensive reality and game shows. As a result, one could argue that there is less room for more modestly budgeted scripted entertainment. Furthermore, in the present industry climate, there are far fewer young writers being hired to staff these big shows. One young TV writer said it was a disservice to the longevity of the industry that the head writers don't hire more new writers so as to cultivate the next generation of TV creators; however, given the huge economic stakes involved in keeping these TV franchises on the air, large, multiformat shows like *Lost* and *Heroes* are hiring primarily senior writer-producers. The general attitude is that it is worth paying the added cost to hire established executive producers (EPs) who bring double the experience, and hence efficiency, to the process.

At the center of the storm and navigating "the mother ship" that is *Lost* are Lindelof and Cuse. While a virtual army of writers and producers has worked on the show since it first aired in 2004, the current list of senior executive producers who are contractually tied to *Lost* until the completion of its final season in 2010 include: EP/co-creator/showrunner Lindelof, EP/showrunner Cuse, and EP/co-creator J. J. Abrams as well as EP Bryan Burk, EP/director Jack Bender, co-EP Edward Kitsis, co-EP Adam Horowitz, and co-EP/director Stephen Williams.[8] Notably, as a result of the stringent Writers Guild protection governing creative authorship, Jeffrey Leiber still receives a valuable (and lucrative) co-creator EP credit even though his early draft of the pilot was deemed unusable. However, Lindelof and Cuse, the executive producers who are in charge of the writing staff in Los Angeles, are conceived of as "the brain trust that keeps the series' epic plot twists and stop-or-you-might-miss-'em little details coming."[9]

Defining TV Authorship Today

Before launching into an interrogation of the specific circumstances associated with the production of the *Lost* brand, it is important to consider the significance within the TV production community of the term "author" as it relates to the role of the head writer or showrunner. One of the primary objectives of this chapter is to use situated fieldwork (i.e., observation and interviews with production personnel) to consider the revised meanings associated with the term "TV author" in the new postnetwork environment. Previous top-down TV production studies have tended to isolate a single author or, at most, a writing partnership.[10] For a show of the scale of *Lost*, it is not enough to focus exclusively on the two showrunners or even the six to eight senior personnel holding the top title of executive producer or co-executive producer, without also giving some consideration to the role and responsibilities of the hundreds of production personnel associated with the show, as well as the networks and studios, talent agencies, advertising agencies, freelance production companies, and the countless other bureaucratic organizations that contribute to the production of a big-budget, multiplatform TV franchise. Despite this obvious collectivity, each of the industry insiders who participated in the research for this project tended to emphasize the creative power and potency of the "singular" voice of the authors, Abrams, Lindelof and Cuse. While it is understandable why industry professionals would adhere to this hierarchy to simplify issues of credit and payment set by the WGA, it is less clear why media scholars persist in attributing authorship to the show creators and/or showrunners given that the theoretical category of the auteur has been largely overturned by the post-structuralist, postmodernist theories of Barthes, Foucault, and others.[11] In reality, the humanist literary tradition that ascribes authorship to a single writer based on whether or not his/her work registers a modernist intervention in the dominant hegemonic tendencies of the mass media is now paradoxically maintained through the coordinated efforts of a platoon of bureaucratic personnel and interlocking media corporations that constitute today's heavily conglomerated, globalized, and convergent TV industry.

Network television publicists have long understood the value of reinforcing the image of the TV author, a development that can be traced to the 1980s when not just media scholars but popular critics began celebrating a group of TV writer-producers (e.g., Steven Bochco, David Lynch, Michael Mann, etc.) associated with "quality TV" shows that exhibited a shared stylistic, structural aesthetic, and the type of socially relevant themes favored by the older, sophisticated audience of big spenders that advertisers prefer.[12] The reasons for the industry's reverential regard for the potent figure of the showrunner may seem obvious at first glance. After all, most young TV writers working on staff hope one day to have enough power and leverage to create and run their own show. Furthermore, networks and their sister studios are dependent on talented and experienced show creators to fill their distribution pipelines. However, none of these pragmatic realities explains why industry insiders, who are acutely aware of the institutional obstacles to unfettered creative autonomy, rigorously uphold the illusion of the TV showrunner's ultimate power over the TV production process both inside the TV writers' room and outside it.

Given the magnitude of the job and their eagerness to replicate the economies of scale at which the Hollywood system has historically excelled, one Hollywood insider observed that some studios have pondered the question of whether they could set up a more cost-effective system by adding a "second writers' room," much like a "second-unit" on the production side, which would allow them to have two separate writing staffs writing at the same time. The same source concluded, however, that "the problem with [trying to have two separate writing staffs] is that at some point the buck has to stop; and there's only one Damon and his producing partner Carlton Cuse." Reluctantly conceding to the studios' dependency on a few, potent members of the talent pool while simultaneously reinforcing the auratic power and potency of the singular TV authorial voice, the source added: "So we're forced to deal with the fact that you don't know what your next episode is going to be until you finish writing the episode that you're currently writing. That's the biggest challenge that Damon and Carlton have as they try to map out the mythology and the stories and the character development." Before launching a close analysis of the corporate and creative forces that contributed to the making of the *Lost* pilot, I turn next to a brief analysis of early 1980s production studies and some of the methodological pitfalls they exposed.

Production Studies Methodologies and Precedents

Production studies are still a relatively new phenomenon given an ongoing pre-occupation in media scholarship with texts and audiences or, alternatively, with political economic trajectories. The few, early instances of American media schol-arship devoted to production studies and, in particular, those that focused on top-down studies of television's most powerful creative personnel—the head writer-producer—ran counter to the Marxist-inspired cultural studies project. Those scholars conducting early production studies focused on the writer-producer therefore risked incurring the ire of their colleagues in the field. However, even these early attempts to engage in situated fieldwork shed light on the often unintended insights (as well as the pragmatic hurdles) associated with scholarly encounters with real people working in Hollywood. One of the more promi-nent of the early, top-down production studies is Horace Newcomb and Robert Alley's oft-cited 1983 interviews with several prominent TV writer-producers in *The Producer's Medium*.[13] This book-length study sought to elevate the contribu-tions of the TV writer-producer by giving each the designation of "creative artist" working within a complex industrial system; in that respect, Newcomb and Alley's definition of "auteur" is closer in spirit to Walter Benjamin's definition of art in the age of mechanical reproduction than the critical category derived from literary studies that was applied to certain directors in the late 1950s by like-minded critics and filmmakers contributing to *Cahiers du Cinéma*.[14] Assigning the term "creative artist" to television writer-producers was a deliberate and no doubt controversial step in the early 1980s given the general reluctance among academics at the leading American research institutions to sanctify television as a suitable object of study. Since then, as television studies have made slow but steady inroads in American universities, most scholars have lined up on one side or the other of the cultural/industrial divide.

As the early production studies conducted by Newcomb and Alley and others have demonstrated, the showrunner or TV show creator, while often celebrated as a singular author, is in fact notoriously buffeted by conflicting obligations to his/her own creative compass *and* to the many corporate players involved in maintain-ing the commercial engine and bureaucratic constraints of the network television industry as a whole. Newcomb and Alley's early efforts to integrate first-hand accounts from production personnel into cogent scholarly analyses paved the way for more recent efforts to include situated fieldwork in TV studies by invoking the need for critical commentary as a necessary adjunct of situated fieldwork; in other words, it is not enough to simply provide raw, unmediated transcriptions of interviews with production personnel. For instance, in *Convergence Culture*, Jenkins foregrounds these two discursive registers by juxtaposing the comments of media makers (signaling their importance to his discussion by printing them in bold font) alongside his more scholarly discourse (printed in regular font), creating a dialectical counterpoint of theory and practice visually on the page. In *The Producer's Medium*, Newcomb and Alley's use of the phrase "self-conscious creative television producers" to describe the shared affinities between professional and scholarly communities foresees the more nuanced designation of "industrial reflexivity" or "low theory" advanced by John Caldwell's *Production Culture*.[15] The latter view invokes the self-reflexive discursive systems adopted by industry personnel to describe their implicit understanding of the industrial and cultural constraints limiting their creative activities. For example, shows like *Entourage* (2004–) or *Extras* (2005–2007) provide ironic commentary about the state of the industry and point to the explicit and implicit hierarchies and power dynamics operating among production personnel in the film and television industries being portrayed. Notably, Cuse and Lindelof allowed "The Book Club" episode of *Lost* to mock the creative process by having several characters debate the literary value of sci-fi impresario Stephen King, a major influence for many of the series' writers; furthermore, the writer-producers didn't flinch at the obvious breech of the "fourth wall" when the Disney-owned Hyperion Press decided to carve out additional profits by publishing a novel purportedly written by the show's fictional Oceanic airlines' crash victim, Gary Troup.[16] A similar knowing, self-reflexive, and ironic tone infuses much of the show's auxiliary content as well, including: various cross-platform stunts and several of the "DVD bonus extras."[17]

One of the challenges facing scholars engaged in production studies is the reluctance of most production personnel to speak candidly about their shows. For instance, on-the-record conversations with network personnel require official clearance from an executive in charge of corporate publicity. Another practical hurdle facing media scholars is the need to separate the candid comments made by above-the-line production personnel during a formal interview from the type of pre-approved comments present in most press packages (i.e., the type of materials prepared by network publicists and distributed to popular media journalists during press junkets). Given the ubiquity of this type of behind-the-scenes reporting, many media scholars share Henry Jenkins, Tara McPherson, and Jane Shattuc's secret fear that critical analyses of contemporary media developments sometimes blur the line between scholarly and popular, journalistic styles of writing.[18] To counter this tendency, it is useful for academics to unpack these opaque institutional systems by viewing interviews with above-the-line and below-the-line TV talent as cultural artifacts containing evidence of an intricate, interlocking system of heavily codified, discursive knowledge. As longtime producer Peter Guber likes to say, "There are no rules in Hollywood, but you break them at your own peril." It becomes incumbent on the media scholar to intuit from the industry insider's behavior and comments whether or not he/she is succumbing to any of these self-imposed, disciplinary activities—i.e., if he/she is self-censoring certain information that may provide the scholar with meaningful insights into how the industry actually works.

Elana Levine provides a useful primer on how to integrate critical analysis with situated fieldwork to examine the workplace struggles among divergent members of the production community responsible for the television series, *General Hospital*.[19] While Levine organizes her study along rather conventional lines, examining "the continuities among production, texts, audiences, and social contexts," the essay also demonstrates how situated fieldwork can produce unintended insights into previously unexplored workplace power dynamics. For example, despite the difficulty Levine had accessing the writers on the show, her conversations with various other production personnel provided her with the consensus view that "writers held a mysterious and somewhat revered, place within the organizational hierarchy."[20] This example shows how a theoretical construct like auteurism infiltrates the production community in several precise ways. Writer-producers of primetime series are among the most powerful and well-paid individuals in the television industry, which when translated to the workplace means that the nonwriting personnel at *General Hospital* treat their writers with a certain reverence even though daytime soap operas operate at decidedly lower budgetary (and lesser critical) levels. In fact, as seen thus far in the case of *Lost* and *General Hospital*, this lofty view of the "author" tends to permeate the television production community. One of the unintended insights received while interviewing two *Lost* writers at the same time was the rigid hierarchies that exist among members of the writing team, in this case, a low-level staff writer and his supervising producer. The newer writer consistently deferred to the more senior writer, allowing the latter to dominate the conversation; nevertheless, his fears that he might have overstepped his place were so great (even though neither writer currently works on the show) that he called the day after our interview to reassert that the more senior writer-producer's explanation of how things worked should always take precedence over his own remarks.

The Producer's Habitus/Habitat

Despite the challenges associated with production studies that rely on interactions with above-the-line talent as outlined above, my interviews with TV showrunners Cuse, Tim Kring (*Heroes*, 2006–), and others were greatly facilitated by the apparent symmetries between the academic and industrial settings and the shared affinities between media scholars and media practitioners.[21] Both sets of individuals, professors and showrunners, have deliberately chosen professions that provide them with relative autonomy despite the fact they also must operate in highly bureaucratic settings. For instance, while interviewing Cuse and Kring, I discovered that both had humanities degrees.[22] Furthermore, both understood that their previous commercial success as the creators of rather conventional episodic series had given them considerable leverage with their respective networks to create their expensive, innovative, heavily serialized shows, *Lost* and *Heroes*, respectively.[23] Kring started out working in various "blue-collar," below-the-line positions (e.g., production assistant, camera assistant, etc.) and Cuse began as a development executive; both had quickly realized that the most expeditious route to the top creative jobs in TV would be through writing TV scripts (just as the publish or perish rule grants academics the power and privilege of tenure). As film producer and media scholar Adam Fish explains, "There exists a fluid play in the field between academic and media industrial institutions that is predicated on the producer's habitus while mediated by different forms of intra-field or inter-institutional fluidity."[24] An even more profound sense of the shared affinities between the academic and industrial communities resulted when *Heroes* creator Tim Kring described how he prepared for his role as brand manager of a major television franchise. He explained that he had researched media convergence and peer participation models by reading *Wired* magazine editor-in-chief Chris Anderson's *The Long Tail* and Jenkins' *Convergence Culture*.[25] Anderson's landmark treatise, heralding the substitution of an old way of doing business with a new, 2.0-universe of low-tech production and distribution strategies, was designed to celebrate niche marketing via the Internet. Authors of emerging platforms like *Lost* and *Heroes* are obvious target audiences for this book given their role in creating new, participatory platforms in the context of the traditional TV industry. In contrast, Jenkins presumably did not intend for his book to function as a "how to" guide for successful above-the-line media personnel eager to capitalize on this new business environment. However, the utility of Jenkins' book for television powerhouse Kring *and* for academics speaks to the shared affinities binding scholars researching industry practices and media professionals researching new business models in the still largely uncharted waters of a globalized, conglomerated, convergent media industry.

In view of the shared affinities binding media scholarship and media production, media scholars engaged in production studies have discovered that the cultural anthropology of Clifford Geertz and others, by involving ethnographic fieldwork, helps provide a holistic approach to analyzing complex systems, in this case the TV television industry and production community.[26] One cannot get an accurate portrait of the showrunners' work world without gathering different perspectives on the same issue; furthermore, one must learn to evaluate the institutional context in which these views are expressed. Media scholars implicitly understand how they tailor their own speech according to the venue, avoiding the specialized jargon used at academic conferences when delivering an undergraduate lecture, for instance. By extension, media scholars must learn to decipher the institutional goals implicitly at work in the showrunner's various habitats—at trade shows like NAPTE in Las Vegas, in front of sponsors at the network "upfronts" in New York (an annual staged extravaganza in which the network heads and a handful of television celebrities fly to New York to announce the next season's fall line-up to the advertisers), or at fan conventions like Comi-Con in San Diego.[27] The Comi-Con comic book convention, for instance, has become a favorite location for network marketing teams, in consultation with the showrunners, to stage outrageous publicity stunts; one such event took place at the July 22, 2006 Comi-Con, when the actress playing Rachel Blake in *The Lost Experience* Alternate Reality Game (ARG) warned the fans attending the convention about the conspiracy taking place at the fictional Dharma Institute, a central theme of the Internet-based treasure hunt. In some instances, the scholarly and promotional worlds merge, such as when Cuse used a speaking engagement at UCLA on July 18, 2006 to launch the viral word-of-mouth campaign, telling the hundred or so graduate students in attendance to go to Comi-Con the following weekend to check out the surprise he and the network had planned (i.e., Blake's stunt).

Cultivating the Corporate Brand

The complex, multivalent, bureaucratic rituals involved in creative authorship in a corporate setting provide an alternate type of origin story to the contemporary television series. One of the early creative and industrial models for *Lost* is the phenomenally successful "cult show-turned-mainstream hit," *The X-Files* (1993–2002). Media scholars Sara Gwenllian-Jones and Roberta E. Pearson write: "Perhaps more than any other single phenomenon, it is the success of *The X-Files* that ensured that from the early 1990s onward, cult television has become an industry in and of itself."[28] Yet unlike *The X-Files*, however, *Lost* was not the singular vision of a TV writer and avid fan like Chris Carter, who created his show in large part to replicate the fear and excitement he felt growing up and watching *Kolshak: The Night Stalker* (1974–1975). Rather, *Lost* represents something of a corporate fabrication. A close read of the development process will show this. The idea for *Lost* literally originated at a network retreat when Lloyd Braun, then-chairman of ABC Entertainment Television Group, told the group of executives that he'd always wanted to do a show about people stranded on a desert island, a show that depicted desperate people thrust together due to some cataclysmic event and forced to figure out how to live together in order to survive.[29] Eager to assign greater significance to this water-cooler program, some media analysts trace the show's origins to a post

9-11 zeitgeist; however, Braun had a more banal vision in mind. His brainchild was to hire someone to create a scripted version of the hugely successful reality show, *Survivor* (2000–), a desire exacerbated, no doubt, by the fact that the reality juggernaut was airing on a competitor's network.

Once the ABC executives returned to Los Angeles at the end of the summer retreat, they began pitching their "scripted *Survivor*" concept to each of the major talent agencies, which in turn sent all of their most promising writers to pitch their take. One of those writers, Jeffrey Leiber, who at the time had a deal with Spelling Television, pitched his idea and later, in December, delivered a pilot script for the network. Braun read it and hated it, saying, "It's … such a bland ordinary take … It's exactly what I didn't want." At that point, Braun brought in writer-producer extraordinaire J. J. Abrams, who, as the creative force behind *Alias* (2001–2006), was perceived, then and now, as the network's "go-to guy," known for his ability to solve irresolvable story issues. The power and potency of certain TV showrunners, like Abrams, is a function of their implicit understanding of the corporate ethos inherent in creating and selling a successful multiplatform TV brand. Abrams accomplished this early in his career when he created *Alias*, and the networks took note. That is why he and his production company, Bad Robot, are considered so valuable within today's conglomerated, globalized, and convergent entertainment industry. Because it was by now already January, Abrams reminded the executives at both ABC and ABC TV Studio that they needed to start shooting the pilot within the month if they were to deliver the show in time for the May up-fronts. Given the time constraints, and given his unique take on the story, Lindelof was brought in to co-create the pilot for *Lost* and is credited, along with Abrams, with "breaking the story."[30] Being seasoned pros, the writers used the much maligned (but frequently employed) technique of describing their project by juxtaposing two successful antecedents that telegraphed both the tone and business model being employed simultaneously. According to one journalist, "Working off their original 20-page outline, Mr. Abrams and Mr. Lindelof had ideas about the show's vibe—'Gilligan' meets 'X-Files'…"[31] Abrams recalls, "I met Damon for the first time on a Monday." He continued, "By that Friday we had written a twenty-page outline. And they green-lit the pilot on Saturday. At that point, we didn't even have a script, but in less than twelve weeks we had to start shooting."[32]

The intractability of the TV pilot production schedule, coupled with Lloyd Braun's determination to inaugurate a new, more expensive type of TV franchise, factored heavily into every step of the production process during the making of the *Lost* pilot. Braun felt that not only was his own future tied to the success of the *Lost* pilot, but that of the network as a whole. Notably, Abrams left the day-to-day operations of the series shortly after the pilot was completed, further evidence that his value to the studio-network complex is a function of his ability to launch and oversee a number of franchises at once, multitasking within a highly bureaucratized environment. Abrams is not the first writer-producer to create and manage several TV franchises at once (others include Aaron Spelling, Dick Wolf, etc.); however, in the face of an eroding broadcast television audience, he is one of a handful of successful writer-producers that advertisers associate with the type of "engagement TV" that lends itself to network-designed "360 media campaigns" meant to bombard consumers with advertising messages 24/7 using a multitude of new technologies ranging from website banner ads to cell phone mobisodes to digital bulletin boards displayed while unwitting customers pump their gas.

The WGA Strike: Redefining TV Authorship in the 2.0 Workspace

Whereas earlier production studies have tended to celebrate independent-minded showrunners like Bochco, Brooks, and Norman Lear, who were perceived as "TV auteurs" at odds with the network's corporate agenda, the authors of many of today's television franchises reveal a more cooperative (if not completely amicable) relationship with their network counterparts. Given the expanded definition of TV authorship in the age of the Internet, head writer-producers or "showrunners" like *Lost*'s Lindelof and Cuse not only fulfill the typical activities of writing, producing, and delivering twenty-two to twenty-five weekly episodes of a series annually—already a herculean task—but also steward a vast array of auxiliary media products and promotional activities in order to activate fan interactivity online, all while negotiating the sibling rivalry between sister companies. While the networks are embracing their new status as content providers not just for broadcast but for digital distribution outlets, it is only recently that certain show creators have begun to recognize the need to become more involved in manufacturing promotional web content for their shows to keep them on the air. For instance, during the 2005–2006 season of his show, *The Wire* (HBO), author and executive producer Eric Haney wrote:

> I am one of the last of the low-tech dinosaurs. In creating and producing our show, I thought it was pretty funny that we needed to have a blog, but I'm one of the owners. When you take your pigs to market, you have to tell people about them.[33]

According to Steve Andrade, Vice President of Interactive Development for NBC,

> I've been in this job for ten years. For the first time, all the creative people in town are finally realizing how advantageous it is to work in this space. They all know it's going to be part of their future. There is no model. We're all trying to figure this out.[34]

The increased corporate responsibilities associated with the job of the TV writer-producers of transmedia TV franchises are still in a state of evolution as the networks respond to the social-cultural-industrial implications of the Internet. That said, the WGA strike shifted the line in the sand that previously existed between content-creators and their counterparts at the network in charge of selling. In May 2007, Lindelof and Cuse took a leadership role in crafting the language used to define the new workplace responsibilities for TV writer-producers who create these content-promotion hybridizations. The deal they forged with ABC Studios on *Missing Pieces* (2000) made sure the writers of *Lost* (including Cuse and Lindelof) would be paid to create the series of new two- to three-minute shorts released on ABC.com that reveal background information and missing clues about the marooned residents of the island. The webisodes also feature the show's regular actors and characters and hence could end up serving as a prototype for future deals with the Screen Actors Guild as well. According to *New York Times* journalist Edward Wyatt, "The writers, actors, and others involved in the production were paid specifically for their work on the Web episodes and will earn residual income, just as they do for the broadcast show."[35]

One of the primary issues dividing the WGA leadership and management at the studios and networks was the proper definition of these quasi-entertainment ventures that straddle the once firm line dividing art and hype. Whereas the WGA and its members insisted on calling their creative contributions "content," the networks and studios insisted they functioned primarily as "promotions," thereby limiting their need as corporate owners to pay residuals to talent.[36] The guild claimed that a fair licensing fee should be linked to the amount of advertising revenue a given website can secure for its web content. The studios dismissed the idea that advertising revenue should be part of the discussion.[37] In other words, the studios were using the traditional models of TV series authorship to protect their financial back end; however, they were eager to have these same showrunners now take responsibility for their shows' viral marketing content. These distinctions lay at the heart of the strike as both sides debated the future of network television and the extent to which it will segue from traditional definitions of series television to include online promotional content.

In the months leading up to the strike, the WGA balked at their writers' new duties in the face of the new digital technologies. According to Patric Verrone, President of the Writers Guild's western division, writers were not only "being asked to finagle all these branded products into the scripts without getting any reward for it," but to help create "branded entertainment" on television by engaging in network-sponsored websites and interactive marketing gambits. Verrone continued: "In their race to the bottom line to create the so-called new business model, network and advertising executives are ignoring the public's interest and demanding that creative artists participate in stealth advertising disguised as a story."[38]

On the one hand, guild members said they were "in effect being drafted against their will to pitch products ..." and complain that "networks and studios have built this lucrative $1-billion-a-year business without paying actors and writers their fair share;"[39] on the other, writers like Lindelof and Cuse, and their counterpart Joe Davola, executive producer for such WB shows as *Smallville* (2001–), *One Tree Hill* (2003–), and *What I Like About You* (2002–2006), "defended the practice as a financial necessity in today's tight-fisted TV business." Davola noted that "budgets were especially tight at smaller networks, such as the [now defunct] WB, which still want first-rate production levels." He shot back defensively to his critics: "I don't pimp Pringles," and continued: "My arm is not being twisted to do this."[40]

Conclusion

A cynical observer of popular culture in the postnetwork era might argue that Lindelof and Cuse and other showrunners engaged in these new practices have forged an overtly commercial pact with the corporate suits by agreeing to create, manage, and promote multiplatform, corporately conceived franchises of the scale and magnitude of *Lost*. On the one hand, the showrunners' consistent efforts to interact with fans on multiple fronts (via fan web-blogs, fan conventions like Comi-Con, and alternate reality games like *The Lost Experience*) invoke a new era of populist and peer-participation entertainment. On the other hand, "big footprint" film and TV franchises like *Lost* also invoke a vision of an Adorno and Horkheimer-styled capitalist takeover in which "advertisements [or in this case the programming-marketing hybrids] are the voice of big industry, a voice that instills consumer fantasies into the minds of the masses."[41] However, neither of these disparate readings of the significance of this innovative, expansive "text" seems appropriate. Rather, Lindelof's response to accusations that he and Cuse are mere dupes of the system is more subtle and suggestive of the revised power dynamics and symmetries binding today's TV authors and their supposed adversaries, the network suits. Lindelof states: "We obviously come up with these ideas based on the storytelling, what's cool to us ... But then our masters will provide us with resources to do this stuff if there's a potential revenues stream down the line. So we're scratching each other's backs."[42] Despite the ascendancy of certain writer-producers to the top of the Hollywood food chain given their facility with the expanded 2.0 TV universe, the power dynamic binding "talent-for-hire" to their network "masters" remains uneven, as Lindelof asserts here. That said, Lindelof (like Cuse and *Lost* co-creator, Abrams) is equally aware that his street credentials among fans as a talented "auteur" and his corporate value as a brand manager in the eyes of Disney shareholders give him considerable leverage in his negotiations with ABC. Many analysts see *Lost* as a model for a new media age, "one that has far-reaching financial and ethical implications for artists and producers as new technologies and viewing practices almost demand that they produce original content for internet sites and blogs, DVDs, podcasts, and books."⁴³ It is left to media scholars to assess the cultural cost of these highly calculated corporate byproducts of postnetwork conglomeration, convergence, and globalization on the creative process. As the previous pages attest, the lingering fascination that even jaded and seasoned TV production personnel maintain for the critical category of the TV author is so pervasive that the heroic futurology forecasting the end of network television appears to be somewhat premature.

Notes

1   Carlton Cuse, Q&A with the author, "Greenlight Speaker Series," UCLA, July 18, 2006.
2   Ibid.
3   *MTM: 'Quality Television'*—an impressive, early production study that explores the independent TV production company MTM—helped perpetuate the troubling designation of "quality TV" used by many contemporary media scholars to justify their object of study. By championing MTM shows for "their creative 'difference', their 'progressiveness', their 'reflexiveness'," the book's co-editors were drawing in part on a modernist literary critical tradition that focuses on stylistic innovation, formal experimentation, multiple perspectives, and oppositional narrativity. However, Feuer et al. did not limit their study to textual analyses of the shows but rather, included a consideration of "context" (i.e., the production realities associated with MTM shows). Jane Feuer, Paul Kerr, and Tise Vahimagi, eds., *MTM: 'Quality Television'* (London: BFI, 1985), ix–x.
4   Henry Jenkins, *Convergence Culture: Where Old and New Media Collide* (New York and London: New York University Press, 2006).
5   Cuse, Q&A with the author. Cuse stated that he and Lindelof were excited about the expanded creative opportunities represented by viral formats like *The Lost Experience* ARG videogame, or *The Lost Diaries* mobisodes. According to Cuse, "… this is all uncharted [territory]." "Branded entertainment" (often associated with "product integration") refers to any media format that is linked effectively to a particular brand. For instance, *The Lost Experience* required viewers to closely examine Sprite TV ads for clues to solve the alternate reality game.
6   Whereas a typical budget for a one-hour TV drama is $2.0–2.5 million per episode, *Lost* episodes tend to cost over $3 million per episode. The total budget for twenty-two episodes of *Lost* in 2006–2007 was $65 million, according to Lorne Manly, "Running the Really Big Show: Lost Inc.," *The New York Times*, October 3, 2006.
7   For a discussion of the feature film blockbuster, see Eileen Meehan, "'Holy Commodity Fetish, Batman!': The Political Economy of a Commercial Intertext," in *The Many Lives of The Batman: Critical Approaches to a Superhero and His Media*, eds. Roberta E. Pearson and William Uricchio (New York: Routledge, 1991), 47–65.
8   Abrams left to create and run other shows after co-writing, producing, and directing the *Lost* pilot but remains tied to the series via his production company, Bad Robot. Whereas most showrunners don't know whether their show will be picked up year to year, Lindelof, Cuse, and the networks agreed upon a final air date of May 2010, which gave them greater control over the narrative's evolution.

9 Natalie Finn, "Producers Stay 'Lost' Next Season," eonline.com (April 6, 2006), archived by: gertiebeth, http://lost-media.com/modules.php?name=News&file=article&sid=1751.

10 David Marc and Robert J. Thompson, *Prime Time, Prime Movers: From 'I Love Lucy' to 'L.A. Law'—America's Greatest TV Shows and the People Who Created Them* (Boston, Toronto, London: Little, Brown and Company, 1992).

11 For a discussion of Foucault's theories of the author, see Mary Klages, "Michel Foucault: 'What Is an Author?'," November 15, 2001, http://www.colorado.edu/English/courses/ENGL2012Klages/foucault.html.

12 John Thornton Caldwell, "Unwanted Houseguests and Altered States: A Short History of Aesthetic Posturing," *Televisuality: Style, Crisis, and Authority in American Television* (New Brunswick, NJ: Rutgers University Press, 1995), 32–72.

13 Horace Newcomb and Robert S. Alley, *The Producer's Medium: Conversations with Creators of American TV* (New York and Oxford: Oxford University Press, 1983).

14 Ibid., 37.

15 John Thornton Caldwell, *Production Culture: Industrial Reflexivity and Critical Practice in Film and Television* (Durham, NC: Duke University Press, 2008), 35.

16 Gary Troup, *The Bad Twin* (New York: Hyperion, 2006).

17 "Bloopers on the Set," "On the Beach with Evangeline Lilly," "The World According to Sawyer," in "DVD Bonus Features," *Lost: The Complete Second Season—The Extended Experience* (USA: ABC Studios, September 5, 2006).

18 Henry Jenkins, Tara McPherson, and Jane Shattuc, eds., *Hop on Pop: The Politics and Pleasures of Popular Culture* (Durham, NC: Duke University Press, 2002), 3–42.

19 Elana Levine, "Toward a Paradigm for Media Production Research: Behind the Scenes at *General Hospital*," *Critical Studies in Media Communication* 18 (2001): 66–82.

20 Ibid.

21 See Sherry Ortner's chapter in this book, which gives other examples of overlaps and tension between producers and academics who are part of the same knowledge classes.

22 Cuse has a BA in American History from Harvard University. Kring has a BA in Religious Studies from University of California, Santa Barbara and an MFA from the University of Southern California.

23 Cuse was with *Nash Bridges* (1996–2001) and Kring was with *Crossing Jordan* (2001–2007).

24 Adam Fish, "Media Anthropology and the Democratization of Television," unpublished seminar paper, UCLA, Los Angeles, CA, November 2007.

25 Chris Anderson, *The Long Tail: Why the Future of Business Is Selling Less of More* (New York: Hyperion, 2006).

26 See, for instance, Caldwell's discussion of Clifford Geertz and the relevance of media ethnographic methodologies for media production studies in *Production Culture*.

27 Amanda D. Lotz, "The Promotional Role of the Network Upfront Presentations in the Production of Culture," *Television & New Media* 8, no. 1 (2007): 3–24.

28 Sara Gwenllian-Jones and Roberta Pearson, *Cult Television* (Minneapolis: University of Minnesota Press, 2004).

29 Joe Rhodes, "How 'Lost' Careered into Being a Hit Show," *The New York Times*, November 10, 2004.

30 Leslie Ryan, "Damon Lindelof," *Television Week*, August 2, 2004.

31 Ibid.

32 Ibid.

33 Ibid.
34 Ibid.
35 Edward Wyatt, "Webisodes of *Lost*: Model Deal for Writers?" *The New York Times*, November 20, 2007.
36 This is true for writers, certainly, but also for the actors and directors, who threatened to go on strike in 2008. John Scott Lewinski, "Strike Over 'New Media Pie' Could Cripple Hollywood,"*Wired*, September 18, 2007.
37 Wyatt, "Webisodes of *Lost*."
38 Meg James, "In-Show Product Pushing Chided," *Los Angeles Times*, November 14, 2005.
39 At an investor event, Disney CFO Thomas Staggs told the audience that "*Lost* and [*Desperate*] *Housewives* will account for approximately $1 billion in profits over 5 years. He indicated that ABC is focused on new platforms for future profits (not traditional syndication dollars) even though, at present, the revenue streams for digital content are still modest." Elizabeth Guider, "Mouse House Striking Up the Brand," *Daily Variety*, January 19, 2006.
40 James, "In-Show Product Pushing Chided."
41 Lynn Spigel, "Introduction," in *Make Room for TV: Television and the Family Ideal in Postwar America*, ed. Lynn Spigel (Chicago: University of Chicago Press, 1992), 7.
42 Maria Elena Fernandez, "ABC's *Lost* Is Easy to Find, and Not Just on a TV Screen," *Los Angeles Times*, January 3, 2005, 3.
43 Ibid.

Chapter 8

Showrunning the *Doctor Who* Franchise

A Response to Denise Mann

Christine Cornea

The focus of Denise Mann's previous chapter on contemporary television authorship in connection with the *Lost* (2004–) franchise identifies and questions an emerging model of production and marketing that applies to a number of recent big-budget US drama series. At a time when "must see" television has become crucial to the branding strategies of TV channels in the US and beyond, together with the competitive struggles to both retain and acquire audiences in a multichannel and multiplatform era, I am prompted to offer comparative comment from a UK perspective. While buying in a big-budget, US-produced drama series/serial has certainly operated to shore up the corporate identity of UK channels,[1] high-end, home or co-produced dramas are increasingly adopting and adapting the kind of US model outlined in Mann's chapter. Perhaps the most obvious example of this trend in British television can be witnessed in the BBC, BBC Wales, and the Canadian Broadcasting Company's big-budget relaunch and end of *Doctor Who* (2005–2008), currently at the finish of the first run of its fourth season.[2]

The success of the new *Doctor Who* can be measured with reference to BARB's UK audience figures: episodes have repeatedly topped the eight million mark, clawing back Saturday night viewers to the BBC from its terrestrial rivals ITV, Channel 4, and Five. The new *Doctor Who* has also spawned several spin-off series, the more adult and "edgy" *Torchwood* (2006–), an animated serial *The Sarah Jane Adventures* (2007–), *The Infinite Quest* (2007–), which aired as part of the children's television series *Totally Doctor Who* (2006–2007), as well as what I would call the promo-documentaries, *Doctor Who Confidential* (2005–) and *Torchwood Declassified* (2006–). Alongside regular reruns of *Doctor Who* and *Torchwood*, which now air at various times across both the BBC's terrestrial and digital channels, the franchise has reached out to an international audience with sales, for instance, of *Doctor Who* to the Sci-Fi Channel assuring a US audience and broadcasts of the series in Canada, Australia, and New Zealand. BBC Worldwide has also profited from DVD sales to the US and Canada as well as novelizations, games, and various other licensed merchandise. Together with examples like *Star Trek*, *The X-Files*, and more recently *Battlestar Galactica*, *Lost* and *Heroes*, *Doctor Who* now functions as a global franchise.

As I have argued elsewhere, it was no accident that science-fiction film moved into the mainstream with the arrival of a new Hollywood and the later emergence of the blockbuster. The genre's propensity for spectacle, special effects, ensemble casts, and complex, layered, sometimes ambiguous narratives certainly made it a most suitable vehicle for the global marketing of feature films from the 1970s onwards.[3] Likewise, television series/serials that have been variously categorized as "Science-fiction-genre television," "telefantasy" or "cult TV" have also proved eminently suitable for a growing global television market and the most recent of the series mentioned above have received serious and celebratory criticism from both academics and journalists alike. In large part this can be put down to the adoption of a "quality" gloss that not only marks these series apart from the usual "flow" of programs but also from earlier television forerunners. Here *Doctor Who* provides the perfect example of a shift from the low-budget, cult status of Science Fiction television to high-budget, "quality" fare, as the use of designer digital effects and well-crafted costumes and sets distinguishes this latest series from its earlier incarnations.[4]

A further signifier of the BBC's intended "quality" status for the series is the assigning of an American-style showrunner role to Russell T. Davies.[5] From the outset Davies' involvement with the new *Doctor Who* was trumpeted in press releases and he seemed to provide a surprising pedigree as the writer of the controversial Channel 4 drama serial *Queer as Folk* (1999–2000) and *The Second Coming* (2003). Although not strictly the "creator" of the series (unlike, say, Chris Carter for *The X-Files*), Davies was clearly set up as the authorial voice of the new *Doctor Who* and like many an American showrunner repeatedly spoke for the series in television and newspaper interviews. His promotion as figurehead and "creative force" behind the entire franchise was further cemented in his role as interpretative anchor in the accompanying *Doctor Who Confidential* and *Torchwood Declassified* series (versions of which were also made available in later DVD box sets). While episode writers, performers, directors, and technical personnel frequently detail their involvement in quasi-vox-pop style interviews, it is typically Davies' more measured remarks that frame each promo-documentary. Also, from the second season onwards, Davies is usually featured in the *Confidentials* in what looks to be a more isolated domestic or office setting, calmly declaring the meaning of the narrative or situating an episode within the wider context of the series. This is opposed to the more rushed, on-set/between takes approach adopted for other personnel interview segments. Interview responses from the "people on the ground" in the *Confidentials* will commonly mention Davies' contribution and their reliance upon him. Likewise, the Davies interviews will often praise the work of an episode writer or actor. However, his designation as controller is quite forcefully constructed here. Having said that, this construction is also offset by the consistent portrayal of the production and creative team as "happy family."

In his comprehensive account of industrial practices in American television, John Caldwell highlights shifts in how the writing process and writing teams have been represented, from a 1960s model of "cohesive and supportive family" to the more competitively stressful, divisive, and macho conditions that have come to dominate the industry.[6] Borrowing this model and applying it more broadly to the personnel who appear in the *Confidentials*, what is interesting is the way in which they appear to travel back in time: while the pace of work appears energetic, the producers of the *Confidentials* portray the making of episodes as predominantly protected from the rigors of contemporary corporate media production.[7] This is directly stressed with, for example, the return of Elizabeth Sladen as the "Sarah Jane Smith" character (who appeared as regular "companion" in the series from 1973 to 1976).[8] Sharply intercut with her work on set, Sladen comments in the accompanying *Confidential*, "The mood on set is just totally *Doctor Who*. Everyone is enjoying being here. That feels totally the same—it's just bigger."[9] Also, various actors and other personnel are regularly portrayed like excitable children. For instance, John Barrowman (Captain Jack) excitedly chatters about how he is "being paid to play" and, intercut with the shooting of an action sequence,[10] Doctor actor seasons two to four David Tennant playfully states, "The mind of Russell T. Davies is a very strange and curious place and it conjures up these extraordinary scenarios, which we get the great joy of acting out. It's a hoot."[11] Not only does the editing style firmly embed these comments within the *Doctor Who* working world, but workers resolutely play out these rather retro corporate personas for the audience. At the same time much is made of the bigger budget expectations of the new series in the *Confidentials*: like the bonus features on a DVD film, the performance of physical affects and the design of digital effects are foregrounded and personnel frequently make aside comments like "I have to get that money on camera today."[12] But, even though there is some evidence in these promo-documentaries of a rather more pressured corporate environment, it is notable that Davies is repeatedly referred to by editors as "head writer" in the undertitles, emphasising his creative rather than business role as co-executive producer and some effort seems to go into his construction as benevolent patriarch.

Of course, the Davies persona performs for the *Doctor Who* franchise on a number of levels; while the new *Doctor Who* works hard to foreground familiar London landmarks and tourist spots in its promotion of this decidedly British franchise, Davies' Welsh heritage is played out in the Cardiff setting for *Torchwood*. Further, this aspect of his persona activates associations with the writer Terry Nation (born in Cardiff, Wales), as creator of the Daleks for the "classic" *Doctor Who*, and even the highly contentious 1960s science-fiction-fantasy series, *The Prisoner* (1967–1968), famously filmed in Portmeirion in Wales.[13] Also, while the BBC may portray Davies as fatherly in the *Confidentials*, a rather more alternative, parallel identity emerges in connection with the *Torchwood* series (which features the bisexual "Captain Jack" character, played by the British-American actor John Barrowman) alongside Davies' growing status as gay icon for fans.[14] Via the centrally placed Davies, this BBC franchise is therefore able to attract both a niche and broader audience. In addition, the Davies persona operates in conjunction with efforts to attract a local audience (answering to the BBC's historical remit for public service broadcasting) at the same time as it opens up its "content" to an international audience and simultaneously celebrates British television's past achievements.

Although the advent of the writer-executive producer as powerful authorial figure might be viewed as a relatively new turn in the US, British television has a long and well-established tradition of elevating the importance of its writers as central creative figures.[15] With roots in theater and literary adaptation, as well as early aspirations to disseminate "high culture" to the masses, British television drama has tended to place a great deal of importance on the creative agency of the writer. Moreover, in comparison to the US, 1950s and 1960s British television science fiction was more often aimed at an adult audience, where the kudos that a well-respected writer could bring was emphasized in the commissioning of existing stories or dramatists. For instance, anthology series like ABC's *Armchair Theatre* (1956–1974) had featured science fiction and the BBC's *Out of the Unknown* (1965–1971) actively promoted those plays adapted from novels or short stories by esteemed writers like E. M. Forster and John Wyndham. Likewise, the genre's association with serious and valued television drama secured the skills of respected television writers such as Nigel Neale, who delivered the vast majority of the scripts for BBC's *Quatermass* serials (1955–1958). More recently, one of the most acclaimed television dramatists, Dennis Potter, revived this tradition with the four-part science-fiction serial *Cold Lazarus* (1996). So it is possible to see how Davies can be associated with this longstanding British tradition at the same time as he boasts a new-style authorial voice, guaranteeing "quality" for an overseas market, as well as marshaling the franchise into the twenty-first century. Indeed, Davies eagerly draws upon these associations in a recent interview television appearance with Mark Lawson:[16] as if ticking off a list of appropriate links, Davies manages to mention renowned television dramatists Stephen Poliakoff and Potter, the serial dramas *I, Claudius* (1976) and *Pennies from Heaven* (1978), as well as respected children's television shows such as *Blue Peter* (1958–) and *Magpie* (1968–1980). By placing himself within this tradition he is simultaneously aligning himself with well-respected television auteurs as well as alluding to his own past in television. From apparently "humble" beginnings in Swansea, Davies graduated from the University of Oxford with a degree in English Literature. With early work experience in theater he later undertook a director's course with the BBC. After this, he soon moved into production and writing positions with children's television prior to his more recent success as the writer of high-profile dramas. So, on the one hand, Davies appears to style himself with reference to previous "working-class lad made good" auteurs, like Potter,[17] on the other hand he places his past television work within a tradition of British television that spans children's light entertainment/educational programs to the thoroughly adult and serious drama. His careful crafting of his persona thereby emphasizes a breadth of past experience that is not only entirely appropriate to the new *Doctor Who* franchise, but that also provides relative freedom in terms of his future association with a range of possible projects.

Perhaps recognizing that the term and function of the showrunner is relatively unfamiliar to the British public,[18] the Lawson interview also opens with Davies' description of his role for *Doctor Who*: "It's that sort of American showrunner position, where you don't just script, where you oversee it ... It needs someone, it needs streamlining ... and the showrunner does that."[19] Davies calls attention to his authorial status by describing himself as "bolshie" and briefly detailing his control over the visual style of the *Doctor Who* series.[20] While he readily admits to being approached by the BBC to undertake the job he also stresses the degree of autonomy and trust he commands, as well as his earlier attempts to have the series relaunched. However, the authenticity of Davies' commentary is undermined when, during the closing discussion, he takes issue with the post-Hutton pressures on television not to mislead the viewing public.[21] Irritated by these pressures as they apply to the science-fiction genre, Davies jokingly states: "Never think I tell the truth in an interview ... it's rubbish when you come to drama ... I lie through my teeth ... it's a big media game."[22] Davies sees lying to the press as part of his job in protecting ongoing storylines and creating interest in the *Doctor Who* franchise. While readily admitting a willingness to "play the press," Davies has repeatedly stressed his lack of engagement with hardcore "Whovians" and is disparaging of American writers who pander to pressure from fans: "I think it's a huge mistake. If you came to me and said 'You've made a brand new programme, I'd like to run it past a focus group of 2,000 people,' I'd say, 'No way, no good drama has ever been made that way.'"[23] This would seem to differentiate the Davies persona from, say, the *Lost* showrunners who cater to their fan audience. As Henry Jenkins puts it, fans have moved "from the invisible margins of popular culture and into the center of current thinking about media production and consumption."[24] *Lost* provides a clear example of "quality TV" that is vehemently designed to play to fan participation on a number of levels. In this sense, although Davies' function as showrunner may be portrayed as pioneering for British television, this seems to be in tension with a new breed of showrunner whose role and function is increasingly and more obviously dispersed. In fact, it was recently announced that Davies is stepping down as showrunner and passing the reins of power for the *Doctor Who* franchise on to Steven Moffat (writer of award-winning episodes for the series) and co-executive producer Julie Gardner is being replaced by Piers Wenger. Presumably, like Davies before him, Moffat will be required to promote an authorial signature for this new, new *Doctor Who*, but he will also be charged with upholding the familiar principles and doctrines of the series. It will be fascinating to watch how the Moffat persona develops and how the *Doctor Who* franchise will regenerate in answer to ongoing "quality" competition from the US. Indeed, I would say that this is a particularly interesting juncture as already existing tensions between old and new are brought to the fore; the tension that has always been evident between old and new *Doctor Who* series; the tension that has been present in Davies' dual role as a kind of neoromantic auteur and as corporate figurehead; and the tension between the old-style ethos of British television and a new-style global age of media production.

Notes

1 I use the term "buying in" to indicate not only the purchase of a US series, but the ways in which a British channel can tap into the kudos of a quality US series as part of its own branding policy. For example, Channel 4 has made particular use of "quality" US series, such as *ER* (1994–), *Friends* (1994–2004), and *The West Wing* (1999–2006), frequently outbidding other channels for exclusive British first run rights for both the terrestrial channel and the digital E4 channel. Also, albeit to a lesser extent, Channel 5's re-branding as Five in 2002 has been recently marked with the buy up of flagship series like *House* (2004–) and *Grey's Anatomy* (2005–).

2 While UK press and academics tend to use the term "series" to refer to the separate runs of episodes that appear each year, for the purposes of this piece I am adopting the American term "season."

3 Christine Cornea, *Science Fiction Cinema: Between Fantasy and Reality* (Edinburgh and New Brunswick, NJ: Edinburgh University Press/Rutgers University Press, 2007).

4 *Doctor Who* was in continuous production from 1963 to 1989 at the BBC. Alongside the series, two spin-off films were produced in the mid-1960s: *Dr. Who and the Daleks* (1965) and *Daleks' Invasion Earth* (1966), which attempted to cash in on the "Dalek mania" sweeping Britain at the time. This was followed by a BBC Worldwide/Universal Television produced *Doctor Who* feature-length film in 1996. Although the low-budget sets and clunky costumes have long been celebrated as a feature of the "classic" series amongst fans, as the series moved into the 1980s it became increasingly difficult to compete with the higher budget production values of American series like *Star Trek: The Next Generation* (1987–1994). For James Chapman, the relative failure of the bigger budget 1996 film to relaunch the television series at this time can partly be put down to the difficulties of dealing with a "flashy" American sci-fi aesthetic that did not marry well with the quaintly British and eccentric "Heath Robertson" look of the earlier series. See James Chapman, "Millennial Anxieties: 1996," *Inside the Tardis: The Worlds of Doctor Who* (London and New York: I.B. Tauris, 2006), 173–183.

5 Along with Julie Gardner (Head of Drama for BBC Wales and BBC Television Controller of Drama Commissioning), Davies is executive producer, as well as being "head writer" of the series.

6 See John T. Caldwell, *Production Culture: Industrial Reflexivity and Critical Practice in Film and Television* (Durham, NC: Duke University Press, 2008), 214.

7   From 2005 to 2008, the series producer of the *Confidentials* has been Gillane Seaborne, with executive producers Russell T. Davies, Julie Gardner, and Mark Casey.

8   "School Reunion," *Doctor Who*, Season 2, Episode 3, directed by James Hawes (England: BBC, August 26, 2006).

9   "Friends Reunited," *Doctor Who Confidential*, Season 2, Episode 3, directed by Adam Page (England: BBC, August 29, 2006).

10 "Special Effects," *Doctor Who Confidential*, Season 1, Episode 9, directed by Tony Lee and Rupert Miles (England: BBC, May 21, 2005).

11 "The New, New Doctor," *Doctor Who Confidential*, Season 2, Episode 1, directed by Adam Page (England: BBC, April 15, 2006).

12 Comment by the director James Hawes, "Backstage at Christmas," *Doctor Who Confidential*, Episode 14, DVD (England: BBC, 2005).

13 See Catherine Johnson, *Telefantasy* (London: BFI, 2005), 42–67. Interestingly, *The Prisoner* was also stamped with the mark of quality by 1960s standards, in terms of its hybrid series/serial format, its recording onto film, designed with both UK and US markets in mind, and, as Catherine Johnson has argued, marketed as the creative brain-child of the actor-executive producer Patrick McGoohan.

14 Davies can be found at the top of the list of influential gay men in Britain. See Hugo Eyre-Varnier et al., "The pink list 2007: The IoS Annual Celebration of the Great and the Gay," *Independent on Sunday*, May 6, 2007, http://www.independent.co.uk/news/uk/this-britain/the-pink-list-2007-the-iiosi-annual-celebration-of-the-great-and-the-gay-447627.html.

15 For Caldwell a distinctive look and authorial signature mark the emergence of what has come to be seen as quality TV in the US from the 1980s onwards. John T. Caldwell, *Televisuality: Style, Crisis, and Authority in American Television* (New Brunswick, NJ: Rutgers University Press, 1995).

16 *Mark Lawson talks to Russell T. Davies*, directed by Helen Partridge (London: BBC Four, January 16, 2008).

17 Potter's father was a coal miner in Gloucester and Wales. Following National Service, Potter managed to secure a scholarship to attend New College, Oxford. After Oxford, Potter joined the BBC, initially working in radio and television journalism, before moving on to become a television playwright.

18 Anecdotal evidence would suggest that it is also relatively unfamiliar within television production circles in Britain. When asked to write this piece I hurriedly phoned around a number of television producers and executive producers that I am in contact with (who primarily work in television drama or "factual entertainment') and all stated they were unfamiliar with the term "showrunner." However, I suspect that this will change soon.

19 Ibid.

20 In this context, Davies uses "bolshie" as a common colloquialism that indicates his argumentative and belligerent nature.

21 The Hutton Inquiry was set up in 2003 to investigate the circumstances surrounding the death of Dr. David Kelly, after he had been named by BBC journalists as a source in reports that claimed the government had deliberately exaggerated Iraq's military capabilities prior to the second Gulf War. Following the Hutton report, as well as more recent debacles surrounding misconduct and dishonesty in television phone-in quizzes, there has been an ongoing concern within the BBC about anything that could be construed as misleading the public.

22 Ibid.
23 Ciar Byre, "Russell T. Davies: The Saviour of Saturday Night Drama," *The Independent*, April 10, 2006.
24 Henry Jenkins, *Convergence Culture: Where Old and New Media Collide* (New York: New York University Press, 2006), 12.

Part III

Production Spaces:
Centers and Peripheries

Figure 9.1 Broadcast Tower and Palms. Photo by John Caldwell, 2002.

Chapter 9

Liminal Places and Spaces
Public/Private Considerations

Candace Moore

While researching the production and consumption of Showtime's hit lesbian-themed series *The L Word* (2004–2009), my fieldwork alternatively brought me to the show's set in Vancouver, BC to interview and observe producers, writers, and actors, and to public viewing venues in multiple cities, to do the same with the show's fans.[1] One particular boundary-crossing moment happened not across national borders, rather when I witnessed "media people" from the set and "ordinary" audiences of *The L Word* converge in the same space: Hollywood's lesbian nightspot *The Falcon*.[2] On the night of the show's second season premiere, I observed *The L Word*'s showrunner, Ilene Chaiken, and co-executive producer, Rose Troche, inconspicuously eating dinner at *The Falcon*, a popular LA screening spot for the series, watching hundreds of fans responding to the episode as it aired. As behind-the-scenes producers, rather than recognizable stars, these two participant-observers went largely unnoticed by the fans around them.[3]

In his discussion of media pilgrimages, British cultural studies scholar Nick Couldry cautions that media consumers should consider "moments when, instead of us journeying to places in the media, the power gradients that structure the media landscape suddenly pass close to us."[4] *The Falcon*'s independently promoted screening parties have become a part of a "real" queer female culture in Los Angeles that *The L Word* seeks to both describe and fictionalize, and thus this site participates in a feedback loop between the community that gathers and socializes there—a community also *constructed* by and around the television show—and its representation.[5] This incident at *The Falcon* in 2005 inspired me to further explore the *L Word* screening party phenomenon with an eye to how audience research, branding, viral marketing, manufactured points of contact between show executives and fans, and virtual world-building attempt to unite and harness this fan public.[6] Drawing from 2000 Census Bureau statistics on gay and lesbian couples, I chose to observe viewing parties in three of the zip codes in America with the highest numbers of same sex couples (as compared to married and unmarried heterosexual couples): West Hollywood, Los Angeles, CA (90069); Andersonville, Chicago, IL (60640); and

Park Slope, Brooklyn, NY (11215).[7] I conducted the bulk of my research in Los Angeles from 2005 to 2008 and traveled to Chicago and Brooklyn in 2007. I engaged in conversations with participants after and before screenings, openly introducing myself as both a fan and scholar of *The L Word*. Emerging from my notes, this essay interrogates four different *L Word* screening party environments and one particular virtual space as peripheral sites of production, where queer female consumers become incorporated into the production process (through audience surveillance and interaction) and where lines between private/public, producer/consumer, and insider/outsider are blurred.[8] I first consider useful approaches to screening parties; second, I examine independently produced gatherings around *The L Word* in bars and restaurants; next, I turn to screening parties co-produced by Showtime Networks; and lastly, I analyze OurChart.com, a networking site owned by Showtime, Chaiken, and cast members of *The L Word*.[9]

Responding to Couldry's scholarship on media rituals, this chapter considers liminal places and mediated spaces that emphasize the myth of social cohesion through media.[10] Media rituals, as Couldry describes them, seem to "integrate" consumers and producers of media, while they "[mask] social inequality," given that they rely on the "uneven distribution of symbolic resources."[11] Boundaries between consumers and producers of *The L Word* become seemingly permeable, only to be capitalized on and more effectively reinscribed.

The L Word changes narrative and representational strategies season by season, acting in a quick relay with audience response in order to maintain profitability and cult draw.[12] Writers and producers keep the show topical and timely, trading on star personalities and pulling from current events and trends in mainstream and queer culture. *The L Word* also has a ravenous reflexivity and self-referentiality, taking itself to task for its own idiosyncrasies, problems, or failed representations, exhibiting an awareness of potential critiques, and incorporating them into the show. Keeping things contemporary and appropriately self-critical allows queer female audiences particularly to feel that they are being "accurately" represented and that their input is being "heard," while the show is simultaneously designed and multipurposed to cater to straight tourists.[13] Showtime's prefiguring of diverse audience groups for *The L Word* is underscored by the network's commercial for season four, which flaunts and parodies the concept of "everyone" watching *The L Word* and, through their tourism, becoming "honorary lesbians." In the promotional ad, various (stereo)types are depicted, including Italian mobsters, male soldiers, and an elderly, heterosexual African American couple on a porch, all proclaiming themselves "lesbians." The advertisement is capped with the statement: "This Time of Year, Everyone Is. *The L Word*, Coming Soon." The producers of *The L Word* market the show to both a broad crossover audience and a specific queer female niche—the fan contingent arguably in the majority at *L Word*-themed events and screenings.

Social gatherings organized around watching TV in bars, restaurants, and similar venues have been a part of television viewing culture since the medium was introduced, as media historian Anna McCarthy explores. Her analysis of sports television spectatorship in late 1940s American taverns interrogates the press coverage of this phenomenon, including snapshots of bar patrons, eyes glued toward a common spot just outside the photographic frame. McCarthy notes reporters' tendencies to equate the audience's location (as TV gazers within the bar) with its identity (as sports fans). These "speculative links," McCarthy argues, "illustrate a wider ideology that continues to define much commercial discourse about television outside the home, namely, that there is a direct correspondence between social space and social subjectivity."[14]

As scholars analyze the twenty-first-century phenomenon of group television viewing outside the home, McCarthy's caution is worthy of further consideration. For instance, there is no way to accurately correlate an attendee's mere presence at an *L Word* screening party with the intensity, sincerity, loyalty, or significance of their fandom, nor extrapolate from the queer-centric gathering spaces that these fans inhabit their likely sexual preferences. However, perceived correlations between these spaces and personal subjectivity surely relate to the draw of the screening site as a place for fans to express their affiliation with the public (however imagined) constructed by the circulating discourse of *The L Word*. Screening party attendees, part of a fluctuating sub-viewership, seek a semblance of social cohesion with others who, if not like them, certainly *watch* like them and are joined by the very fact of their receivership of the discourse. Through attendance at screening sites where strangers can congregate, members of this fan public define themselves *as members*, and play an embodied role in a group dynamic, acting out physically a relationship to the text of *The L Word*. Attending screening parties resembles the interactivity of responding to Internet fan message boards; however, the intentions at the heart of this ritual may differ slightly, given the attendant urge to "make it real," to perform a relationship to the community depicted on-screen in a temporally and spatially distinct way from the virtual, even as the cohesiveness of such a public is, of course, still altogether imaginary.

In *Publics and Counterpublics*, Michael Warner argues that publics are always indeterminate and the only requirement membership in a public entails is one's attention.[15] Yet, attention is fleeting and difficult to chart, especially with regard to television. Public screening parties further underscore the unquantifiable nature of television consumption and fandom. Given OnDemand, DVRs, TV-on-DVD, online viewing technologies, as well as group screenings, consumption of *The L Word* cannot be estimated simply by determining how many Showtime subscribers tune in to watch episodes when originally broadcast. Network-sponsored screening parties seek to borrow the charge (and sometimes the locales) of screening parties that are grassroots or independently produced, to condone these viewing rituals and spaces and authoritatively mark them as "official," while simultaneously conducting qualitative audience research.

Collaborative viewing with strangers involves a dynamic of performance that domestic viewing alone or with family members or friends lacks; presence at a public viewing site attempts to articulate a fan's allegiances within a broader social realm. Why did a culture of outside-the-home viewing sprout up with such geographic scope around *The L Word*? As the first longstanding serial drama about a diverse queer female community featuring a lesbian dating and bar scene, the show consciously reflects queer female cultures and, due to its popularity with young people particularly, the styles, tropes, and perhaps even sexual ethics foregrounded by the show have been further reflected and refracted in lived queer cultures. Producers of the series encourage the fantasy of an off-screen lesbian public connected by degrees of separation that can be surpassed through fan practices. While not all of the fans that view the show socially are queer or female, much social interaction around *The L Word* potentially happens as a result of this fantasy. Most of the regular participants of screening parties cite the atmosphere of the surrounding party as on a par in importance with, if not exceeding, their experience of viewing the show. The ability to make timely, snarky comments as an episode is broadcast is also highly valued among members of most *L Word* screening party communities.

Such parties began from both local/grassroots expressions and corporate/capitalistic interests. Conceiving of television spectatorship outside of the home as embodying "a particular sense of the relationship between the public and private," rather than taking place in distinctly "public sites," McCarthy describes the tavern screening site as a "cultural arena in which liberatory ideals of democratic socializing met the privatizing forces of commerce and insular expressions of community."[16] *The L Word* screening parties are not events that discretely belong to or solely represent the fan public, nor are the spaces in which they are held unconditionally public. Indeed public and private distinctions are blurred by the corporate and entrepreneurial forces involved at *L Word* screening parties, particularly in those cases where Showtime has sent delegates or has some relation with the event, whether as facilitator, sponsor, participant-observer, or silent partner.[17] The screening party is also structured by private interests in the form of bar owners, bartenders, and promoters. How much an event is advertised locally (through print media or flyers), online, or through word of mouth also affects how insular the community that gathers there is likely to be. Furthermore, certain devices are used by event promoters to determine who "deserves" entry more, such as RSVP lists and entrance monitors that quantify and qualify participants.

At *The Falcon*, for example, the weekly events, which include two screenings every Sunday night the show airs, often reach "full capacity" and throughout the night lines form outside of hopefuls waiting to get in. However, VIPs (whose status is determined by promoter's lists or sometimes judged on-the-spot by the doorperson) are allowed expedited entry. Similar to the stereotypical bouncer who lets well-dressed participants into a club first, the doorperson at *The Falcon* polices status within the Hollywood industry or the local lesbian club culture. Once inside, seating arrangements are determined based on whether one's party is eating dinner in the restaurant or not. The event staff offers the best seats to those who make dinner reservations ahead of time, thereby creating a hierarchy of seating in which patrons with more money to spend are placed in good hearing and viewing range of the screens. While Showtime is not acknowledged as a partner to the parties at *The Falcon*, a note on the promotional company's website declares that their seasonal Sunday event "recently featured Showtime's 'L WORD' episode each week, with regular attendence [sic] by the cast and creative team."[18] FUSEevents might very well have a tacit agreement with Showtime; their events further brand *The L Word* and Showtime and offer the creative team free audience research, while the increased likelihood of star sightings (potentially manufactured) raises this event's cache for fans and brings more people in to spend money. Although the screening party is a free event, put on by independent promoters rather than the network, it is negotiated by questions of access, status, and privilege.

Contrast this atmosphere with that of *Cattyshack*, a two-story lesbian pub in Park Slope in Brooklyn, New York, where attendance of the weekly *L Word* screenings is considerably lower—capping just under a hundred people. Park Slope, as previously mentioned, is a diverse neighborhood with a large queer population; it is even known by some as "Dyke Slope." Access based on class and status operates very differently in this Brooklyn viewing space than at *The Falcon*. There is no doorperson counting attendees at *Cattyshack*, nor "sorting" them, and thus screening party participants flow in and out without any major oversight. The screenings are held in a bar area and adjacent room upstairs, so neighborhood patrons uninterested in *L Word*-related festivities can enter the establishment freely and enjoy themselves downstairs. Regular screening party participants also provide a weekly community pot luck, spread outside the screening room for pre- or post-screening snacking. This reduces the cost of the experience considerably for those who might not be able to afford the cost of going out for dinner on top of going out for drinks. Somewhere between these two screening party models, *Joie de Vine* in Andersonville, a community on the north side of Chicago, tends to attract a smaller audience culled from the local neighborhood. However, purchasing a glass or a flight from the wine bar's drinks menu, which features organic wines, is politely encouraged if one wants to take a seat. The wine bar is located in a middle-class commercial district with a significant LGBT patronage. There is no doorperson in this long, one-room bar, and although non-*L Word* fans seem equally welcome, a hush (except for reactionary exclamations to the show) takes over the bar at screening time.

Interestingly, at each of the three venues so far discussed—the independently promoted party at Hollywood's *The Falcon*, the more communal-style gathering upstairs at Brooklyn's *Cattyshack*, and the intimate *L Word* wine event hosted by *Joie de Vine*'s owners—audience members' interaction with the screen and with each other differs. Depending on their settings, participants cite varied reasons for attending and acknowledge a range of levels of fandom. For many attendees at larger venues, the purpose of the screening party does not seem to revolve around watching the episode (in fact, at *The Falcon* it becomes hard to hear dialogue over the crowd's din), but has more to do with socializing, mirroring the night life depicted on screen; in these cases, the show acts as a device for bringing a specific public together. The screening does not merely serve as mediated "wallpaper," however; the brand names of *The L Word* and Showtime, projected onto the screens and emblazoned on flyers and signs, appear and circulate throughout these spaces. By associating themselves with the screening party public, participants, perhaps unintentionally, link themselves to the Showtime brand. The smaller venues with less audience surveillance and mechanisms of crowd control provide meeting places for active viewers who concentrate on the show as it is broadcast while alternating at providing running commentary, often talking back to the screen in sarcastic or campy ways.[19] Yet, these smaller venues also propagate the Showtime brand. Patrons at both *Cattyshack* and *Joie de Vine* mentioned lack of premium cable at home, positioned as a "luxury," as a main reason for attending *L Word* screening parties. Such parties allow participants to catch the show over drinks without doling out a monthly subscriber fee to Showtime. This financial reasoning seems aligned with discourses about the initial public gatherings around television when the technology was first introduced and not yet affordable for most Americans. The tavern was considered popular as a place to watch television not only because of camaraderie or a cold pint of beer but because a majority of its patrons could not afford a set at home or a ticket to the game. As of September 2007, 98 percent of households have one or more television sets, 58 percent subscribe to basic cable, and under 8 percent subscribe to Showtime.[20] The choice not to purchase premium cable for these viewers occasionally includes a defined anticorporate sentiment—attendees at *Joie de Vine*, for instance, mentioned they would rather spend their money at local establishments than offer that money to cable providers. Such statements slightly sidestep questions of affordability and class. They also minimize the pull of the social atmosphere as a factor in participation. By emphasizing the necessity of attending public screenings in order to keep up with the show, this reasoning subtly downplays participation in a public. Similarly, "talking back" and "talking over"[21]—two relationships to the screen that participants often demonstrate at screening parties—express forms of engagement, ambivalence, and also disavowal: the fan public both links themselves to the fiction (by their very presence) and surprisingly resists it (by exhibiting critically distanced or even disinterested forms of attention).

Recognizing fans' attraction to the "rhetoric of social togetherness" that the *L Word* screening parties represent, Showtime partnered with the Human Rights Campaign (HRC) to create network-sanctioned screenings in over thirty-five cities nationally for the premieres of seasons four and five.[22] While locally sponsored or grassroots screening parties that take place at bars, restaurants, and people's homes tend to be free (except for the cost of drinks), these HRC co-sponsored screenings double as charity events with recommended donation fees (as high as $20) that in practice act as charges for admission. HRC and Showtime mutually benefit from this arrangement, in that these events collect funds for and spread the word about HRC, at the same time that HRC, an organization that lobbies for LGBT equal rights, lends its stamp of real-world "social relevance" to the show. For fans, the assurance that admission fees are "going to a good cause" buttresses the notion that the social culture developed around *The L Word*, which they perform and purchase participation in, is an ethical one. For lesbian and queer fans, this cross-promotion thematically links representational and real politics; subtly hinting that "positive" images of queer sexualities on the smaller screen might be translated into, or help lead to, real-world transformations in civil rights for LGBTQ Americans.

In advertisements for these special screenings, Showtime offers those who arrive early an advance copy of the season's next episode on DVD, giving participants the sense of getting a special, insider's look at the upcoming season and a souvenir to take home, while suggesting that "it is 'exciting' to get standardized promotional material."[23] At one of these "official" premiere parties for the fifth season, held on January 8, 2008 at *The Factory*, fans were additionally rewarded with the chance to see their favorite *L Word* stars in the flesh. On an uncharacteristically stormy night in West Hollywood, hundreds waited in the rain for over an hour before gaining entrance to the premiere of season five, introduced by Chaiken and stars Jennifer Beals, Pam Grier, Mia Kirshner, Leisha Hailey, Rose Rollins, Rachel Shelley, Daniella Sea, and Laurel Holloman. Event workers patrolled the line of fans huddled under umbrellas, passing out free raffle tickets, clipboards, and pens. Each ticket offering the chance to win an *L Word* season four DVD set requested personal information in exchange: name, home address, phone number, and email address. Presented as an opportunity for attendees to get lucky and win show merchandise, the raffle doubled as an information-gathering opportunity for Showtime about *The L Word*'s loyal consumer base. The promotional DVD and raffle both functioned as "opt in" forms of viral marketing.[24] As Henry Jenkins has pointed out, media executives are increasingly turning attention to loyal fan constituencies who attend such network-sponsored or endorsed fan events for their favorite media brands.[25] Tracking dedicated fans who participate in larger worlds created around the content of a media franchise and offering varied points and modes of affective contact for fans proves extremely lucrative for producers. Diversifying the places and spaces for media rituals to play out provides exponential opportunities for advertising as well as multiple forums that encourage fans to feel as if they have agency within the production process.

Data-mining of these "loyals" happens through self-disclosure, as producers lure fans with chances to feel special, included, and knowledgeable about media content. While any number of attendees of such events may already regularly subscribe to Showtime's email listservs, receive promotional materials, or participate in online fan communities, fans on the data-grid will likely bring untracked and potential fans along with them. Thus, network-produced screening parties gather enthusiasts, budding enthusiasts, and strays, all the while collecting information used to expand marketing databases. Such events also stage content popularity contests, as participants are encouraged to vocalize their responses to stars, on-screen scenarios, and to the show itself as a brand.

Producers stage instances where they seem to be "asking for help" or require fan consensus on a subject at promotional events. For instance, when Showtime president Robert Greenblatt spoke at the season five premiere screening, his presence there cast him into the role of the godhead that could alone judge whether *The L Word* would be greenlit for a sixth season. The crowd was summoned by actresses Leisha Hailey and Kate Moennig to make their emotional appeal to Greenblatt:

Hailey: We could do another season of *The L Word* …
Moennig: The only way we could do another season of *The L Word* is if you [referencing the audience] want to do it? [audience cheers and screams]. So is that a yes? [louder cheers]. You guys got to do us a favor, you've got to tell Showtime [referencing Greenblatt offstage] that you want to do it [loud cheers and screams, again]. Come on, Come on. I can't hear you! [audience vocalizes at earsplitting decibels].

Producers of *The L Word* rely upon such staged engagements with fans, offering to them a rhetoric of democratic agency. Such network sanctioned screening parties reproduce the sense that the show's fan public has a group agency by addressing the audience with verbal requests for response, cuing the illusion that any power differential between producer and consumer is a gap that can be filled through "talking back." The message to fans is that publicly emoting enthusiasm, desire, or even dismay, if enunciated almost univocally for producers, has the power to inform or change institutional decision making. Fan opinion *does* influence network opinion, but it may not often dramatically sway it. Of course, these dramatized interactions between media people and audiences function quite differently than the "stealth" observation tactics described earlier, even as they may be used similarly to cater media content and marketing materials to maximize consumer affect.

Taking place in face-to-face environments that pretend to give fans "access" to behind-the-scenes executives, these ritualized interactions often serve to make fans feel essential to the fate of the show—they perform fan agency. However, this is mostly illusion: rarely are they integrated into the production or corporate decision making process. In "Industrial Geography Lessons," John Caldwell uses the term "contact zones" to describe such "half-way spaces" where Hollywood executives meet with and "mentor" industry hopefuls, whom they seldom actually take into the fold: "These contact zones provide one of the few points of human contact, and promise to help aspirants achieve more effective 'skill-sets', but they exist at the furthermost ring of the studio/network maze."[26] Fans who wish to affect the production of their favorite show are industry aspirants of a type that reside outside even this furthermost ring. Producers journey to them because they wish to entice (and learn how to entice) these fans to consume their brand consistently and in multiple ways.

As Henry Jenkins has found, social fans—those who tend to watch television in group settings—are also "more likely to access program-related web sites. Of course, as those viewers move onto the Web, some are choosing to discuss their interpretations and assessments of the programs via online fan communities. Social viewing, then, would appear to be an important driver behind brand and content extension."[27] At the same time as Showtime trades on the erotic and ethnographic appeals of lesbian sex scenes and the exoticism of queer culture to market *The L Word* beyond the queer female niche, the network has devised a part of their marketing campaign to specifically target this audience. The social networking Internet site OurChart.com is based on the character Alice's chart of "connected" lesbians depicted on *The L Word*. Acting as a "real" simulacrum of a fictional chart, OurChart.com is advertised as similar to "sites such as MySpace," in that it "helps you find others with your same interests and promotes connections of all kinds, but is aimed directly at lesbians, their friends and family."[28] In creating OurChart.com, Showtime and partners cashed in on the grassroots social networking that was already happening "analog" style, acknowledged the network's chief executive Matthew Blank: "Everyone I know who watches that show and is gay watches it with their friends … It makes for a natural extension."[29] Since launching in 2007, OurChart.com has drawn approximately 500,000 visits monthly, and has become a queer female hub on the Internet that serves as more than simply just a networking site or a fan site.[30] The site includes "celesbian" blogs and editorial pieces; webisodes and original video content; behind-the-scenes features on *The L Word*; message boards and other user-generated content; photo galleries; reportage on night life, lifestyle subjects, and humor writing; and links to content on other featured queer media outlets. OurChart.com's president, Hilary Rosen, former head of the Recording Industry Association of America, explained that OurChart.com's design featured hybrid online formats because "we felt we had something unique to offer. There were lesbian news sites, there were lesbian travel sites, there were fledgling lesbian dating sites, but nothing that, in our view, combined the stickiness of a social network with original content." She added that "the corresponding piece [to what *The L Word* portrays] is people's individual L Worlds."[31] Rosen used the same "world" metaphor with Elizabeth Jensen of *The New York Times*, in describing how the site's *L Word*-based content will eventually be replaced by more user-generated content: "Every lesbian has their own L world. We thought it would be really interesting to let go of the show in this environment and bring other people's L worlds into the mix and let them share with each other."[32]

Through OurChart.com, Showtime Networks and their partners (including CBS) proctor and promote a ritual media space, cordoned off for lesbians (mostly), and yet following Couldry's logic, since on the Internet there are no "ritual bodies," anyone can declare him- or herself a "lesbian," or indeed a "friend of."[33] Furthermore, queer female cyber-identities are "charted" (i.e., organized) on the site, and thus made ever more accessible to Viacom, the conglomerate that owns Showtime Networks, as a marketing demographic for tailored advertising from its companies. In fact, OurChart.com is the first Showtime Networks venture to be supported by ad revenue, since like other premium cable networks, Showtime does not sell ad time.[34] Yet, fans seem enticed to participate by the "opportunity" to chart *themselves*. Practicing in "mediated self-disclosure," OurChart.com members individually design, provide content for, and maintain their own profile spaces within what is at root an institutionally controlled, monitored, and profit-based network.[35] Ilene Chaiken and *The L Word's* actresses Jennifer Beals, Leisha Hailey, and Katherine Moennig lend the value of their celebrity names to this project; in fact they are financial partners in the endeavor.[36] Thus, fans gain a charted relationship to these stars within the ritual space. Participants may also have the chance, through their individualized profiles and participation on message boards, to draw attention to themselves or to become net-celebrities.[37]

The cross-promotion between OurChart.com and *The L Word* is staggering. In a transmedia stunt, OurChart.com launched the season five premiere of *The L Word* a week before the show premiered on Showtime, reportedly raising the audience by 36 percent compared to the previous season's premiere, according to *Hollywood Reporter*.[38] Close-ups of laptop computer screens featuring OurChart.com on the browser have become nearly weekly fare on *The L Word*, as characters Alice (Leisha Hailey) and Max (Daniella Sea) extol the newest features on the fictional/real site. Product placement of the website within the show first occurred on the season four premiere previous to the site's official launch. In the context of updating her friends on her latest project, Alice rattled off OurChart.com's selling points.

One of the first blogs on OurChart.com was "Come on, Ilene," Chaiken's weekly podcast commentary on the behind-the-scenes decisions of each episode.

The video blog includes a forum for fans to respond "directly" to the show's executive producer with disgruntlements, savored moments, and wishes. This format corresponds with Chaiken's description of her vision of OurChart.com in press accounts as a place where fans can "weigh in" on the show and see their desires worked into storylines.[39] The first "Come on, Ilene" video podcast, released on January 7, 2007, depicts Chaiken curled up on a living room sofa in her tube socks. The second, from January 14, 2007, found her wearing skull-patterned pajamas while discussing the composition of "Livin' la Vida Loca" with the episode's writer Alexandra Kondracke, who appeared in sweats. Later installments of Chaiken's cutting-room-floor perspective, entitled "The Secret Ingredient," found her at a kitchen counter, perched over mixing bowls as she vigorously stirs. Below each podcast appears the recipe for the dish she's concocting for anyone who wants to "try this at home." Chaiken humbly positions herself as just like fans "at home," seeking to dispel the boundaries between media and ordinary people; rather than addressing the fan public in an executive's suit from her office, she portrays herself as a homey domestic, getting comfy in PJs or cooking in the kitchen. These podcasts also parody television past. The PJs in "Come on, Ilene" echo Oprah's 1997 televised pajama party with Maya Angelou, while "The Secret Ingredient" updates the key workhorse of classic TV—the female gendered cooking show—with a twenty-first-century twist. In "The Secret Ingredient, Episode 504," posted on January 27, 2008, Chaiken whips together "triple berry muffins" while discussing how she cast the show's behind-the-scenes personal trainer, Leah, as a self-defense instructor on the show, who will soon be offering a weekly diet and fitness advice column on OurChart.com. Somehow, Chaiken's upbeat tone while confidently spooning muffin batter into molds smoothly naturalizes this exchange between the actual, the fictional, and the virtual. It is, frankly, the exchange that *The L Word*'s media rituals proclaim possible.

Joining with FanLib, a company that promotes and capitalizes on fan-generated fiction in the name of fan liberation, Showtime offered *L Word* script-writing contests in 2006 and again in 2007. These contests have produced a full-length, collaboratively-generated "fanisode" script, distributed online, as well as a Charlie's Angels-themed scene shot in Vancouver and included in season five's "Lady of the Lake" episode. This "teaser" scene, written by 2007 contest winner, Molly Fisher, was revised by the show's writing staff and lasted only a few minutes, appearing as a dream sequence in the greater episode; however, it generated its share of publicity and fan enthusiasm, free audience research for Showtime, along with online ad revenue for both companies.

Claiming to believe that "audiences own TV shows these days," Chaiken has made a display of giving fans some hold on her reins.[40] However, the question remains: are these just token gestures, politely framing fan agency in order to keep better control of fan attention, or are they genuinely part of a contemporary production strategy of fan incorporation, of shared input? Perhaps both are true. In defining a public as "the social space created by the reflexive circulation of discourse," Michael Warner acknowledges that feedback loops between addressee and addressed have world-building results.[41] According to Warner, "[c]irculation also accounts for the way a public seems both internal and external to discourse, both notional and material ... Writing to a public helps to make a world insofar as the object of address is brought into being partly by postulating and characterizing it."[42] Warner's discussion of publics focuses on how written discourses construct publics. In the current "information age," however, public address is, for the most part, mediated entirely differently and travels quickly and broadly by way of digital forms. While reading publics are already indistinct, digital media publics are doubly so.[43] Although a public is always in flux, it is still practiced and promoted as if it were stable. A social engagement, however slight, with the text of The L Word participates in a dialogic process between cultures of production and consumption that not only inspires fodder for a continuing serial, but also creates an L World (or perhaps L worlds). Insomuch as fans identify themselves as properly addressed by the show and relate themselves to other self-identified fans, they provide the possibility for subsequent cycles of address and response.

As members of an idealized and constructed public, queer female fans are acknowledged by producers as cultural "insiders," experts on the efficacy of the fictional representation of themselves. Producers are "insiders" in a different way— the true arbiters of what gets portrayed, they must scramble to keep up with, to stay "in" on sea changes within the culture they seek to describe. As a result of this knowledge and power exchange, producers seemingly incorporate fans into the production corpus. Through forms of audience collaboration and surveillance used to shape the show, and by establishing network sanctioned (and thus always already colonized) queer female cyberspaces, the producers of The L Word and executives of Showtime wield their symbolic power to enact the "comforting sense that 'we' are all involved in the process of constructing 'our' reality through media rituals."[44] While producers indeed hold symbolic power, they are dependent upon fan identification, recognition, and at least partial belief in the notions of identity and community which the show founds itself upon and also "works on." Thus, The L Word's viability as a cultural form is also predicated on the fan culture it has promulgated.

Notes

1 Though The L Word is set in Los Angeles, Showtime shoots most of the show's content in a studio in Vancouver and cuts in external footage from LA. Many Hollywood-based production companies shoot films outside the US because foreign subsidies, cheap labor, and other economic incentives bring costs down; this phenomenon is known as runaway production.

2 Please see Nick Couldry's description of the "media/ordinary boundary" in *Media Rituals: A Critical Approach* (New York and London: Routledge, 2003), 31–35, 120. For further discussion, see Couldry's *The Place of Media Power: Pilgrims and Witnesses of the Media Age* (New York and London: Routledge, 2000).

3 I describe these producers as "participant-observers" since they engage in audience research resembling my own ethnographic method. Chaiken, Troche, and I are not outsiders to the queer female communities of LA looking in, however: we inhabit multiple roles inside and outside this culture. I write for a national lesbian magazine *Curve* and have lived in LA for eight years. Both producers are out lesbians who live and work in LA. Note: Chaiken has since become the visible star of "Come on, Ilene," discussed later in this chapter.

4 Couldry, *Media Rituals*, 93.

5 By "'real' queer female culture," I refer to a lived and ever-changing local culture, which includes a variety of affiliated queer female members, who may call themselves lesbian, gay, bisexual, transgender, or by another term, and straight and gay male allies. Because this culture is difficult to define in any fixed way, scare quotes remain around "real." Note: for mention of "feedback loops" see Couldry, *Media Rituals*, 69.

6 For elaboration on "branding," "viral marketing," and production "contact zones," see John Caldwell's *Production Culture: Industrial Reflexivity and Critical Practice in Film and Television* (Durham, NC: Duke University Press, 2008).

7 These figures are likely undercounted and inaccurate; however, they helped me focus my overwhelming choice of research sites. Gaydemographics, "2000 Census information on Gay and Lesbian Couples, by zip code," http://www.gaydemographics.org/USA/2000Census_Gay_zipcode.htm.

8 Michel Foucault describes *surveillance* as a form of oversight that seeks to obtain information about individuals without their knowledge of when, or even if, information gathering is happening. See Michel Foucault, *Discipline and Punish: The Birth of the Prison* (New York: Vintage, 1995; originally published in French in 1975).

9 My larger work includes research conducted in San Francisco, CA and Provincetown, MA and addresses international consumption of the show.

10 As Couldry explains, the term *liminal*, from the Latin for threshold, is used by anthropologists like Victor Turner to describe rituals of "boundary crossing." Turner argues these rituals work to reaffirm the social order. He prefers *liminoid* to describe voluntary rituals like TV viewing; however, since I use *liminal* metaphorically, I retain the more commonly used word. See Couldry, *Media Rituals*, 31–34.

11 Ibid., 3–4, 38.

12 *The L Word* shares many of the characteristics of cult TV as defined by Matt Hills, "Defining Cult TV: Texts, Inter-Texts and Fan Audiences" in *The Television Studies Reader*, eds. Robert C. Allen and Annette Hill (New York and London: Routledge, 2004), 509–523. These characteristics include: a clearly positioned TV author (Ilene Chaiken); the implication of a "broader narrative world than that shown on screen" (ibid., 520); fan creativity; a narrative that plays with its own rules; an attraction never consummated; and most clearly, the idea that "cult TV is centrally important to cult fans' lifestyles and identities" (ibid., 517). *The L Word* does not fit with all of Hills' suggestions about cult TV, therefore here I use the term "cult" loosely.

13 For a discussion of *L Word* audiences as tourists, see my essay "Having it All Ways: The Tourist, the Traveler, and the Local in *The L Word*," *Cinema Journal* 46, no. 4 (2007): 3–23.

14 Anna McCarthy, *Ambient Television: Visual Culture and Public Space* (Durham, NC and London: Duke University Press, 2001), 32.

15 Michael Warner, *Publics and Counterpublics* (New York: Zone Books, 2002), 73–89.

16 McCarthy, *Ambient Television*, 3, 33.

17 A list of *L Word*-related events sponsored or co-sponsored by Showtime is available on the fan site The L Word Online, "Events," http://www.thelwordonline.com/events.html.

18 FUSEevents, "Who We Are," http://www.fuse-events.com/index-wwa.html.

19 See note below on "talking back."

20 This analogy between the contemporary era and the 1940s is not illogical given that both eras are noted for the introduction of marked technological changes in media delivery systems ('40s: broadcast television, contemporary era: digital). Data from National Cable and Telecommunications Association, "Cable Industry: Statistics," http://www.ncta.com/Statistic/Statistic/Statistics.aspx and Peter Lauria, "It's Showtime: Channel's Program Strategy Takes Aim at HBO," *New York Post*, September 17, 2007.

21 When *L Word* fans "talk back" at screening parties, they stand a good chance of being heard by other participants. The function of "talking back" is thus performance-oriented, social, and potentially reciprocal. The phenomenon of "talking over" demonstrates that media stimuli can go ignored, even in contexts that seem predicated on media. These social spaces may contain more gratifying interactions for fans than those with the screen. This may be especially true for fans with other options for viewing episodes; thus, class may factor into "talking over."

22 Couldry, *Media Rituals*, 9.

23 Ibid., 97.

24 These chances to "win" promotional materials operate similarly to other "opt in" viral marketing forms. See Caldwell, *Production Culture*, 274–315.

25 Henry Jenkins, *Convergence Culture: Where Old and New Media Collide* (New York and London: New York University Press, 2006), 1–24.

26 John Caldwell, "Industrial Geography Lessons," in *MediaSpace: Place, Scale and Culture in a Media Age*, eds. Nick Couldry and Anna McCarthy (New York and London: Routledge, 2004), 186.

27 Jenkins, *Convergence Culture*, 82.

28 Showtime, "The L Word: Find out about OurChart.com," email to the author, December 18, 2006.

29 Elizabeth Jensen, "*The L Word* Spins Off Its Chart," *The New York Times*, December 18, 2006, C5.

30 Candace Moore, "Screw MySpace!" *Curve*, November 2007, 58.

31 Moore, "Screw MySpace!" 58–59.

32 Jensen, "*The L Word* Spins Off Its Chart," C5.

33 Couldry, *Media Rituals*, 130.

34 Gail Schiller, "Our Space: Net Gain for 'L Word,'" *The Hollywood Reporter*, December 18, 2006.

35 Couldry, *Media Rituals*, 115–133.

36 Moore, "Screw MySpace!" 58.

37 Couldry, *Media Rituals*, 130.

38 Again, such numbers cannot accurately account for how many people viewed the premiere. Note my use of "reportedly." See Andrew Wallenstein, "'L Word' Gets Online Peek," *The Hollywood Reporter*, January 27, 2008.

39 Daisy Whitney, "Nets Tinker With Social Networking; Broadcast, Cable Channels Launching More Sites to Compete with MySpace," *Television Week*, January 15, 2007, 60.
40 Jensen, "*The L Word* Spins Off Its Chart," C5.
41 Warner, *Publics and Counterpublics*, 90.
42 Ibid., 90–91.
43 The differences between "writing to" and "televising to" a public need to be further teased out (along with differences in their world-making effects).
44 Couldry, *Media Rituals*, 39–40.

Chapter 10

"Not in Kansas Anymore"
Transnational Collaboration in Television Science Fiction Production*

Jane Landman

Otherworldly science-fiction series conventionally reference urtext *The Wizard of Oz* (1937), and some such intertexts allude to the production of many of these big-budget adventures at some geographic remove from the media entertainment "command and control" center of Los Angeles.[1] The 200th episode of *Stargate SG-1* (1997–2007), for example, suspended the usual plot structure in favor of a comedic special episode that riffs on a fan's gift to the production of a framed drawing of the SG1 team depicted as Dorothy's companions.[2] In the background of many scenes of this self-reflexive celebration, set dressers move about carrying potted exemplars of the distinctive Canadian pines that forest each and every distant world visited through the "Stargate" portal. There was no precedent for big-budget science-fiction television production, local or offshore, when another sci-fi series *Farscape* was made in Sydney (1998–2002; 2004).[3] The series concerns an American astronaut, John Crichton, and his adventures in attempting to return home after being inadvertently catapulted into another galaxy, and generated predictable punning about "Oz," and the "not in Kansas anymore" displaced experience for both American and Australian cast and crew.[4]

There is jarring dissonance between such sly in-text or extratextual acknowledgments of substitute locations that invite audience recognition and complicity on the one hand, and the totalizing political economy critique of current production practices developed in Toby Miller et al.'s *Global Hollywood* on the other.[5] In this account of Hollywood imperialism, Miller and his co-authors argue that the leverage created by the hypermobility of US production is deployed to exploit and "discipline" labor in the cultural industries, both in the US and in foreign locations. This is part of the broader structure of global power where, "It is not the threat of invasion but rather the *threat of non-invasion* of investors … that constitutes the means of coercion."[6] Miller et al. describe how nations, or subnational territories, become in some measure dependent on income generated by such "offshore" or "runaway" US productions, and compete against one another in offering incentives that discount local labor, cultural assets, and taxes, with the incongruous result that public recourses contribute to the profits of multinational entertainment conglomerates. They propose that "the real Hollywood" now actually lies in this division of labor, which they call "The New International Division of Cultural Labour" (NICL). This division sees creative control and copyright rest with the center while "semi-periphery" industries, such as that in Australia, risk being locked into a vulnerable and compliant state of "dependent underdevelopment."[7] Local investment—of money or civic pride—in contributions to such offshore production is, in this account, a very sad joke indeed.[8]

This polemic provides a Marxist perspective on continuing and vigorous debates in Australia about the balance and interrelations between industrial and economic goals on the one hand, and cultural policies aimed at supporting and protecting local film and television production on the other, in light of the growing significance of foreign production.[9] In respect of the recently introduced "Australian Screen Incentive" which grants refundable tax offsets of between 20 and 40 percent to qualifying productions (with the more generous incentives needing to meet local input requirements) and which extends to large-budget television as well as film, industry representatives remain divided about "whether the package is a business or a cultural initiative."[10] In the context of the complexly interconnected realms of economic and cultural activities in the screen industry, this chapter investigates *Global Hollywood*'s characterization of local participation in American productions as courting "cultural oblivion."[11] Does the production of *Farscape* offer a different perspective?

The chapter first outlines the deal that brought to Australia a production looking to experiment and differentiate itself in its generic field, and then considers the dynamics and dimensions of this production in the accounts of key personnel, along with the relative proportions of local and international labor on the production. There is extensive coverage of the making of this critically acclaimed cult series in printed and online sources and I expanded on key themes in this coverage in interviews with two of the Australian producers, Sue Milliken (producer or executive producer for sixty-six episodes) and Andrew Prowse (who worked on the series throughout in senior production roles), as well as the principal local writer, Justin Monjo (who also worked as a creative consultant), all of whom generously and willingly discussed their work. These interviews focused on the nature of the local input and on the experience of making genre television, and suggest that *Farscape* is better described as a "co-venture" and as a creative collaboration, than as piecework production under the tight fiscal and creative control of US interests.

Milliken uses the descriptive term "co-venture" to distinguish *Farscape* from "official" co-productions where respective partners qualify for subvention on cultural grounds.[12] The series can also be described as transnational television: set in the intergalactic reaches of the Uncharted Territories, it nevertheless remains *located* in ways that testify to the cultural and creative contributions of the peripheral host nation, so that the displaced location of the series significantly shapes the ways in which "American" science fiction is decentered and repositioned in the series. The series constitutes an industrially mediated dialogue between nations with differential production stakes and capacities, but common cultural and historical investments in this genre of popular culture.[13]

Farscape Faraway

Four seasons of *Farscape* were made over the period 1998 to 2002, after which it was abruptly canceled, then revived in 2004 for a four-hour miniseries that concluded major plot lines. The series was a flagship production for the now NBCU-owned Sci Fi Channel (a subsidiary of General Electric), and was commissioned as part of an expansionary drive that sought to rebrand the channel by stamping its mark on the genre, staking a proprietorial claim through commissioning original production.[14]

In the early 1990s, experienced science-fiction writer-producer Rockne O'Bannon and Brian Henson, co-head of the US- and UK-based "Creature Shop" (specializing in animatronics, puppetry, and special effects), were encouraged to consider shared interests by their mutual agent.[15] Henson was looking for a showcase vehicle, with a view to repositioning his family-owned company for work outside the ambit of children's entertainment, and he asked O'Bannon to write some episodes for a series then titled "Space Chase." O'Bannon then sought assistance from David Kemper, with whom he had previously worked on the television series *Star Trek: Voyager* (1995–2001), and they later added another *Trek* writer, Ricky Manning, to the team. All three shared an interest in developing a series that worked against the tropes of this vast science-fiction franchise, such as the tidy weekly resolutions, and the repression of affect ensuing from the inviolate professionalism of the disciplined military crew. O'Bannon put character realism at the center of his vision for generic reinvention.[16]

Henson experienced some delay in finding an investor prepared to commit to a full season, which he needed to cover extensive start-up costs. His project was, finally, attractive to the relatively new Sci Fi Channel (launched in 1992), which was looking for "edgy" and "really alien" programming as part of an agenda to "unlock the power of sci fi," in other words to broaden out the appeal of genre programming that had proven potential in a fragmented market of niche tastes.[17] At this time, Sci Fi and "parent" USA Network were owned by Barry Diller (then taken over by major stakeholder Vivendi in May 2001).[18] Henson successfully organized a co-production deal that included Hallmark, who helped bring in minor Australian partner the Nine Network, following "tortuous negotiations."[19] Sci Fi contributed US$44,000 per episode (including rerun rights for two years), with Henson, Hallmark, and Nine making up the rest of the estimated budget of US$1.2 million per episode.[20]

Favorable currency exchange at the time ensured that a cost saving of about 30 percent resulted from locating production and postproduction in Australia. Matt Carroll, who set up *Farscape* in Australia and produced the first season, figures this as the amount needed to provide the incentive to bring work to Australia.[21] An indirect subsidy was also available, in that for the first season it utilized the Fox Studios, built as a public-private partnership (though it then, like much other local production, moved to convert a warehouse at Homebush Bay to its needs) and the series qualified as part of the local content quota mandated of Australian television license holders, providing an incentive for the Nine Network. Some minor tax concessions were also available.[22]

In the account of series creator Rockne O'Bannon, the cost savings granted by the rate of exchange ensured that this series was always intended for production in Australia. However, O'Bannon also insists that the move was not purely "deal driven," citing the draw of local FX expertise, and suggesting that a certain off-centeredness that assists in creating the sense of being in another galaxy ensued from the location, for example in the use of unfamiliar—at least to non-Australians—actors and settings. This decision in the interest of mild exoticism for non-Australians generated unanticipated effects. O'Bannon instructed actors to use "mid-Atlantic accents" (neither American, Australian, nor British), yet this blending is unevenly realized, especially on the part of the wide pool of weekly guest actors, and from Milliken's perspective the fact that these actors were *not* required to use American accents was "a major breakthrough in US production in Australia."[23] Jes Battis's textual investigation of the series reinforces her point in describing these aliens as "definitely Australian."[24]

The Plasticity of Place

Film production has always depended on geographical substitution, but the current mobility of production represents both an extension of and a shift from earlier practices. Ausfilm is an LA-based joint industry and state government funded group that facilitates production in Australia, and lobbies the federal government over financial incentives to foreign production, and its website advertises Australia's "plasticity" in publishing a map inscribing the nation with the names of the locations for which it has substituted.[25] Location shooting is a privileged tradition associated with cultural authenticity in Australia, and overlaying or repressing the local meanings of place can readily be seen as a form of colonial and cultural reterritorialization, which touches on sensitive ground in a colonial-settler society wracked by contestation over colonial narratives of nationhood ("history wars"), and historically dominated by American film and television. Intense and fraught investments have played out in complex ways in respect to representational politics of national cinema, adding layers of potential for affront in respect of offshore practices.[26] Further, few local film or television productions can afford to make use of high-end studio spaces, the construction of which has been publicly subsidized in commercial partnerships with state governments. Such inhibiting budgetary constraints persist notwithstanding the discounted rental rates offered with the intention that large-budget international productions cross-subsidize local production.[27]

Issues of authenticity and territory are complicated in the location practices of fantasy genre productions, where substitutions often represent imaginary places that may nevertheless bear traces of their specific cultural origins, such as the Britishness of Narnia in *Chronicles of Narnia: Prince Caspian* (2008), shot in the Czech Republic, for example. As a long-running series with exile and flight at its narrative center, *Farscape* works its way through many studio-based settings and exterior locations, many which make allusions or pay homage to previous generic exemplars. Such textual remaking is characteristic of this self-conscious genre.[28] This generates few opportunities for local traces, but the series does draw on the iconography of later films in the *Mad Max* series. For example, in episodes set on a planet where the crew stop for ship repairs, acts of betrayal and theft end in car chases in pared back buggy-like vehicles, across bleached sand dunes (season three, episodes fourteen and fifteen). The flamboyantly disreputable dress and hairstyles of various visiting characters also draws on *Mad Max*'s imagining of the social fringes of the postapocalyptic future—such as seen in the style of the "garbologist" character in the season one episode "The Flax" (episode thirteen).

In a first season return-to-earth story, Crichton lands in Sydney (episode sixteen, "A Human Reaction") while later return-to-earth stories are set in his homeland of the US, but these (substitute) locations are usually revealed to be virtual environments, constructed from memories extracted from Crichton's tortured or manipulated psyche (e.g., "Won't Get Fooled Again," season two, episode fifteen). The point to be made about these examples is that the look of the series neither privileges nor disguises its Australian site of production: the mythological Australian landscapes of *Mad Max* are interspersed with iconic tourist sites (Sydney beaches and the Opera House), with local exteriors standing in for various planetary stopovers, and with studio sets and psychic spaces rendered by special effects. This is a location practice that supports Ben Goldsmith and Tom O'Regan's contention that the contemporary global studio's range of locations offerings blur distinctions between "reality, artifice, superficiality and verisimilitude." This suggests that whilst place remains meaningful, a new logic applies where the meanings of place must take into account specific production and postproduction services such as effects specializations.[29]

Local Labors and Inputs

Milliken says that *Farscape* "provided the rarest thing of all in the Australian film and television industry—continuity of employment."[30] Continuity necessarily underpins successful collaboration, and Prowse accredits the ongoing employment, along with the satisfactions of working with an enabling budget, with generating a base of worker loyalty and commitment that minimized staff turnover and added to the quality of the production.[31] Milliken, who has been working as a producer since the 1970s, and is a past President of the Screen Producers Association, contrasts this example of four years of reliable, ongoing, and fairly remunerated work with the expectation of some Australian productions that crews subsidize costs by discounting their own labor.[32] While Nick Herd's study of "runaway" production and film studio development in Australia concedes the validity of such economic advantages, his concerns echo those of Miller et al. in pointing to a lack of worker agency and the subservient order of work done under the control of foreign heads of departments and other "key creatives" such as writers, directors, and producers.[33]

The Nine Network had no tradition of working in the generally unaffordable genre of action science fiction, and entered into this co-production on the strength of a prior association with Hallmark, and a pioneering interest in making internationally oriented programming. Yet this sole Australian stakeholder had a conflicted relationship with the experiment undertaken in investing in this production.[34] The point to be made here is that the network was the agent of its own relative lack of involvement and influence whilst in other respects Herd's argument about limited creative control for Australian crews is simply not borne out by the case of *Farscape*.

A good starting point is the breadth of the Australian labor contribution: About 90 percent of the production was performed by Australians, and with the exception of lead actor Ben Browder (Crichton), all the actors in this ensemble drama are Australians or New Zealanders. From the outset Australians occupied "key" positions:

> All the directors were Australian. We hired as many Australian writers as we could find—this generally amounted to about one third of the writing team on each season. The producer designer, director of photography, music composer, costume designer, key make-up, puppeteers and all the film editors were Australian.[35]

A significant consideration in thinking about the dynamics of this production is its duration over four years (not including the miniseries). In season two, Australians took over from those Creature Shop staff that had seen the series into production: for example, Tim Ferrier took over production design from Ricky Eyres, and Tim Micville became lead puppeteer after John Eccleston returned to the UK.

The flexible positions occupied by key production crew, who were rotated and promoted and repositioned over the four years, reinforces Milliken's claim that *Farscape* provided a valuable training ground for both experienced and inexperienced members of the Australian crew. Justin Monjo, who had written only four hours of television when he started on *Farscape*, and had little knowledge of the genre, became one of the core writing group with Manning and Kemper. The production worked its way through a succession of others—both Australian and American—who either did not "get" the show thematically and tonally, or failed to work well in the ensemble.[36] Monjo wrote scripts for thirteen episodes, and was also employed as executive producer, script consultant, and creative consultant. Director Andrew Prowse was also co-producer for periods of production, responsible for supervision of postproduction and special effects. O'Bannon describes him as "the most critical person to the overall look and sound of the show."[37] Rowan Woods, better known locally as a director of intense realist low-budget cinema, meanwhile made a quirky *auteurist* guest appearance as a "fat ugly blue guy."

Creativity and Science Fiction

Conventionally, a distinction is made between below-the-line workers, such as location managers, set designers, props manufacturers, wardrobe and make-up artists, and above-the-line workers, such as directors, writers, and producers, in whose work the "creative" side of the production inheres.[38] Yet accounts of this production reiteratively reference the creative contributions of below-the-line workers, such as in the ideas for plot lines that emerged from possibilities suggested or enabled by designers, props, and effects.[39]

When O'Bannon, describing the high quality of Australian below-the-line workers involved in *Farscape*, for example, singles out hair and make-up artist Lesley Wanderwalt as someone with whom he particularly wants to work again, it is clear that her hairstyles are not *mere* set dressing, but are central to the creative process involved in the imaginative evocation of imaginary places and cultures.[40] Set design, set dressing, and costumes and hair are narratively significant in all visual media, but in science fiction, where "backgrounds" are part of the foreground of the story, they carry particular importance.[41] Props and settings create the materiality and the difference of the imaginary worlds on which the generic premise rests.[42] They form part of the accumulation of rich detail germane to the development and elaboration of the "cosmologies" at the heart of the creative endeavor of fantasy and science fiction.

The importance of contributions from all levels, and the invested commitment generated through the openness of the project to suggestions, forms part of the discursive particularity of this collaborative process as stressed in reports, interviews, and DVD commentary. While O'Bannon commuted between Sydney and LA, Kemper and Browder both moved to Sydney and in the second year, the writing department was also moved to Australia, and O'Bannon became executive consultant with Kemper taking on the role of executive producer. The production started with "north" and "south" writers' rooms, with stories broken in the States, but this unwieldy arrangement was abandoned so that production and postproduction were substantially based in and run from Australia, as "having everyone in the same place ... allows for the best creative cross-fertilization."[43] Monjo says that Kemper had overall responsibility for arc narratives and the continuities of the series history, while he wrote more or less standalone episodes, experiencing no network interference (in contrast to his experience of Australian network production). O'Bannon reinforces the point about local control, saying there was no direct interference, though Sci Fi later cited increasing concerns about complex serial storylines excluding new viewers amongst their reasons for canceling the series.[44]

Prowse attributes the success of the collaboration to Kemper's early realization that he could not maintain control of all elements of the production and his decision to run with a situation where the series would not ultimately be just his creation, but a deep collaborative interaction between key production crew. In Prowse's view, the sheer scale, complexity, and expense of the series' components (prosthetics, animatronics, puppetry, and visual effects) "meant that in order to keep up the production values of the show, the production simply had to find Australian collaborators in a way that no previous show [US series made in Australia] needed to."[45] He describes a production culture that prized imaginative solutions and risk taking.[46] Unusually for television, the four regular Australian directors—who each came to specialize in particular types of episode—contributed to each other's work as well. Browder, who also wrote a few scripts, says of this directorial interaction: "There was tremendous input there, creatively."[47] Scripts worked as starting points, modified and contributed to by the directors, and other crew, as well as the actors, and this loose collective exchange contributes to the show an improvisational and eclectic quality that feeds into the rather lurching, erratic, seemingly unplanned adventures of the characters.

The narrative structure of *Farscape*, where one lonely American astronaut has to learn to live amongst aliens, echoes the conditions of production: Crichton is a "symbolic reservoir of uniquely American ideologies and practices" whose perspectives and assumptions are confronted and moderated in the face of his experiences.[48] The Australian workers drew on their varied cultural experience of US popular culture as well as on interests and experiences established at some remove from the American industry. Woods, for example, speaks to shared cultural ground in his comment about his interest in working on this project:

> You have a very, very simple original spin on a guy that's lost in space but in this case he's a contemporary Gen X'er. He sees things in space, and encounters situations in space, and he doesn't really have any reference points except to planet Earth—the sort of reference points we all have.[49]

Yet at the same time, Woods treated the series as social realism, pushing hard against what is expected from "archetypal writing" and instead going "fat and ugly."[50] Monjo, describing his work as including selecting and developing from Kemper's vast reservoir of ideas, also discussed resisting "American TV" tendencies to focus on the hero or central couple, or on idealized heroic struggle. Prowse comments that "it's not a science-fiction show, it's a character show with science fiction added to it."[51]

Such contributions combine distance and proximity in productive ways within the architecture of the series as established by O'Bannon and overseen by Kemper. In discussing contrasting organizational modes O'Bannon says the "friction created interesting things … by us pushing in our direction and the Australian producers in theirs we found a really appropriate place."[52] Prowse nevertheless points out that *negotiating* industrial compromise was a "political minefield [and] a power struggle between US and Australian models of production … for its entire production period."[53] Ben Browder testifies to the positive contribution of distance from "those who control the mood of television" in the comment below, which whilst reinforcing much of the previous discussion of the collaborative process, also adds further insight into the contribution of a specifically Australian decentered perspective:

> The Australian approach to work is more egalitarian … Hollywood is founded on a star system … They create franchises and they create stars … I don't think you could make this show in the US or even Canada because you are too close to the normal powers who control the mood of television. There is an irreverence and a sense of humour infused in the show that I think is particularly Australian … there is an acerbic wit, sarcasm, irony and ability to take a jab at the conventions of science fiction, while at the same time paying homage to them that *Farscape* does.[54]

Generic Collaboration and Transnational Reinvention

What can be concluded from and about the local Australian contribution to *Farscape*? To briefly recapitulate: this was a project conceived and overseen in America (the Henson Company is originally American though also based in the UK), financed in large part due to opportunities within that niche television market, and brought to Australia for production due to a combination of factors in which exchange rates played the driving role. Yet this example demonstrates that dynamic cultural collaboration can occur in unexpected places. The "key" creative positions occupied by Australians, the extent of the Australian above- and below-the-line contribution, the collaborative nature of the production process and the absence of attempts to repress or efface the local combine to produce a series very evidently marked by its site of production. It is production that has in turn marked some of those cast (and crew) as part of the pool of science-fiction talent recycled in extensive practices of cross-series casting. In all these respects Milliken rightly describes the series as a "co-venture," and it is one that provided an enabling base for the generic repositioning sought by Sci Fi and O'Bannon. Further, the tonal qualities and accented local inflections (such as style, look, voice) to which this genre was particularly open, make this a culturally transnational production.

The largely positive summations of the collaboration by Milliken and O'Bannon do nevertheless overlay "behind the scenes ... contradictions and tensions inherent in a transnational venture of this kind."[55] In Prowse's view, the particular scale and nature of *Farscape* (the budget, its technical ambition, and programming aims) offered some measure of bargaining power to Australian production workers, who enjoyed well-paid work of a sort that could only be done in co-production. In this context, and in the light of many aspects of shared—and differentiated —colonial history existing between the US and Australia, there is something entirely apposite about Australian cultural labor participating in a genre conventionally preoccupied with colonial adventure in "uncharted territories," alien encounters, identity and hybridity, power and territorialization.

Notes

* With thanks to Sue Milliken, Justin Monjo, and Andrew Prowse for generously discussing their work with me. I would also like to acknowledge the contribution made by Ben Goldsmith, Tania Lewis, Tom O'Regan, and Sue Ward in discussing earlier versions of this research with me, and finally, to thank the editors of this collection, for their astute and insightful questions, comments, and suggestions.

1 *The Wizard of Oz*, USA, Victor Fleming, MGM, 1937. Ben Goldsmith and Tom O'Regan, *The Film Studio: Film Production in the Global Economy* (Lanham: Rowman and Littlefield, 2004), 6, 178–179, are amongst those who call Los Angeles the command and control center of the entertainment industry, emphasizing the importance of sophisticated and centralized "back room" coordination in the management of productions taking place at distant locations.

2 *Stargate SG-1*, USA, MGM, 1997–2006 as television series, ongoing as occasional telemovies.

3 This general claim of no local tradition holds true despite the very occasional exception, and those science-fiction/adventure programs made for children, for example the television miniseries *The Girl from Tomorrow*, produced by Noel Price (Australia: Nine Network/Film Australia, 1991) and the television series *Ocean Girl*, produced by Jonathon Shiff (Australia: Jonathon Shiff Productions and Network Ten, 1994–1997). Australia has also been the location site for the production of a number of international science-fiction films, such as the *Dark City*, directed by Alex Proyas (USA/Australia: Mystery Clock and New Line, 1998) and *The Matrix*, directed by Andy Wachowski and Larry Wachowski (USA/Australia: Village Roadshow and Warner Bros, 1999). See Mark Juddery, "The New Science Fictions: An Australian Perspective," *Metro* 135 (2007): 134–137.

4 Series director Rowan Woods, commentary on "Die Me Dichotomy," Season 2, Disc 3, Episode 22, *Farscape*, DVD, produced by Sue Milliken (USA: Jim Henson Company and Hallmark Entertainment, 2003).

5 Toby Miller et al., *Global Hollywood 2* (London: BFI, 2005).

6 Ulrich Beck, *Power in the Global Age*, trans. Kathleen Cross (Cambridge, UK: Polity, 2005), 52.

7 Miller et al. *Global Hollywood 2*, 140. The term "semi-periphery industries" is used by Terry Flew, *Understanding Global Media* (Houndsmill: Palgrave Macmillan, 2007), 79.

8 Some contrasting research on transnational genre television is more equivocal, examining ways in which the local inevitably slips through—or is invited—to shape or inflect production. See, for example, Gaye Naismith, "Locating the Local(e) in *Xena Warrior Princess*," *Metro* 129/130 (Spring 2001): 217–223; Gaile McGregor, "Stargate as Cancult: Ideological Coding as a Function of Location," in *Reading Stargate SG-1*, eds. Stan Beeler and Lisa Dickson (London and New York: I.B. Tauris, 2006).

9 Previous literature on this central problematic of cultural policy is too extensive to enumerate; the Australian Film Commission (recently subsumed under the umbrella body Screen Australia) regularly commissions research into Australian production issues and is a good clearing house for relevant reports and submissions.

10 Michael Bodey, "Shoot and We'll Cough Up," *The Australian*, February 27, 2008.

11 Miller et al., *Global Hollywood 2*, 146.

12 Sue Milliken, email message to author, October 23, 2007.

13 Sue Milliken, interview with the author, October 25, 2007. That the making of *Farscape* constituted a "dialogue" about respective modes of production is evident in the many comments about accommodations and adjustments made amongst actors and production crew. Andrew Prowse describes the genre material—and budget—as a "playground" where the crew could "invent it for ourselves." There are a number of respects in which this dialogue is reflected on screen, that overlay the conventional intertextuality characteristic of the genre. Most obvious are the occasional visual in-jokes that acknowledge the displaced location, and the self- and genre-depreciating humor that Ben Browder considers such a significant influence on the series (see Browder below). Textual interpretation points to particular resonances for Australian audiences, denizens of a "second world" nation and former penal colony, in respect to the series setting on a (seized) prison ship, crewed by the lost, the criminal, and the exiled, all yearning for (an impossible) return home.

14 Alan Frutkin, "Sci Fi Rides First Wave for Three Years," *Mediaweek*, March 29, 1999.

15 These initiators of the series are all Americans; Brian Henson is the son of Jim Henson, whose company is still best known for *The Muppets*. It is worth noting in this context that

the sole Australian writer, Justin Monjo, is an ex-New Yorker, long settled in Australia, but who identifies with the local influence on *Farscape*.

16 Ann Kaplan, "*Farscape*: Season Three," *Cinefantastique*, June, 2001; Jim McConville, "Sci-Fi Enters Warp Speed," *Electronic News*, August 30, 1999; Randal Rothenberg, "Cable's Sci Fi Boldly Builds Fans Outside Its Original Niche," *Advertising Age*, July 22, 2002.

17 Hammer's comment about being directed to "unlock the value" is widely cited in the trade press, including in Porter Anderson, "Bonnie Hammer: She is Sci Fi," *CNN.com*, October 10, 2001; Ann Kaplan, "*Farscape*: Season Three" discusses Sci Fi's search for edgier fare; Catherine Johnson's *Telefantasy* (London: BFI, 2005) discusses catering to niche tastes.

18 Allison Romano, "Jackson Makes Sun Shine in Eye of Vivendi Storm," *Broadcasting and Cable*, November 18, 2002.

19 Brian Henson on negotiations with the Nine Network, in Lauren Martin, "Animator 2," *Sydney Morning Herald*, December 12, 1998. The Nine Network was at this stage a subsidiary of Australian media company Publishing and Broadcasting Limited. One estimate puts Nine's contribution at A$100,000 per episode for the early seasons only, but I have been unable to confirm this figure. Joe Nazarro, "Out on the *Farscape*," *Starlog*, no. 285 (April 2001), provides an account of negotiations with Sci Fi.

20 John Demsy, "Sci Fi Reups Henson's *Farscape* for 2nd Year," *Variety*, July 29, 1999.

21 Australian producer Matt Carroll, in Ann Kaplan, "*Farscape*: Season Three."

22 Sue Milliken, in an annexure reporting on *Farscape* for an Ausfilm report on tax offsets: "The Case for Extension of the 12.5% Refundable Tax Offset to Large Budget Television Series and Bundled Non-Theatrical Films," Moore Park, NSW: AUSfilm, 2003.

23 Ibid.; O'Bannon in Kaplan, "*Farscape*: Season Three." The "mid-Atlantic" accent is a deliberate attempt to refrain from sounding identifiably Australian or British or American, although in general it remains perhaps recognizably closer to American speech patterns than the other two. It tends to avoid the nasal sounds and upward inflections of Australian speech pattern and the diverse elongated or truncated vowels of various British or American regional accents, whilst providing a sort of "middle-ground" amalgam of the idiomatic vocabulary and pronunciations of the most standard versions of all three.

24 Jes Battis, *Investigating "Farscape": Uncharted Territories of Sex and Science Fiction* (London and New York: I.B. Tauris, 2006), 166.

25 The website tag, "Australia: Anywhere You Want to Be," indicates the continent's plasticity in the sense of its being readily molded into convincing geographic substitutions. Ausfilm, "Locations Doubling Map," http://www.ausfilm.com.au/childsplay/cgi-bin/show_page.pl/2/ 201, accessed December 18, 2007.

26 On the history wars and cinema, see Felicity Collins and Terese Davis, *Australian Cinema after Mabo* (Cambridge: Cambridge University Press, 2004). On social and policy debates in the 1920s about the uses of Australian backgrounds in bolstering "Empire" cinema, and the need to compete with the capacity of Californian landscapes to double for a great number of other places, see Jane Landman, *'The Tread of a White Man's Foot': Australian Pacific Colonialism and the Cinema, 1925–1962* (Canberra: Pandanus, 2006).

27 Ben Goldsmith and Tom O'Regan, *Cinema Cities, Media Cities: The Contemporary International Studio Complex*, Screen Industry Culture and Policy Research Series (Brisbane: AFC/Australian Key Centre for Cultural Studies and Media Policy, 2003). In research for the Australian Film Commission, Goldsmith and O'Regan found that many local

productions simply cannot afford to build studio sets, which does offer some support to Miller et al.'s claim, in *Global Hollywood 2*, that states revenues inappropriately underpin the profits of multinational entertainment conglomerates. Their later research offers a more nuanced view in exploring specific *local* motivations behind the development of studios, such as urban renewal.

28 For example, the *Blade Runner* (1982) derived postmodern cityscape was in "The Choice," Season 3, Episode 17, *Farscape*, produced by Sue Milliken and Andrew Prowse (Sydney: Fox, August 17, 2001).

29 Goldsmith and O'Regan, *The Film Studio*, 7–9.

30 Milliken, annexure.

31 Andrew Prowse, telephone interview with author, October 25, 2007.

32 Milliken, email message to author.

33 Nick Herd, *Chasing the Runaways: Foreign Film Production and Studio Film Development in Australia 1988–2002* (Sydney: Currency House, 2004), 88.

34 *Farscape* was the first project of the network's Film and Television Unit, which was established to boost an international, rather than national profile. Author, "Far and Away," *Sydney Morning Herald*, September 14, 1998. As the series first went to air, Noble described the series as "sit[ting] on the world platform of high-concept drama and promises to break through barriers of television production to open up a brand new genre in Australia" (Mike O'Conner, "Horny Aliens Unlikely to Inspire our Desires," *Courier Mail*, May 18, 2000), though other accounts suggest that embarrassment and contempt characterized the reaction of Nine executives (David Hoskin, "TV Eye: Muppets in Space," *Metro* 140 (2003): 110). A conflicted, confused, and unsympathetic attitude of series is also suggested by the erratic, interrupted, disadvantageous scheduling of the series (outlined in Peter Mattessi, "Programmed to Oblivion," *The Age*, January 15, 2004).

35 Milliken, annexure.

36 Justin Monjo, conversation with the author, October 31, 2007; O'Bannon in Kaplan, "*Farscape*: Season Three."

37 Kaplan, "*Farscape*: Season Three," 50.

38 Goldsmith and O'Regan, *Media Cities*. See also Miranda Banks' chapter in this volume.

39 In Kaplan, "*Farscape*: Season Three"; David Kemper and Rowan Woods, commentary on "Die Me Dichotomy," Season 2, Disc 3, Episode 22, *Farscape*, DVD, produced by Sue Milliken (USA: Jim Henson Company and Hallmark Entertainment, 2003).

40 Wanderwalt left the production to work on *Moulin Rouge* (2001) and *Star Wars Episode 2: Attack of the Clones* (2002).

41 Jan Johnson-Smith, *American Science Fiction TV: Star Trek, Stargate and Beyond* (London: I.B. Tauris, 2005).

42 Adam Roberts, *Science Fiction* (New York and London: Routledge, 2006).

43 Series writer Ricky Manning in Kaplan, "*Farscape*: Season Three."

44 Monjo, conversation; Rockne O'Bannon in Jo Nazarro, "Farewell to *Farscape*," *Starlog*, no. 308 (March 2003), 25.

45 Andrew Prowse, email message to the author, September 12, 2008.

46 Prowse, interview.

47 Browder in Kaplan, "*Farscape*: Season Three," 49.

48 Battis, *Investigating "Farscape"*, 14.

49 Woods in Kaplan, "*Farscape*: Season Three," 68.

50 Woods, "Die Me Dichtotomy." Woods' account of going "fat and ugly" can be linked to the series' commitment to character realism, and takes form in a focus on low body humor and the grotesque.

51 Prowse, interview; also see comments in Kaplan, "*Farscape*: Season Three"; Monjo, conversation with the author.

52 Prowse in Kaplan, "*Farscape*: Season Three," 35.

53 Andrew Prowse notes: "[Conflict] reached a head at the end of Season One, simmered through the second and third seasons and burst into flame again halfway through season four. In fact my own elevation to a producer role was to act as a kind of mediator between the US creatives and the Australian producers ... The other task of the Australian producers was to keep the cost of labor at Oz rates, which created conflict with the crew (particularly on Season One), who thought (reasonably) that if they were working on a big-budget show, they should be paid more ... We refused to work on the show unless our rates were substantially lifted. The Oz producer wanted to fire us, but the US creatives knew that the quality of the show would suffer. We won a substantial pay rise. Another anomaly occurred in the script area. *Farscape*'s scripts were written under WGA rules ... there was a situation in which one group of Australian creatives (writers) did a lot better than another roughly equivalent group (directors)."

54 Ben Browder in Sharon Rainsbury, "Out of This World," *Herald Sun*, May 28, 1998, TV Extra.

55 Prowse, email to the author.

Chapter 11

Crossing the Border

Studying Canadian Television Production

Elana Levine

As scholars of media and culture continue to explore the significance of place, of the geographies—both virtual and actual—of communities and identities in a globalized world, questions of location have become increasingly significant to media studies.[1] Such matters have long been central to debates around cultural imperialism, which concern themselves with the imposition of the cultural products of one geographic entity (typically the US, or the west) upon less dominant places worldwide.[2] Questions of place are also vital in revisions of the cultural imperialism thesis that seek to understand negotiations of power and identity across local, regional, national, and global planes.[3] While studies of global media culture often focus on the presence of tensions between the local and the global in media texts, or in practices of reception, these matters are equally vital concerns for media production.

This chapter considers the significance of geographies of media production by examining the question and relative importance of geography in media production studies. In other words, in this chapter I explore the significance of place not only in the media production process but also in the practice of media production scholarship. I do so through a case study of my own media production research, an examination of the production and distribution of a half-hour Canadian scripted television series, *Degrassi: The Next Generation* (*DTNG*). Produced in Toronto by Epitome Pictures, *DTNG* debuted in 2001 as the latest iteration of a twenty-five-year-old Canadian franchise that combines comedic and dramatic elements to narrate the lives and loves of its teenage ensemble cast. The series, along with its franchise predecessors, has been on the whole well regarded both within and outside Canada for its age-accurate casting and unflinching, open-minded treatment of social issues from teenage pregnancy to multicultural identities, winning multiple Gemini Awards (Canada's highest TV industry award), International Emmy Awards, and a Teen Choice Award in the US.

My study of *DTNG* is a useful case for an inquiry into questions of identity and place for several reasons. For one, the series is both a product of the Canadian television industry and the particularities of its history, economics, and structure *and* a product of a global television market. First-run episodes of *DTNG* are licensed to approximately seventy different broadcast networks and cable stations worldwide and these global sales are vital to the production's economic viability.[4] Thus, the show's production is both bound to its specific national location and connected to a distribution system that spans national and continental borders. My study also raises questions of place and identity because of my own relationship to the production. I am an American researcher whose work has focused largely on American television. For this project, however, I spent time at the Toronto-based set of *DTNG*, observing production and interviewing a number of the series' creative personnel.[5] My own research process thereby involved a border crossing, not only through my physical visit but also through my efforts to become familiar with the Canadian television industry and the contexts of *DTNG*'s production.

The case of my *DTNG* research is additionally an apt example through which to consider questions of place, identity, and production because my project was initially concerned with the role of Canadian identity in the program's creation. As a result, I questioned multiple members of the *DTNG* staff about their show's "Canadianness." Across the board, these questions yielded answers that were vague and conflicted. What it meant to produce a Canadian show was never straightforward or simple. For example, actor and producer Stefan Brogren pondered, "What would you actually do to be a Canadian show?"[6] Similarly, director Phil Earnshaw told me, "Well, we have Canadian flags, we don't hide them, which is Canadian but ... that's a good question. [Pause] I don't know. I mean it's hard to distinguish on television the difference between American and Canadian in a way because Canadians are so ... [shifts topic]."[7] At first, executive producer and creator Linda Schuyler told me, "I don't feel the show is any different than if I would be an American doing it," but she later speculated, "I suppose the one way being Canadian influences our storytelling [is] that as a country and as a nation we are probably more small and liberal than America ... and there certainly is a lot of liberalism in our storytelling."[8] Executive producer and head writer James Hurst also mentioned the left-leaning tendencies of Canadians as compared to Americans, but denied that they alone could explain the show's Canadianness. He suggested, "I don't think you could do *Degrassi* in America but ... it's not exactly for the obvious reasons; it's very complex."[9] The vagueness and ambivalence of these answers point to a multifaceted process of geographic identification for these media producers. They also point to some of the chief challenges of this sort of "cross-border" media production research and of media production research of any kind that seeks to grapple with questions of identity and its role in the production process.

In what follows, I explore the case of *DTNG* and its creators' uncertain responses to the question of their program's Canadian identity. In so doing, I argue that the matter of a place-based identity is inevitably a conflicted one in a global media culture. That conflict takes particular shape in the case of Canada and a globally circulating product like *DTNG*. While I believe it would be impossible to ever fully transcend these sorts of identity quandaries, I also argue that production scholarship offers us a means of attending to the specificities of place and identity that is essential to an understanding of globally circulating media products and the people who create and consume them.

Identity and the Canadian Context

The ambiguity and vagueness that marked my interviewees' responses to the question of the Canadian identity of *DTNG* require analysis and contextualization, for the significance of place in media production is rarely straightforward. Geographic specificity may shape media production in numerous ways. As Allen J. Scott has argued, "Producers in any given cultural-products agglomeration [or geographic space around which production clusters] … will always tend to draw to some extent on local social traditions, mental associations, and icons."[10] Yet there is not necessarily a clear causal link from place to product. The complexity of geography and production may be especially great in the case of Canada, where ideas about national identity are foundational to the history, structure, and funding of the broadcasting industry but where the specific dimensions of this foundational national identity are rather ambiguous and ill-defined.

In her work on the Vancouver television production industry, Canadian media scholar Serra Tinic has explained that, "The search for Canadian identity has often been regarded as a defining national characteristic in and of itself."[11] This uncertainty may be largely due to the fact that Canadianness is most often defined in the negative, by what it is not. As American sociologist Seymour Martin Lipset writes, "Canadians have tended to define themselves not in terms of their own national history and traditions but by reference to what they are *not*: Americans. Canadians are the world's oldest and most continuing un-Americans."[12] Tinic adds that a perception of marginalization pervades Canada, generated by a sense of subordination not only to the US, but also to "the legacy of Britain's imperial past" or, for many regions of the country, to the national power centers of Toronto and Ottawa.[13] With a national identity defined at best by Canada's difference from and perceived marginalization in relation to the US, it is not surprising that the *DTNG* producers had a difficult time asserting what exactly makes their show Canadian; ambivalence about Canadian identity is central to their experience as Canadians, and thus to their work on *DTNG*.

At the same time, however, the *DTNG* creative team clearly wanted to identify their work as Canadian; they were happy to embrace its national roots. This is in part because the question of Canadian identity, even when that identity is defined as the not-American and the marginalized, has been particularly central to the country's television history, and especially to the cultural policy that has shaped it.[14] Canadian broadcasting policy has sought to preserve distinctly Canadian programming as a means of preserving Canadian national identity and protecting it from US dominance, as well as encouraging Canadian economic health. Indeed, the Broadcasting Act of 1968 declared that the country's national broadcasting service, the CBC, should "contribute to the development of national unity and provide for a continuing expression of Canadian identity."[15] This sentiment has gathered even more force over time, as the 1991 Broadcasting Act declared that the entire Canadian broadcasting system—both its public and its private elements—"provides ... a public service essential to the maintenance and enhancement of national identity and cultural sovereignty."[16]

This stance is not merely one of official state rhetoric; it penetrates all manner of discussion of television in Canada. For example, the Writers Guild of Canada declared that, "television shows us what it means to be Canadian by reflecting our history, values and sense of humor," in a 2006 statement submitted to the Radio-Television Commission (CRTC).[17] In a 2006 address, *Globe and Mail* television critic John Doyle argued that every country "with the vaguest notion of culture" needs stories of itself reflected back at itself and thus that homegrown television was, "like ensuring health care and safe drinking water," vital to the nation's very existence.[18] While such concerns are present in many national contexts, they are particularly heightened in Canada, where American-produced media and culture pervade the nation's television screens and its cultural consciousness.

The rhetoric that connects television production to national identity and sovereignty is further reinforced in the funding structures for Canadian TV. Canadian production funding comes from a range of public and private sources. Independent film and television production first became viable in Canada in 1983 with the government's creation of Telefilm Canada as an independent production funding source. In 1996, the Canadian Television Fund (CTF), a private-public partnership supported in part by Telefilm, was created, and it eventually became the central funding venue for Canadian TV. CTF support is dependent upon a given production receiving ten of a possible ten points in the Canadian content requirements established by the Canadian Audio-Visual Certification Office. These points are not dependent upon the narratives or characters presented in a Canadian production, rather they are awarded by virtue of the number and kind of Canadian personnel a given production employs (e.g., 2 points for a Canadian director, 1 point for a Canadian lead performer or music composer). The CTF also requires that productions be shot and set primarily in Canada, that the producers are Canadian, and that significant portions of the budgets are paid to Canadian individuals and firms. In addition, only certain kinds of programming are funded by the CTF; genres such as sports, news, reality, and talk are not eligible.[19] Instead, CTF support is divided amongst documentary, drama (fictional programming, either comedic or dramatic, in series or special form), children's/youth, and variety/performing arts categories, and is shared between English-, French-, and Aboriginal-language productions. The CTF declares its mission to be supporting "the production and broadcast of a specific type of culturally significant television production. These productions speak to Canadians about themselves, their culture, their issues, their concerns, and their stories. These productions reflect the lives of Canadians across the country and reveal Canadians and their society to the viewer."[20] The CTF's policies and practices are thus rooted in a rhetoric of Canadian national identity, although, practically speaking, that identity and the funding it allows is predicated more upon a given production's employment of Canadian labor and ability to substitute for the kinds of programming that Canadian broadcasters can buy relatively cheaply from US producers than it is upon any kind of essential national character.

Even as the notion of a Canadian national identity may be imagined, mythic, even ideological, the discourse of national identity has a powerful place in the Canadian television industry.[21] The fact that funding structures, regulatory policy, and industrial and critical discourses echo one another in their assertion of a link between Canada's national identity and its television productions provides a strong incentive for the *DTNG* producers to claim their program's Canadianness. At the same time, however, the ambiguity of that identity makes explaining just what that Canadianness entails a problematic effort. Still, these were not the only reasons why my interviewees expressed some ambivalence about the connection between national identity and the program they produce, for *DTNG* is as much a part of a global television culture as it is a Canadian one.

Identity and Global Television Culture

The producers of *DTNG* understand the importance of their show appealing to audiences beyond Canada. Indeed, *DTNG* depends upon its income from international sales; the license fee from its domestic broadcaster and the various public/private production funds from which it draws cannot alone cover production costs. Because of this reliance on the series' global circulation, the producers have an investment in creating a program that has universal appeal and that is not tethered to a particular geographic place. This basic economic motive may help to explain some of their hesitation to commit to a concrete description of the show's Canadianness.

It is especially important to *DTNG*'s economic viability that the program sell well in the United States, which it does through its appearance as the flagship series of digital cablecaster The N.[22] The significance of the program's placement in the

US market is related to the positioning of US media as globally desirable. In the global market, the national origins of television programming play an important part in establishing a hierarchy of desirability for those productions. Data from 2006 reveal that US sales make up 70 percent of the total hours sold to foreign broadcasters while UK sales make up 10 percent. The distant third-place TV exporter is Canada, with 3.7 percent of the market.[23] Because US television is omnipresent and favored worldwide, any association with the US benefits a program's fortunes. Thus, the fact that *DTNG* is produced in English and that its actors have accents difficult to differentiate from those of US performers works in its favor. So, too, does the program's generic and narrative similarity to US teen series. Finally, as the number of Hollywood-based productions that shoot in Canada makes clear, a Canadian location—especially an English-language metropolis like Toronto—can stand in for the US on screen, offering yet another advantage to Canadian productions seeking success on the international stage.[24]

All of these factors make Canadian programming sellable within the US as well as around the world. This even further advantages the program purchased in the US, as a US sale makes sales elsewhere in the world all the more likely. As one Canadian entertainment executive has explained, "Around the world, one of the first questions a Canadian selling a product will hear is, 'Who is buying it in the United States?'"[25] Another Canadian TV distributor adds, "We can get a great review anywhere in the world—it won't matter as much as a great American review."[26]

The economic significance of the placement of *DTNG* on US television may be matched by the psychological validation that success south of the border brings to the *DTNG* workplace, another reason the creators may not want solely to identify the series as Canadian. The program's success in the US is a point of great pride for the Epitome staff. Studio hallways are papered with photos from the cast's summer 2005 US shopping mall tour, where the thousands of fans screaming with excitement at meeting their idols surprised and somewhat overwhelmed the cast, who were used to the more decorous responses of Canadian viewers. Many Epitome staffers told me about the remarkable turnout of fans during that mall tour, suggesting their sense of pride and accomplishment in the show's transnational appeal. This pride is clearest in a story told by Stepahnie Cohen, Epitome's communications and marketing vice-president, about the company's efforts to acquire the surfboard trophy awarded to *DTNG* at the 2005 US Teen Choice Awards, where the show was voted Choice Summer Series. Although winners do not typically take home their trophies, Epitome happily paid to have their own board shipped to Canada, where it is now displayed in Cohen's office, signifying, as Cohen laughingly put it, "Oh my God, we're good! They like us!"[27] The emotional component of The N's involvement—and the success with US viewers that involvement has brought—is a significant matter in the culture of the Epitome workplace. In the Canadian context, achieving the admiration of Americans is seen as a victory, even while maintaining one's difference from Americans; one's identity as the "not-American" is equally prized.

DTNG's success in the US offers the production direct economic and psychological benefits. Its popularity south of the border signifies a kind of global acceptance; it secures the series a status of universality that flatters the participants in its production for its ability to overlook, efface, and conceal—or at least not be deterred by—the program's Canadian roots. Because this validation means so much to the *DTNG* production team, it is logical that they would not be eager to define their program as a distinctly Canadian one. If that were the case, the series might not be able to claim the kind of universal—and, especially, American—appeal that has helped it succeed and, just as importantly, that has given its creators a sense of achievement.

The relationship of Canadians to the United States, and especially of Canadian television workers to the US television industry, also complicates those workers' motivation to declare their show to be distinctly Canadian.[28] It also complicates my ability as researcher to locate the series and its creators in any particular geographic space.[29] Canadian media culture is nearly synonymous with US media culture. As many Canadians live close enough to the US border to receive the signals of US broadcasters over air, they have long watched US television that way. In addition, Canada's simultaneous substitution policy allows domestic broadcasters to air US-produced series simultaneously with their US first-run airings. This preserves the advertising revenue of Canadian broadcasters by drawing viewers to their stations rather than those picked up from across the border. And Canada's private broadcasters, including *DTNG*'s network, CTV, invest most of their money in those series acquired from the US. In 2006, for example, those networks invested $478.6 million in foreign-produced scripted programming compared to $70.9 million on Canadian produced scripted fare.[30] While the implications of such a situation are manifold, my point is that all Canadians, including those whose livelihood depends upon a vibrant Canadian television production industry, are regular *consumers* of US TV. US television is as much a part of their culture as it is of their southern neighbors'.

US media also inform the creative process in Canadian television. For example, *DTNG* head writer James Hurst told me about his admiration for various US films and television shows, including *The Sopranos* and *Lost*. He also cited the first season of the BBC series *Cracker* as "the best television, period." But he had little good to say about Canadian TV; in fact, he had harsh criticism for a number of "successful" Canadian series, which he argued were well reviewed in Canada "because [they] were] Canadian, and because [reviewers] felt they had to."[31] It is not just that Canadians, including Canadian TV writers, are exposed to US (and British) fare; it's that they often see such fare as the ideal to which they aspire in their own work (in part due to their envy of the larger budgets US productions are allowed). As Canadian TV writer Denis McGrath wrote of *Mad Men*, a US cable drama, "I hope one day to be able to write something one-tenth this good."[32]

At the same time, however, writers such as Hurst and McGrath have a strong investment in the viability of Canada's domestic production industry and champion it as having value in and of itself. Thus, McGrath has written that

> Good work in Canadian television] will come from a growing community of people … who think that Canadians do have a unique and different view on the world. A generation who believes that "telling Canadian stories" simply means "Canadians telling stories (and not stories they think Americans want to hear)."[33]

Meanwhile, Hurst has argued that without greater Canadian investment in domestic TV production, "We will lose our identity."[34] These writers deliberately tap into the rhetoric of Canadian broadcasting policy to argue for the significance of Canadian-created television, yet they are also arguing for their livelihood. At times, Canadian television creatives may identify themselves and their work as distinctly Canadian. Yet at other times, they may seek to disassociate themselves from a culture in which they find little inspiration, preferring instead to model their efforts—and their senses of themselves as artists—upon non-Canadian works. For such reasons, assigning any given production a particular geographic identity is an inherently frustrated act. *DTNG* both is and is not Canadian from the perspective of those who produce it, a position they accept as a fact of life in Canada.

Identity and Production Research

Many aspects of *DTNG*'s production may be identified as Canadian and yet, as we have seen, many other aspects are more appropriately identified as dependent upon or resulting from the US-dominated global media culture within which the series, its creators, and its viewers circulate. Because of the complications inherent in questions of geography and media production in general, as well as to the particular situation of a Canadian-produced and globally circulated series like *DTNG*, media production research that takes on matters of place and identity faces a significant challenge. My own experience researching the production and distribution of *DTNG* has had to confront such challenges. The previous sections have outlined some of the ways I have been able to make sense of *DTNG*'s multiply located, multiply identified status and the ambiguous responses I received to my questions about the show's Canadianness. But the ambiguity of the answers the *DTNG* staff offered must also be understood as by-products of media production research in general, and of the specificity of my research in this instance.

It is important to remember here that all efforts at on-site production research, interviews, and observations alike, have limits to the insights they can offer.[35] While the benefits of speaking directly with those involved in media production are great, these sorts of interviews are still subject to all of the shortcomings inherent to any such situation. Interviewees may be short on time, or concerned about their public image, or eager to please the interviewer—all circumstances that may shape their responses to questions in ways that guide the conclusions one can draw. Thus, a prominent Canadian television producer such as *DTNG*'s Linda Schuyler would be understandably concerned with presenting herself and her company as invested in their status as Canadian, but also as fundamentally committed to a level of quality work that transcends any nationalistic considerations.

In addition, my interviewees' responses to my questions about the Canadianness of their work may have caught them off-guard, in that they are much too wrapped up in the daily business of their jobs to spend much time thinking about such matters. While questions of geographic location and place-based identity may be pressing ones for media scholars, to media production workers they are surely no more prominent a concern than are other aspects of their identities—how their work is a product of their maleness, or their whiteness, or their age, for example. Similarly, media production workers are typically far removed from the motivations and interests of academia. Even when those interviewed or observed want to be as open and forthcoming as possible, they may not understand a researcher's specific interests. In the case of my *DTNG* research, the very welcoming Epitome staff steered me away from a production meeting about music, as well as a location shoot, because they thought such matters would be of little interest to me. I have no doubt that this was a genuine effort of accommodation, but it was one that arose from a mismatch between their perception of my interests and my actual interests.

Fortunately, on-site media production research need not solely rely upon interviews. Observational data can also be an important component of such scholarship. Yet the connections between a place-based identity and the "hurry up and wait" work of television production are difficult ones to determine by observation alone, suggesting that production research might ideally be combined with textual analysis, amongst other methods. In the case of my research, my sense of the *DTNG* staff's connection to American popular culture was confirmed by a few of my observations. For example, when a crew member's cell phone rang during a shot setup, his ringtone—the *Mission Impossible* theme song—was recognized by everyone on set; this Hollywood product is as much a part of Canadians' cultural landscape as it is Americans'. Similarly, the CTV posters papering the offices of *DTNG* staff featured publicity images of American series that air on CTV, such as *CSI*, rather than Canadian-produced series.[36] The choice to put such programs on their posters is, no doubt, the network's, but the Epitome employees' willingness to display such posters in their offices suggests their sense of cultural ownership of such programs, regardless of their national origin. In these ways, my observations did yield some insight into the presence or absence of Canadian specificity in the culture of the Epitome workplace, but these brief glimpses can hardly be seen as definitive evidence of a matter as complex as the role of a place-specific identity in media production.

My research experience also makes clear some of the specific challenges of "cross-border" production study. My status as an American examining the production of a Canadian series surely shaped the kinds of information offered to me. For example, staff members' regular efforts to tell me of the cast's enthusiastic reception by American fans or to ask me whether young people in the US really do seem invested in the show shaped my understanding of the relationship between the production and its US distribution. Yet a Canadian researcher, or a researcher from elsewhere in the world, may not have been a part of these sorts of conversations. At the same time, however, the aspects of my identity that I held in common with various members of the *DTNG* staff—my age, my role as the mother of a young child, my enthusiasm for television—surely also shaped my interactions, providing me with access to certain kinds of information and keeping me from other kinds. Thus, many facets of my identity, including but not limited to my nation of birth and residence, had an impact upon my research.

In all of these aspects of media production research, the connection between a place-specific identity and the resulting media text is an elusive find within a complex quest. Yet the complexities of cross-border production study need not halt its pursuit. It is only through such a research effort that I have come fully to grapple with the ways that the competing and merging flows of the Canadian and the American, as well as of the local, the national, and the global, are operative in the production of *DTNG*. The increasing pace of the globalization of television industries and the television cultures they produce make such attention to the local specificities of production all the more imperative. As challenging as such efforts can be, production studies will continue to benefit from ongoing efforts to cross borders in order to better understand the role of geographic place in the creation and circulation of media.

Notes

1 See, for example, Lisa Parks and Shanti Kumar, eds., *Planet TV: A Global Television Reader* (New York: NYU Press, 2002); Allen J. Scott, *On Hollywood: The Place, The Industry* (Princeton: Princeton University Press, 2005); Joseph D. Straubhaar, *World Television: From Global to Local* (Los Angeles: Sage, 2007).

2 For example, see Jeremy Tunstall, *The Media Are American: Anglo-American Media in the World* (New York: Columbia University Press, 1977).

3 Tunstall, for example, rethinks many of the ideas about media imperialism set forth in his 1977 work in Jeremy Tunstall, *The Media Were American: U.S. Mass Media in Decline* (New York: Oxford University Press, 2008).

4 Etan Vlessing, "Today Canada, Tomorrow the World," *Playback*, April 16, 2007, http://www.playbackmag.com/articles/magazine/20070416/mip.html.

5 My first encounter with the program, however, came via its appearance on the American cable network, The N, and was thus framed by that network's specific positioning of the text for its market context. I came to the series first as an enthusiastic viewer, watching for pleasure, and secondly as a researcher. This study is not centrally concerned with The N's marketing strategies, although these are crucial to an understanding of *DTNG*'s cross-national circulation. For more on my *DTNG* research, see Elana Levine, "National Television, Global Market: Canada's *Degrassi: The Next Generation*," *Media, Culture & Society*, forthcoming.

6 Stefan Brogren, interview with author, August 2, 2006.

7 Phil Earnshaw, interview with author, August 2, 2006.

8 Linda Schuyler, interview with author, August 2, 2006.

9 James Hurst, interview with author, August 3, 2006.

10 Scott, *On Hollywood*, 7.

11 Serra Tinic, *On Location: Canada's Television Industry in a Global Market* (Toronto: University of Toronto Press, 2005), 20.

12 Seymour Martin Lipset, *Continental Divide: The Values and Institutions of the United States and Canada* (New York: Routledge, 1990), 53.

13 Tinic, *On Location*, 134.

14 Bart Beaty and Rebecca Sullivan, *Canadian Television Today* (Calgary: University of Calgary Press, 2006), 18.

15 "Broadcasting Act, March 7, 1968," in *Documents of Canadian Broadcasting*, ed. Roger Bird (Ottawa: Carleton University Press, 1988), 375.

16 "Broadcasting Act, February 1, 1991," Canada Department of Justice, http://laws.justice.gc.ca/en/showdoc/cs/B-9.01/bo-ga:l_I-gb:s_3//en#anchorbo-ga:l_I-gb:s_3.

17 Maureen Parker, correspondence to Diane Rhéaume, September 27, 2006, http://www.wgc.ca/files/WGC%20OTA%20Submission%20CRTC%202006-5.pdf.

18 John Doyle, "One Thing about Television and Ten Things about Canadian TV" (keynote address, Two Days of Canada: Television in Canada conference, Brock University, November 2, 2006).

19 The exclusion of genres such as sports, news, reality, and talk from the CTF is due to the fact that Canadian broadcasters are already motivated to produce and air such programs, as they draw large Canadian audiences (think, for example, of the popularity of *Hockey Night* broadcasts). In contrast, drama is more expensive to produce and less likely to draw audiences (and advertiser dollars). Because dramatic fare is the kind of programming most likely to be imported from the US and elsewhere, the CTF focuses its support there. However, the goals of the CTF are not always supported by the government's requirements for broadcasters. A 1999 Canadian Radio-Television Commission policy made it easier for broadcasters to substitute cheaper forms of programming (such as reality or talk) for drama to meet the government's quotas of Canadian-produced content.

20 Canadian Television Fund, "Introduction to the Canadian Television Fund: Spirit and Intent," *Broadcaster Performance Envelope Guidelines 2007–2008*, http://www.canadiantelevisionfund.ca/producers/bpe/.

21 On the concept of nation as an imagined community, see Benedict Anderson, *Imagined Communities: Reflections on the Origin and Spread of Nationalism* (London: Verso, 1983). On the myth of Canadian national identity, see Eva Mackey, *The House of Difference: Cultural Politics and National Identity in Canada* (London: Routledge, 1999).

22 The N debuted in 2002 as the evening and nighttime programming block of Noggin, a joint venture between the Nickelodeon cable network and the Children's Television Workshop that targeted its programs to preschoolers. On December 31, 2007 the two channels split and The N became its own, 24-hour channel, available on digital cable and satellite services in the US. The N purchased US distribution rights to *DTNG* just as the series was going into production, making the American market an important audience from the outset.

23 Nordicity Group Ltd., *Green Paper: The Future of Television in Canada*, June 8, 2006, http://www.nordicity.com/reports/The_Future_of_Television_in_Canada.pdf.

24 *DTNG* provides something of a challenge to Toby Miller et al.'s conception of the New International Division of Cultural Labor (NICL), which aptly characterizes much of the media production work undertaken in Canada. Because *DTNG* is not a Hollywood-based runaway production but rather a Canadian production subsidized in part by a Hollywood sale, it relies upon Canadian labor to generate Canadian profit. However, the show also helps generate Hollywood profit (via its airings on Viacom's The N) and is globally viable because of its close association with Hollywood-based narratives. Thus the case neither fully supports nor refutes the NICL paradigm. Toby Miller et al., *Global Hollywood 2* (London: BFI, 2005).

25 Leo Rice-Barker, "The Ins and Outs of the International Market," *Playback*, May 20, 1996, http://www.playbackmag.com/articles/magazine/19960520/5350.html.

26 Sean Davidson, "*DaVinci*'s Leads Cancon Pack in US," *Playback*, March 20, 2006, http://www.playbackmag.com/articles/magazine/20060320/syndie.html.

27 Stephanie Cohen, interview with author, August 2, 2006.

28 In 2006 and 2007, Canadian production companies and broadcaster in-house productions directly generated 34,700 jobs. In the same period, foreign location production (productions from other nations taking place in Canada) provided 14,400 direct jobs. Canadian Film and Television Production Association, *Profile 2008*, http://www.cftpa.ca/news/publications/.

29 While there is not space here to engage in a detailed analysis of the *DTNG* text, I would argue that it negotiates the program's Canadian and global/American identities much as do the producers. For more analyses of the *Degrassi* texts, see Michele Byers, ed., *Growing Up Degrassi: Television, Identity and Youth Cultures* (Toronto: Sumach Press, 2005).

30 "Canadian TV artists lament big spending on US programs," *CBC.ca*, May 25, 2007, http://www.cbc.ca/arts/tv/story/2007/05/25/canadian-drama.html.

31 Hurst, interview with author.

32 Denis McGrath, "Year End List 2007: Fuel for Inspiration (Part 3)," *Dead Things ON Sticks*, January 2, 2008, http://heywriterboy.blogspot.com/2008/01/year-end-list-2007-fuel-for-inspiration.html.

33 Denis McGrath, "Capulets vs. Montagues," *Dead Things ON Sticks*, October 12, 2007, http://heywriterboy.blogspot.com/2007/10/capulets-vs-montagues.html.

34 It is unclear whether Hurst is referring to the identity of Canadians as a whole, or to the identity of Canadian television creators. In any case, just what this identity to be lost entails remains ambiguous. "Canadian TV artists lament," *CBC.ca*.

35 For discussion of these and other qualitative research methods, see Norman K. Denzin and Yvonna S. Lincoln, eds., *Handbook of Qualitative Research* (Thousand Oaks, CA: Sage Publications, 2000).

36 The example of the *CSI* poster is not entirely straightforward, however, in that Canadian company Alliance Atlantis is a co-producer of the show.

Chapter 12

Borders of Production Research

A Response to Elana Levine

Serra Tinic

The late communications scholar Dallas Smythe argued decades ago, that if Canadian policymakers had been serious about fostering a continentally independent broadcasting system then they would have adopted a different broadcasting standard from that of the American NTSC model. This would have effectively created a transmission barrier to American cultural influence.[1] The failure to do so, in his eyes, resulted in a situation whereby Canada became a cultural colony, or branch plant, of the American media industries. Although I certainly do not subscribe to such an isolationist prescription, and its basis within the cultural imperialism thesis, it is difficult to argue for a more effective method of escaping the power of the Hollywood juggernaut than to batten down the hatches and close the virtual border to the influence of American popular culture.

However, national media development policies were never intended to deny Canadians the opportunity to engage with American entertainment. Indeed, I imagine such a policy would have been met with outrage as most Canadians living close to the border had already become avid fans of American stories in the early days of radio border spillover. Rather, the central objective of broadcasting policy was to guarantee a space for the production and circulation of culturally specific stories that would allow Canadians to imagine themselves as a national community living within different circumstances than those of their more dominant southern neighbor. Consequently, national public broadcasting was developed according to the loftiest principles within rigid structural constraints. The Aird Commission, which established the CRBC—the 1930s forerunner to the Canadian Broadcasting Corporation (CBC)—saw a national public radio system as so vital to the evolution of the country that the government rapidly built one of the most sophisticated technological systems to connect the far-flung regional communities across the expanse of one of the largest countries in the world.[2] Unfortunately, the expense of this enterprise meant there was little money left over to produce actual content. The end result was that in the early years of the CRBC, Canadians experienced a media culture that the Aird Commission had hoped to resist; one defined by the centralization of production in Ontario and the continued dominance of American popular culture. These issues have continued to plague every successive task force and royal commission on broadcasting. Trying to find a balance between economic contingencies and domestic cultural expression became what Marc Raboy has referred to as a series of "missed opportunities" in Canada defined by the lack of financial investments and political will to fully invest in a truly, publically funded national media industry.[3] This manifested itself not only in the establishment of competing private and public networks, but also within the later structure of CBC TV itself, which has relied on advertising for one-third of its production revenues for the last fifty years.

This somewhat superficial history of Canadian broadcasting policy serves to underline the continuing saliency of the tension between the interests of building an industry (market goals) and the principles of fostering a sense of cultural community through television narratives. Elana Levine's production analysis of *Degrassi: The Next Generation* (*DTNG*) does an exemplary job of illustrating both the continuing industry–culture schism in Canadian television as well as the centrality of the dialectical relationship between cultural difference from, and similarity to, the United States. Her chapter raises fascinating questions for ways to continue to complicate how we study television production and its relationship to local, national, and global spaces. And, equally importantly, her reflexivity compels global media studies scholars to question their own place-based cultural assumptions within the actual process of fieldwork research. Therefore, to extend the conversation with Levine's work, I will consider why the *DTNG* case study is emblematic of the cultural and industrial issues that characterize the national and global aspirations of Canadian television. My intention here is to highlight the connections between production and cultural identification on the parts of both television creatives and researchers. In brief, I consider how our "situatedness," as academics working within national contexts, influences the types of questions and assumptions we bring to our fieldwork. Lastly, I want to conclude with a similar reflection on the imperative of conceptualizing similar case studies of American television production and national identity. Levine's chapter reminded me of how my own assumptions about the relationship between Hollywood productions and an imagined American national community reproduced a "taken for granted" affiliation between the two. This is despite the fact that I have lived for an almost equal number of years in Canada and the United States and study both countries' industries.

As Levine notes, *DTNG* is an apt example of a television product shaped by the specific exigencies of both the Canadian industry and "its history, economics, and structure," as well as the global television marketplace. However, to fully grasp this interconnection requires us to consider the roots of what has become a successful global youth television franchise. Returning to the original series *The Kids of Degrassi* (1982–1986), the foundational hopes and principles of Canadian broadcasting policy were met with almost unprecedented popular success. *Degrassi* was publically funded as an experimental, educational television series that could perhaps be viewed as a form of community intervention. Degrassi is an actual street in Toronto and the young people living within this multicultural, working-class community were auditioned to play the main characters who would dramatize the sociocultural experiences of living in a particular time and place. These were not professional actors, although subsequently some of these individuals developed careers in the television industry. It was, initially, a low-budget project that nevertheless spoke honestly and frankly to a broader youth culture. In this respect, the original *Degrassi* provides an important entry point into any consideration of the nationally specific—in fact, I would say "locally" specific—dimensions of Canadian television and the series' later incarnation as the globally oriented *DTNG*. Produced within a public broadcasting system, and therefore relatively buffered from risk-averse advertisers, *Degrassi* was provocative and delved into topics including teen sexuality, unplanned pregnancy and abortion, and youth experiences of HIV/AIDS. When the original series was sold to the American PBS, a network that identifies itself with educational programming, it had to be extensively edited as it was considered too controversial for the US broadcast market.[4]

The differences between what is "sayable" within the contrasting Canadian and American television structures also speaks to the sociocultural differences between the two countries. Therefore, it is perhaps par for the course that Levine found that "liberalism in our storytelling" became a recurrent definition of national identity within the production process. This response resonates with the cliché of the Canadian identity/insecurity complex as being one of moral superiority in the face of political, economic, and cultural inferiority vis-à-vis the United States. It is the reiteration of the belief that Canada's social welfare system contributes to a more liberal, tolerant society that allows for a greater range of social discourse across media platforms. The connection between political structure and cultural identity is significant to understanding the complexity of articulating a sense of difference from the United States. Herein, institutions and government investment in the public sector, whether it is domestic television, official multiculturalism policies, or universal healthcare, define a separate sense of community from the market-oriented and seemingly individualistic philosophies of the American Dream mythology. As Levine notes, the researcher's own location within the experiences of these cultural formations generates different questions within fieldwork. This is not to say that "outsider" perspectives are less valid or illuminating. Indeed, they provide unique insights that can complement the supposed cultural familiarity of an "insider."

For example, my past fieldwork within the Canadian television production industry parallels some aspects of Levine's project but differs in that I did not begin from the assumption that there could be a unified Canadian identity open to definition and expression in television production. Indeed, Canadian national broadcasting policy was developed as a means to overcome the absence of a monolithic narrative of the nation and to unite a regionally diverse country defined by a range of subnational tensions. In other words, the significance of the cultural experiences of *place* (the local, regional, urban versus rural) and how they intersected with the institutional dimensions of national and global structural processes shaped the direction of my conversations with producers. Consequently, my questions were concerned with how television producers, who were often working on domestic and American series simultaneously, negotiated narratives within the boundaries of federal content regulations, funding imperatives, and/or global market aspirations. My goal was to tease out cultural patterns or themes through the material aspects of industrial practices. I found it quite remarkable, in the end, how the vast majority of creatives spoke about a "Canadian sensibility" in storytelling, one that was repeatedly articulated as an ambiguous or ambivalent style that diverged from the American networks' more explicit genre and formula expectations. This "sensibility" was one that resisted dramatic closure and the conventions of the Manichean dualism in favor of remaining within the gray areas on sociocultural issues. And if the Canadian identity project has been best described as a sense of cultural uncertainty then depicting a televisual style of ambiguity may be a close approximation to how national identity translates into production practices. This is, of course, aside from the direct references to Canadian settings, issues, and hiring based on citizenship as required by Canadian content regulations.

It is also important to note that the American cultural presence is implicit within the Canadian penchant for ambiguity and ambivalence. American popular culture is an integral part of the Canadian cultural landscape and it is because of the many similarities between the two countries that Canadians emphasize difference as a means of cultural defense. Moreover, contemporary Canadian television production cannot be seen as somehow outside of the American sphere of influence. As Levine explains, creatives are also fans and it is, therefore, not surprising that *DTNG*'s head writer admires various American and British dramas and defines them as markers of quality television. The Canadian broadcasting industry developed as an amalgamation of the two systems and I, too, found that many Canadian producers see television from these two countries as touchstones for their own creative projects. It is, indeed, this "in-between-ness" or mimetic propensity within domestic television production that has enabled Canada to become the world leader in international co-production treaties. According to one European media consultant, Canadian productions with universal themes are popular because they speak the lingua franca of a North American television grammar with a "sensibility" that is more European than American.[5] This reference, once again, to an intangible "sensibility" rather than a definable "identity" may be a more productive conceptual path to understanding the ways in which Canadian television often incorporates both *universal* (global markets) and *particular* (domestic cultural expression) themes. As Levine rightly asserts, this capacity to negotiate between transnational and domestic markets is the hallmark of *DTNG*'s success in speaking to youth audiences across borders.

It is a process that I have begun to identify as the "mediation" role that increasingly characterizes Canadian television production in a global, postnetwork era of channel proliferation and multiplatform programming. Herein, Canadian productions are successful "mediators" in the global market to the extent that they reproduce recognizable Hollywood genres but tend to speak to a broader range of social, political, and cultural discourses. This particularly enhances their value to media buyers in countries with similar histories of public broadcasting. To this end, I would perhaps begin with a different set of questions for the *DTNG* creative team: How was *The Kids of Degrassi* made possible in the first instance? How did narrative and storylines evolve or change in the quest for international sales throughout the franchise history up to the contemporary moment of *DTNG*? What might this tell us about cultural specificity in the translation process between different television structures and market considerations? James Hurst, *DTNG*'s executive producer and head writer, provides a telling and incomplete statement to Levine: "I don't think you could do *Degrassi* in America but … it's very complex." It is purely supposition on my part but I wonder if his unfinished thought may have more to do with the renowned Canadian penchant for politeness toward an American academic rather than an inability to articulate the cultural and structural issues at stake. This reticence may be the central challenge to conducting production fieldwork in other countries, the concern on behalf of both participants and researchers to avoid misunderstanding and breeching cultural etiquette in pushing too hard for details or making negative comments.

To bring the discussion full circle, I want to speak very briefly to a particular structured silence in production research that struck me as I considered Levine's study in the context of my own fieldwork recollections—namely, the relationship between Hollywood and an American "national identity." Canadian media studies research has been consumed by questions of cultural identity as it is the defining feature of defensive broadcasting policies and regulations. Countries around the world have similarly expressed concern that "American" culture threatens to overwhelm their own domestic industries. Globally there is a tacit assumption that American television successfully narrates a united and coherent national identity. Despite the range of outstanding television scholarship that critically examines issues of ideological representation in terms of gender, class, ethnicity, and sexuality within dominant network discourses, there has been insufficient consideration given to the ways that Hollywood has framed a *national* culture that elides the tensions, fissures, and cultural contradictions of the United States. Victoria E. Johnson's recent work on television's construction of the American "Heartland" provides an important intervention into understanding the cultural geography or *place* of American national culture as told by Hollywood. Drawing on trade publications, network programming and promotion strategies, and archival documents, Johnson elucidates the ways that the broadcast networks constructed a myth of the American Midwest as an idealized "middle" or "populist mass" that would represent the broader national identity.[6] This convenient fiction served to rationalize the objectives of mass-market programming in search of an unknowable audience. The saliency of the "Heartland" myth continues into the postnetwork era. In my fieldwork, many Canadian producers who sought to enter the American market were surprised at the extent to which presumptions about one region could drive network decision making. This was best summarized to me by one producer who had successfully sold a Canadian television drama to CBS on the condition that all cultural references were altered to follow the "Heartland" formula Johnson described: "I was told a long time ago that this is American television, the audience is rural Ohio or Indiana—the Midwest … And they homogenize things for that audience."[7] While it is beyond the parameters of this chapter to fully develop the significance of this strategy, suffice it to say that production research needs to continue Johnson's trajectory of deconstructing American television's depiction of an uncontested "national identity." Although research such as Levine's and mine attempts to complicate the expression of a distinct Canadian sense of cultural community in television production, it does so in constant reference to an assumedly coherent American televisual "other." This, in turn, reinforces the dominance of an industrially produced and preferred American national narrative. Therefore, in an era of intensified global production and distribution strategies, it is worth questioning the value of continuing the cultural homogenization debate (when read as "Americanization") and to, instead, begin exploring the possibility that an imaginary "Heartland" may actually be the transnational referent for producers in search of international audiences.

Notes

1 Dallas Smythe, *Dependency Road: Communications, Capitalism, Consciousness, and Canada* (Norwood, NJ: Ablex, 1981).
2 In 1928, the federal government formed the Aird Commission as the first official task force to advise on the future structure and financing of Canadian broadcasting.
3 Marc Raboy, *Missed Opportunities: The Story of Canada's Broadcasting Policy* (Montreal and Kingston: McGill-Queen's University Press, 1990).
4 Serra Tinic, *On Location: Canada's Television Industry in a Global Market* (Toronto: University of Toronto Press, 2005), 181.
5 Tinic, *On Location*, 108.
6 Victoria E. Johnson, *Heartland TV: Prime Time Television and the Struggle for U.S. Identity* (New York: New York University Press, 2008).
7 Tinic, *On Location*, 115.

Part IV

Production as Lived Experience

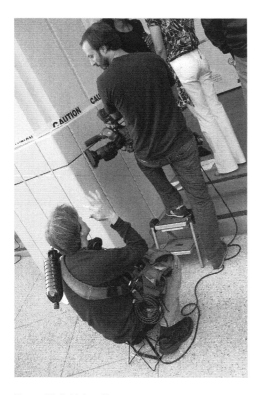

Figure 13.1 Video Shooters in Los Angeles. Photo by John Caldwell, 2007.

Chapter 13

Studying Sideways

Ethnographic Access in Hollywood[1]

Sherry B. Ortner

Hollywood the "dream factory." Hollywood the icon for the entire "culture industry." Hollywood in the twenty-first century remains one of the major sites for the shaping of American, and even global, discourses, identities, and subjectivities. Yet Hollywood has only been studied once by an anthropologist, Hortense Powdermaker, who conducted fieldwork in Hollywood for about a year between 1946 and 1947. She wrote a monograph, *Hollywood the Dream Factory* (1950), which probably remains her best-known book.[2]

There are no doubt many explanations for the lack of continuing anthropological attention to this important site of cultural production, but I will focus in this chapter on one particular factor: the problem of "access." As I will discuss below, anthropologists have always had access problems; it is part of the very nature of fieldwork. But in the case of Hollywood, the problem of "access" seems to be particularly acute, and has bedeviled most outsiders (including Powdermaker herself) who have tried to get "inside" for the kind of research anthropologists want to do.[3] Ethnographers have had more luck with television, but most of the quasi-ethnographic work on the movie industry has been done by journalists and Hollywood insiders themselves.[4] A recent ethnographic success story—John Caldwell's study of "cultures of production" among below-the-line workers in Hollywood—also indirectly underscores the problem of access.[5] While Caldwell's project on the unsung technical workers of Hollywood production is extremely important, it also suggests that a scholar is more likely to get "inside" if that inside is, as with so much classic anthropological work, among the less powerful.

There are really two distinct issues of access for the anthropologist. One has to do with the possibility of participant-observation; the other with obtaining interviews. While in classic fieldwork the two are part of a single package, in a situation like Hollywood they have emerged as quite distinct, and in what follows I will visit them separately. With respect to participant-observation, I will discuss what might be called "interface ethnography," doing participant-observation in the border areas where the closed community or organization or institution interfaces with the public. And with respect to interviews, I will explore the proposition that much of what is called studying up is really "studying sideways," that is, studying people like scientists, journalists, and Hollywood filmmakers—who in many ways are really not much different from anthropologists and academics more generally.

Hollywood and Secrecy

"Hollywood" in spatial terms is an entity that is spread discontinuously across and beyond the city of Los Angeles. But its spatially discontinuous nature should not be confused with the question of whether there is in fact a "community," and in this case the answer would very definitely be yes. The grounds for saying this include at least the following: (1) there is a relatively small number of insiders and, for the most part, they all know who they are; (2) there is a well-known and well-trodden urban geography punctuated visually and symbolically by the various studio lots scattered across the city; (3) there are newspapers and magazines directed toward this community that insiders read compulsively to stay abreast of current developments; (4) there are ritual occasions (most notably the Academy Awards but there are others as well, and these are proliferating all the time) when the community comes together to celebrate itself; and more. It is ironic that this site of high- or even post-modernity is also one of the few places in America where "community" in a relatively classic sense really exists.

Although the community is delocalized, it has a very strong sense of its boundaries. It is deeply invested in discourses and practices that both define and constantly construct insideness and outsideness. One might go so far as to say that the inside/outside binary is an "elementary structure" of Hollywood life.

There are some practical reasons for this. For one thing, Hollywood is a business involving quite cutthroat competition; information is managed for competitive advantage as it is in any business.[6] There is also the fact that, because this is indeed a real community, people need to sustain their social relationships in good working order. One may hate someone, or think poorly of him/her, but this must not be allowed to circulate (unless there is some deeper reason for allowing it to do so). Further, the products of Hollywood—movies and the larger world of cultural mythology of which movies partake—are all about illusions, and the boundaries around the production process, and especially around actors, are important for maintaining those illusions.

In addition to these and no doubt other practical reasons, there is the sheer clubbiness of the Hollywood community. One screenwriter I interviewed likened it to a country club. Producer Christine Vachon likens it to high school, and writes of a culture of exclusion:

> Lots of writing about the film industry promises to take you "inside" Hollywood. Even *in* Hollywood, most people are obsessed with being even

further "inside," on getting a first-look, the right of first refusal, the hottest invitations. It's a culture that thrives on exclusion.[7]

Or take the TV series, *Project Green Light*, in which actors Matt Damon and Ben Affleck, and producer Chris Moore, held a contest for the best screenplay, with the winner to get $1,000,000 from Miramax to make his or her film. The panel of judges included several high-ranking Miramax executives, including Meryl Poster, Co-President of Production and Jon Gordon, Executive Vice President of Production. Producer Moore is very clear that the show is all about providing access to these otherwise inaccessible personages:

> I think every aspiring director, every aspiring writer, would love to have people like Jon and Meryl reading their scripts … It is impossible for somebody who doesn't have an agent, or contacts, or didn't go to college with one of them, to get a meeting with them. That is the essence of *Project Green Light*: We are giving people access.[8]

The boundaries of Hollywood are maintained in innumerable ways. One might begin at the level of language and information, and consider the trade magazines. The contents of *Variety*, for example, are highly coded at multiple levels. The magazine maintains a made-up alternative vocabulary, a system of abbreviations, and a system of alternative spellings. Then there is the level of content: what precisely gets reported, with how much space, and in what location in the magazine. At both levels the outsider has difficulty reading: even if one can make sense of the language (and it is not that difficult, but it is distracting), one cannot understand the meanings being conveyed. The effect is to strongly reinforce the inside/outside divide, as insiders (they assure me) "get it" and outsiders don't, while at the same time leaking the valuable information that keeps the industry humming.

But most of the construction of the inside/outside divide is at the level of materiality and space. Most visibly, the studio lots have high walls that run on for long distances, impressing one with not only the scale of the physical barrier but the amount of real estate enclosed within.[9] Stars and other major personalities also live in high-walled barricaded houses, and the whole conceit of "star tours" is to take tourists past locations where nothing is visible at all. I have taken one of these star tours and it is fascinating to be sitting in a bus with a group of people outside an enormous wall or hedge, while the guide, in a deep and solemn voice, conjures up an image of the invisible star leading his or her life within.

The set of a movie in production is another kind of space to which it is very difficult for an outsider to gain access. At the beginning of the project I could not get access to sets at all. But after about two years of interviewing, I had gained enough allies to get me "on set" for three different productions. Given contemporary technology, most of the action of the filming is observed (even by the director) through monitors some distance away from where the action is taking place. The monitors are set up in a tent called "video village," which is set up and taken down as the filming moves even relatively short distances. I quickly learned that being "on set" did not mean I was really "inside," unless I were actually in video village. It seems there is always an inside further inside the inside.

Again it is not only the anthropologist who experiences the boundaries of access and the varying degrees of insideness. Christine Vachon, quoted above, was a very well-established, and indeed in certain circles quite famous, producer when she went to the Cannes film festival in the year 2000 to raise financing for some projects. Vachon offers ten funny rules for survival at the festival, of which Rule 6 is "There is always some other great thing happening that you have not been invited to." She expounds:

> Cannes breeds this feeling, no matter how secure you think you are. You walk around sensing that, at any moment, there is a lunch, a party, a press conference, a meeting that you have been excluded from. You try to stay above it, but then someone says, "I'm heading off to the Luxembourg Film Financing Website Lunch!" and suddenly you're back in high school.[10]

With all this, then, it is no surprise that anthropologists (among others) have had trouble gaining access to "Hollywood." This brings me to a very brief version of my own efforts to get inside.

When I first arrived in Los Angeles in 2004 and began telling people I was hoping to do research on Hollywood, almost everyone I met seemed eager to help, and volunteered that they had contacts in The Industry. Many people would give me names and e-mail addresses; others went so far as to contact their contacts on my behalf. I did manage to obtain a few interviews, but they were all relatively marginal to the world of Hollywood movie production. For the most part, however, people simply did not return my calls, or if they did, they passed me on to other people who did not return my calls. One effort after another seemed to start with great hope and then go nowhere, and that first year was frustrating in the extreme.

Yet these dead-end experiences also made me reflect on the question of trying to gain access via "contacts." While it is probably true that some kind of approach through contacts is inevitable, it now seems to me that if the person being contacted is merely doing somebody a favor, they are very unlikely to make something really happen. I am inclined to think that the missing ingredient in these sorts of contacts is the insider's *interest*, in either or both senses of the term. It may be a question of pragmatic interest: the people organizing a "press tour" for a new TV program, who encouraged and then dropped me, were looking for big-time journalists from major media who would give their program important publicity. I had nothing to offer. But there is also the question of interest in the sense of curiosity, of intellectual or "gut" engagement with the idea: somebody needs to *feel*, for whatever reason, that this is an interesting project, and get behind it. I will come back to this point below.

Participant-Observation: Interface Ethnography

At the beginning of this project I had access, through friends, to award-winning producer James Schamus, who I approached for the possibility of doing participant-observation in his production company, Focus Features.[11] Schamus was kind enough to give me an hour of his time on the telephone, and he was sympathetic to my request. But he said that participant-observation at the company offices would be quite impossible because of the numerous confidential conversations, meetings, and deals that take place there every day. He doubted that anyone else would let me do it either.

At the higher levels of the Hollywood scene—conversations, meetings, and workaday practices among high-level decision makers—Schamus was completely correct, and participant-observation deep "inside" has been impossible. Early on in the project I found one producer—I will call her Harriet—who thought it might be interesting, or perhaps just amusing, to let me into at least some limited contexts within her business. I did an interview with her in her office and then she invited me back to sit in on a relatively low-power meeting, a so-called "meet and greet" with a screenwriter she and her partner were cultivating. I was, needless to say, ecstatic. After that meeting, however, she evidently had second thoughts. She never returned another phone call or e-mail again. And no one else has even come close to giving me a similar opportunity.

Other anthropologists doing projects with high-status and/or powerful people (what Laura Nader has called "studying up," to be discussed more fully below) have also grappled with the access problem. Hugh Gusterson did an ethnography of Lawrence Livermore National Laboratory, in which nuclear weapons technology is researched and developed.[12] He subsequently published a paper in which he reflects at some length on the fate of participant-observation in studies such as his. He comments that "in most cases participant observation will be highly problematic, if not impossible," and that "participant observation is a research technique that does not travel well up the social structure."[13]

Yet I did not want to give up on participant-observation so easily, and I began to seek opportunities—any opportunities at all—to enter spaces in which some sort of revelations about insiders' ways of thinking and talking and (re-)presenting themselves might be heard and seen. One of these was the star tour noted briefly above. Let me sketch a few more here.

First, many relatively closed communities (like Hollywood) nonetheless have public events. For example, there is something called "The Writers' Expo" that takes place every year in Los Angeles and caters to the hordes of would-be screen-writers who inhabit the city. Anyone can register and attend the many panels in which successful Hollywood professionals—writers and producers—sit and talk to audiences about the art and craft of writing, selling, promoting, etc. one's scripts. I attended one in 2005 and it was enormously informative in terms of hearing the kinds of discourse professionals use to represent what they do and how they do it, a discourse which may or may not correspond to real practices but nonetheless tells one something about the culture in question.[14] In addition the panelists told personal stories and anecdotes about their own experiences which again constituted a kind of public ethnographic data; I assume they would tell me much the same kinds of stories were I to succeed in getting an interview with them. Moreover the whole Expo was interesting as part of an industry specifically designed to help people break into The Industry. Besides the panels and lectures of the official Expo, the tables in the lobby were littered with flyers for screenwriting classes, screenwriter support groups, and so on and so forth.

Another venue of this sort is the film screening with Q&A afterwards. If one belongs to any sort of film-related organization, one will be invited to screenings at which people importantly connected with the film—producers, directors, or writers—will take questions afterwards about the conditions of making the film. I joined one of these organizations, attended many such screenings, and took copious notes during the Q&As. I also attended several film festivals, and while on one occasion I was able to get a little bit "inside," mostly they represented for me essentially non-stop screenings with Q&As.

I initially viewed my attendance at the Writers' Expo, screening Q&As, festivals and similar events as ethnographic supplements, something to beef up the project which—I could already see—would be heavily interview-based. But in fact critical film and television scholar John Caldwell has argued that such events, among many others, should be seen as part of a "hierarchy of graded spaces" in which significant "professional and industrial rituals" take place, and through which one can learn an enormous amount about the cultural assumptions and social relations of The Industry, even if one never gets to the highest level of "insideness."[15] Writing of what he calls "cultivation rituals," for example, rituals in which the industry seeks to promote a view of itself as "collaborative, personal and humane," Caldwell writes:

> This acting-out … frequently takes place in what might be termed "half-way spaces" that exist between the private and public spheres of the professional: guild halls, film festivals, cinemathèque retrospectives, film/TV museums, summits and panels, industry conventions, trade shows and universities … Cultivation rituals and mentoring activities in these half-way spaces, ironi-cally, often pretend to bring the heretofore hidden secrets of the bunkered practitioner out into the light of day.[16]

The "ironically" in that last sentence suggests that the practitioners do not actually bring the secrets out into the open. At one level this is true, and we are not really privy to all the "budget-busting excess, bad-bet developments, derailed productions, colleague back-stabbing and corporate 'exit-strategies',"[17] except through the heavily coded pages of *Variety*. But it is also Caldwell's point that people in these contexts always reveal more than they intend, especially at the level of the deep background assumptions that shape what they say and what they do not say, as well as the body displays and interaction rituals they perform, in these arenas.

In any event without quite theorizing it so elegantly, I had been enacting at least a part of Caldwell's agenda, showing up in many physically disconnected but structurally/culturally connected—and open to the public—sites around the city of Los Angeles, watching people do their thing and listening to them talk. When I first started conceiving of this project, I was still living in New York, and imagined I could do this project by commuting as I had done for the *New Jersey Dreaming* project.[18] Now that I am here, and realize how much of the social universe and cultural formations of Hollywood are literally soaked into the spaces and events in Los Angeles, I think that would have been a major mistake. Thus, although the meat of the project has continued to be the interviews, doing ethnography at various sites of interface between the inner world of Hollywood and the outer world of "the public" has been important in generating, at the least, enough knowledgeability to conduct better-informed interviews, and at most, some genuine ethnographic insight into "Hollywood."

Interviews: Studying Sideways

In an extraordinarily prescient article published in 1969 entitled "Up the Anthropologist," Laura Nader urged anthropologists to "study up," that is, to engage in the critical study of dominant institutions and what she later called "controlling processes" in powerful nations like the United States.[19] One section of "Up the Anthropologist" is called "Obstacles and Objections," and addresses among other things issues of access.[20] Nader paraphrases objections based on problems of access: "The powerful are out of reach on a number of different planes: they don't want to be studied; it is dangerous to study the powerful; they are busy people; they are not all in one place, etc."[21] While minimally acknowledging these points, she also goes on to challenge them:

> The difficulties are true of the people that anthropologists have studied in many different places. That problems of access are any different, or at least any more problematic, in studying up in the United States is a proposition which has not been adequately tested. Anthropologists have had problems of access everywhere they have gone; solving such problems of access is part of

what constitutes "making rapport." In view of our successes among peoples of the world who have been incredibly hostile, it is rather surprising that anthropologists could be so timid at home.[22]

I am not sure it is a question of anthropological timidity, although some of that may be involved. And I do think, contrary to what Nader says, that contemporary institutions of power have generally been able to surround themselves with rather more impenetrable bastions of enclosure. Nonetheless Nader's general point is well taken: anthropologists seeking to do ethnography in relatively closed communities simply need to get more creative.

If it is hard to get into the inner spaces of Hollywood, it is also difficult to get people to sit for interviews, especially of course people in any sort of powerful position. Despite Nader's dismissal of this point, people like this are indeed very busy (as in academia, busyness is both real and part of the culture), and the anthropologist's needs are of very low priority for them. In the early stages of the project I was extremely frustrated about the possibility of getting to talk to anyone who was actively involved in making films in Hollywood. I conducted a number of interviews with people who were quite interesting, but who nonetheless, and for various reasons, were quite marginal to the art/business of filmmaking. And unlike the arguments in the last section, where the margins of Hollywood spaces could be ethnographically productive, the same is not true of interviews. If the person is not him- or herself "inside," then the interview cannot really pay off.

Eventually I got a break through the good offices of my colleagues in the UCLA School of Theater, Film, and Television. John Caldwell, professor of Film and Media Studies, put me in touch with Denise Mann, who runs the Producers' Masters Program. Denise put me in touch with Cathy Rabin, a screenwriter. Cathy put me in touch with Albert Berger, an independent producer, and Albert put me in touch with more producers as well as some studio executives. And so the ball got rolling.

There are important reasons why folks like Cathy Rabin and Albert Berger were more receptive to my project. Both are part of the independent film scene which is very different from the world of big-studio Hollywood moviemaking. Independent film people pride themselves on making much more challenging and sophisticated films, films that would appeal to more culturally and intellectually sophisticated audiences. For this and other reasons, there was a much better "fit" between my interests and theirs. I will return to this point below.

In addition I want to call attention to the specific nature of the chain of contacts that got me to that point, the (not unrelated) fact that the initial access breakthrough came through academic channels, that is, through professors in the UCLA film school. Both the "indie" connection and the "professor" connection bring me very quickly to my point in this section, which is that, while at one level moviemakers seem very inaccessible, at another level they are very much part of the world that we as academics inhabit. As Elizabeth Traube has astutely written with respect to a series of interviews/lectures with people in entertainment and advertising, we are all part of the "knowledge classes."[23] Similarly, Faye Ginsburg, Lila Abu-Lughod, and Brian Larkin have noted that "media professionals are ... our peers."[24] As I began to interview the folks just mentioned, and the folks they referred me to, it began to dawn on me that—even more than in the New Jersey project—I was studying not only my own social class, but my own—in the old Marxist jargon—class fraction.

The interviews always began with a little questionnaire on the person's social background. I asked people what their parents did when they were growing up and how they would describe the social class in which they grew up. While there was some variation in class background, many of the producers and executives grew up in families rich in material or cultural capital or both. In addition, and even more uniformly, they were almost entirely highly educated. Virtually all had BAs, mostly from prestigious colleges and universities. Some had PhDs or law degrees. I was back in the territory of the PMC, the professional managerial class.

I said earlier that I thought that the important factor in someone agreeing to talk to me was "interest," either practical (not much here) or intellectual. And as I broke through and began doing interviews, it seemed clear to me that that was the main reason people were doing this. On the one hand they were responding to the name of the contact person, but that was rarely enough. In addition people—many of whom had taken an anthropology course in college—would say, oh, an anthropological study of Hollywood, how interesting! Filmmaker Rodrigo Garcia (*Nine Lives*; *In Treatment*) was more specific:

> I thanked him for the interview and said I realized he must do hundreds of interviews and it must get tedious. And first he said, well I am happy if this helps you (which I am beginning to hear as the standard polite answer). But then he said, actually I would rather do this for someone who is interested in taking a longer view of all this, meaning presumably the anthropologist.[25]

There are of course people in every class and culture who can find the ethnographic study of their own world interesting. In an old collection of essays about "key informants," a wide range of anthropologists wrote about individuals who came to share their ethnographic passion in projects throughout the world.[26] More recently, reflecting on his fieldwork in Algeria, Pierre Bourdieu wrote: "My inevitable disquiet was relieved to some extent by the *interest* my informants always manifested in my research whenever it became theirs too ..."[27] But the degree to which shared interest can become the basis for genuine cooperation is magnified when the people being studied have the same kinds of educational background as the anthropologist, the same kinds of cultural and material resources, and particularly, when they are working in the same general cultural zone as ourselves—the world of knowledge, information, representation, interpretation, and criticism. This I think plays a large role in the fact that some of the most active areas in the "studying up" game are the anthropology of (the work of) the knowledge classes: of science, visual media, journalism, advertising, and finance.[28]

Yet if in fact, as a graduate-school classmate once memorably said, "we are all natives," then the label "studying up" is actually a misnomer. These folks are not "up" relative to us, they *are*—with certain modifications that I will return to below—us. Thus the title of this section contains a modest proposal that we call this kind of ethnographic enterprise "studying sideways," which recognizes the relative complicity between us and our informants, and which also acknowledges our own elite status more fully. I can complain about the difficulties of getting access to Hollywood, but ultimately I can traverse the manicured campus of UCLA and tap the resources of excellent colleagues in the film school.

If studying sideways means that we and our informants occupy more or less the same social space, this in turn has a number of important implications. On the one hand, it has obviously played a major role in helping me gain access to film-scene insiders. We all more or less share a habitus, including not least a taste for film, literature, art, and the good life.

At the same time, the fact that they and I are in broadly the same business can also mean that there is potentially a competitive edge to the relationship, an edge that can make its appearance at unexpected moments. This in fact has happened several times in the course of the project, almost always with someone whose position was structurally very similar to mine: a director of a film festival, a director of an organization of filmmakers, an editor of a film magazine. These are all people whose job it is to maintain an overview of the larger system, who pride themselves on having the kind of broad knowledge of the scene and its trends that the anthropologist is also seeking.

In all of these cases there came a moment in the interview where the person would challenge where I seemed to be going. Actually I tried not to be "going" anywhere in interviews. But informants in general and these informants in particular asked fairly sharp questions about what the project was about. I tried to give general answers (especially since I wasn't entirely sure for a long time what the project was in fact about) but occasionally individuals would press the question and I would mention some line of thinking I was pursuing. This was almost always a mistake, as the person would immediately disagree with whatever premise I seemed to be working from.

In most cases this did not totally derail the conversation, but in one case it did. It came during an interview with a personage whom I will call Jake Morley, long-time director of a major regional film festival. I was talking to him about independent cinema ("indies"), and I used the phrase "indie community." For reasons that I can now reconstruct from the transcript (but won't have time to do here), this set him off:

JM: I find that one of the problems I sometimes have with this kind of study, this kind of an inquiry, is that so often the person who's doing that study creates an entity in order to study it. Essentially I'd argue that you probably can't tell me what independent film is and I'm not challenging you, but you probably can't.

SBO: I wouldn't even try.

JM: Yeah but you probably couldn't tell me even how to start to think about it, and yet you're telling me about the community, how it exists, it doesn't exist, so what I'm suggesting to you is that the ways in which you think about it are often times the ways of trying to [validate] its definition …

SBO: Well, let me say first I'm really not trying to impose anything on what I'm seeing. Hopefully as an anthropologist I'm really just trying to hear what is—

JM: Maybe you'll do that, maybe you won't, I kind of doubt [that you won't], I'm not being cynical when I say that, I just kind of doubt it because there's a critical practice in any field by definition …

The whole text—and there is much more—could probably serve as an object lesson in an ethnographic interview gone bad, for an introductory field methods course. But that is not my main point here. Even granting that I did not do an exemplary job as an interviewer, it seemed to me that something else was at work. Morley clearly had no respect for academics who, from his point of view, already know what they will find before they ask the first question.

But I think there is a broader point, namely, that the two of us were in the same arena doing basically similar things. This can work in a pleasurable and productive way, which has been true of most of the interviews, or we can start stepping on each other's toes as happened here. As John Caldwell said when I described this interview experience, "You're both 'framers,' " that is, Morley and I are in the same structural position with respect to the knowledge in question, even if Morley knows infinitely more than I do.[29] Alternatively one could say that we are hearing a version of what Andrew Ross has called "a dialectic of 'no respect' "—I failed to show respect for what was important to him (though in fact, unlike a true "no respect" dialectic, I actually have enormous admiration for what he does), and he in turn made it clear that he had no respect for the way "academics" go about their business.[30]

Yet in the end, as Laura Nader said, all ethnography—in the double sense of both fieldwork and writing—has its obstacles, and it is our job to figure out how to surmount them. This brings me to my very brief conclusions.

Breaking Through

Recall the producer Harriet who initially welcomed my project, but subsequently stopped returning my calls. At the time I was devastated, as she was the only person who had shown any interest in the enterprise and any willingness to let me inside. But there was a fly in the ointment even at the time: I did not have much tolerance for the kinds of movies her company produced, many of which seemed to be about teenage boys drinking beer, talking about "chicks," and trying to get laid. I gave myself lectures about my problem with this: It is not my job as an anthropologist to like or dislike the movies people make; all movies tell us something important about the culture we live in, and any kind of movie is just as good as any other for purposes of this kind of project. If this producer was going to let me do participant-observation in her business, after all the trouble I had been having, what more could I ask? Still I was not entirely happy. A good part of the project would involve not only ethnography, but a lot of film viewing. How much of that genre could I take?

Harriet's company is an independent production company, but it puts together Hollywood-oriented movies which it sells to the big Hollywood studios. At the point at which I made contact with her, I was still trying to gain access to the big studios, in the spirit of Hortense Powdermaker. But, as is widely known by now, there are other kinds of independent production companies, which make films that are independent not just formally but substantively, films that work against the Hollywood thematics and conventions, and that try to say something serious and challenging about the world today. Shortly after Harriet dropped me, I made the happy connection described earlier with some independent film people. They were much more accessible than the studio types, they were generous with their time and their contacts, and they opened my eyes to the world of genuinely independent film which quickly became the focus of this project.[31]

I said earlier I thought there were good reasons why the independent film people might have been more receptive to—and sometimes genuinely interested in—my project than people on the Hollywood (or network TV) side of the culture industry. To understand this we need to go back to the point that people who work on the creative side of the film industry are in many ways not that different from "us," that is, from highly educated academics, journalists, critics, and the like. We are all part of what Elizabeth Traube called "the knowledge classes," a subset of the professional-managerial class or the PMC.

But even here further distinctions need to be made. If we are all members of the PMC/knowledge class, nonetheless there are what Bourdieu has called "dominant" and "dominated" fractions of this dominant class. Bourdieu first explores this distinction in *Distinction* (1984), but develops it more fully in relation to the arts in *The Field of Cultural Production* (1993).[32] There he argues quite convincingly that any field of cultural/artistic production is structured by the opposition between commerce and art, with commerce lining up with the dominant fraction, and art with the dominated fraction, of the *haute bourgeoisie*. These points perfectly describe the relationship between the world of Hollywood movies and the world of independent film, and provide at least part of the answer for my differential access to the two worlds.

At the very beginning of this project, I had asked myself what might be new in Hollywood since Powdermaker's work. At one level Hollywood has changed enormously in the past sixty years. Yet at another level all the changes have been consistent with what Hollywood always was about: commercial moviemaking designed to entertain and please mass audiences, and to make big money. One could argue then that the only thing that is genuinely new in Hollywood is the breakout success, since the late '80s, of an anti-Hollywood, the independent film scene. At least that is what I will argue in works to follow.

Acknowledgments

Thanks to Tony Robben and Hugh Gusterson for helpful information about their access experiences. Thanks to George Marcus, and to my in-house critics Tim Taylor and Gwen Kelly, for helpful and insightful comments on an earlier draft. Thanks to the editors of this volume, Vicki Mayer, Miranda Banks, and John Caldwell, for valuable editorial suggestions as well as for their kind patience with a wayward contributor. As noted in the text, John Caldwell has also provided many other kinds of valuable input at many points along the way and I am particularly grateful for his help. Finally, thanks to Adam Fish for excellent research assistance.

Notes

1 This is a shortened version of a longer paper. Whole sections were cut plus virtually all of the footnotes. The full-length version will be published in another context.

2 Hortense Powdermaker, *Hollywood the Dream Factory* (New York: Little, Brown and Company, 1950).

3 See Hortense Powdermaker, *Stranger and Friend: The Way of an Anthropologist* (New York: W.W. Norton & Company, 1966).

4 On television, see: Todd Gitlin, *Inside Prime Time* (Berkeley: University of California Press, 1983); Barry Dornfeld, *Producing Public Television, Producing Public Culture* (Princeton: Princeton University Press, 1998). Journalist accounts include: Peter Biskind, Easy *Rider, Raging Bulls: How the Sex-Drugs-and-Rock 'n Roll Generation Saved Hollywood* (New York: Simon and Schuster, 1998); Peter Biskind, *Down and Dirty Pictures: Miramax, Sundance, and the Rise of Independent Film* (New York: Simon and Schuster, 2004); John Gregory Dunne, *The Studio* (1968; repr., New York: Vintage Books, 1998); Lillian Ross, *Picture* (1952; repr., Cambridge, MA: Da Capo Press, 2002); Julie Salamon, *The Devil's Candy: The Bonfire of the Vanities Goes to Hollywood* (Boston: Houghton,

Mifflin, 1991). Insider accounts include: Peter Bart and Peter Guber, *Shoot Out: Surviving Fame and (Mis)fortune in Hollywood* (New York: The Berkley Publishing Group, 2002); William Goldman, *Adventures in the Screen Trade: A Personal View of Hollywood and Screenwriting* (New York: Warner Books, 1983); Lynda Obst, *Hello, He Lied—and Other Truths from the Hollywood Trenches* (New York: Broadway Books, 1997).

5 John Thornton Caldwell, *Production Culture: Industrial Reflexivity and Critical Practice in Film and Television* (Durham, NC: Duke University Press, 2008).

6 See especially Joshua Gamson, "Stopping the Spin and Becoming a Prop: Fieldwork on Hollywood Elites," in *Studying Elites Using Qualitative Methods*, eds. Rosanna Hertz and Jonathan B. Imber (Thousand Oaks, CA: Sage Publications, 1995), 83–93.

7 Christine Vachon with Austin Bunn, *A Killer Life: How an Independent Film Producer Survives Deals and Disasters in Hollywood and Beyond* (New York: Simon and Schuster, 2006), 7.

8 "Deciding on the Final Three," Disc 2, Episode 1, Chapter 4, *Project Green Light: First Season*, DVD, produced by Ben Affleck, Matt Damon, and Chris Moore (Burbank, CA: HBO and Miramax Television, 2001).

9 See also John Caldwell, "Industrial Geography Lessons: Socio-Professional Rituals and the Borderlands of Production Culture," in *MediaSpace: Place, Scale, and Culture in a Media Age*, eds. Nick Couldry and Anna McCarthy (New York and London: Routledge, 2003), 171.

10 Vachon, *A Killer Life*, 118.

11 Thanks to Karen Seeley for the contact.

12 Hugh Gusterson, *Nuclear Rites: A Weapons Laboratory at the end of the Cold War* (Berkeley, CA: University of California Press, 1996).

13 Hugh Gusterson, "Studying Up Revisited," *Political and Legal Anthropology Review* 20, no. 1 (1997): 115. See also Antonius C. G. M. Robben, *Political Violence and Trauma in Argentina* (Philadelphia: University of Pennsylvania Press, 2005).

14 Thanks to producer Sheila Hanahan Taylor of Perfect Pictures, who invited me to the event.

15 Caldwell, "Industrial Geography Lessons," 186 and passim.

16 Ibid., 171.

17 Ibid.

18 Sherry Ortner, *New Jersey Dreaming: Capital, Culture and the Class of '58* (Durham, NC: Duke University Press, 2003).

19 Laura Nader, "Controlling Processes: Tracing the Dynamic Components of Power," *Current Anthropology* 38 (1997): 711–737.

20 Laura Nader, "Up the Anthropologist—Perspectives Gained from Studying Up," in *Reinventing Anthropology*, ed. Del Hymes (New York: Pantheon Books, 1969), 301ff.

21 Nader, "Up the Anthropologist," 302.

22 Ibid.

23 Elizabeth Traube, "Introduction," in *Making and Selling Culture*, ed. Richard Ohmann (Hanover: Wesleyan University Press, 1996), xv.

24 Faye D. Ginsburg, Lila Abu-Lughod, and Brian Larkin, eds., Introduction to *Media Worlds: Anthropology on New Terrain* (Berkeley and Los Angeles: University of California Press, 2002), 22.

25 Rodrigo Garcia, author's fieldnotes, June 2007.

26 Joseph B. Casagrande, *In the Company of Man: Twenty Portraits by Anthropologists* (New York: Harper and Row, 1964).

27 Pierre Bourdieu, *The Logic of Practice*, trans. Richard Nice (Stanford: Stanford University Press, 1990), 3 [italics in original].

28 For science studies, see Paul Rabinow, *Making PCR: A Story of Biotechnology* (Chicago: University of Chicago Press, 1996); Gusterson, *Nuclear Rites*; Stacia E. Zabusky, "Ethnography in/of Transnational Processes: Following Gyres in the Worlds of Big Science and European Integration," in *Ethnographic Fieldwork: An Anthropological Reader*, eds. Antonius C. G. M. Robben and Jeffrey S. Sluka (Malden, MA: Blackwell Publishing, 2007). For visual media studies, see Ginsburg et al., *Media Worlds*; Elizabeth Traube, *Dreaming Identities: Class, Gender and Generation in 1980s Hollywood Movies* (Boulder, CO: Westview Press, 1992). For work on journalists or advertising, see Ulf Hannerz, *Foreign News: Exploring the World of Foreign Correspondents* (Chicago: University of Chicago Press, 2004) and William Mazzarella, *Shoveling Smoke: Advertising and Globalization in Contemporary India* (Durham, NC: Duke University Press, 2003), respectively. A collection by Melissa S. Fisher and Greg Downey, eds., *Frontiers of Capital: Ethnographic Reflections on the New Economy* (Durham, NC: Duke University Press, 2006) is about finance workers.

29 John Caldwell, personal communication with the author, April 6, 2006.

30 Andrew Ross, *No Respect: Intellectuals and Popular Culture* (London: Routledge, 1989). For other discussions of anthropologists' struggles with informants for authority and/or respect, see Jeff D. Himpele, "Arrival Scenes: Complicity and Media Ethnography in the Bolivian Public Sphere," in *Media Worlds: Anthropology on New Terrain*, eds. Faye Ginsburg, Lila Abu-Lughod, and Brian Larkin (Berkeley and Los Angeles: University of California Press, 2002), 301–316; Sherry B. Ortner, "Generation X: Anthropology in a Media-Saturated World," in *Anthropology and Social Theory*, ed. Sherry B. Ortner (Durham, NC: Duke University Press, 2006), 80–106; Antonius C. G. M. Robben, "Ethnographic Seduction, Transference, and Resistance in Dialogues about Terror and Violence in Argentina," *Ethos* 24, no. 1 (1996): 71–106.

31 I am grateful beyond words for the successful "contact" help of the following people: My cousin, entertainment lawyer Chuck Ortner; Professors Barbara Boyle, John Caldwell, and Denise Mann of the UCLA film school; screenwriter Cathy Rabin; and producers Albert Berger, Ron Yerxa, Ted Hope, and Vanessa Wanger. All of these people were interested enough in the project to help me in the first place; all in turn put me in touch with people who were similarly interested and thus willing to give me further "access."

32 Pierre Bourdieu, *Distinction: A Social Critique of the Judgement of Taste*, trans. Richard Nice (Cambridge, MA: Harvard University Press, 1984); Pierre Bourdieu, *The Field of Cultural Production*, ed. Randal Johnson (New York: Columbia University Press, 1993).

Chapter 14

Audience Knowledge and the Everyday Lives of Cultural Producers in Hollywood

Stephen Zafirau

In production studies, the question of how producers relate to their audiences has been an important, if implicit, issue in understanding why producers make the decisions that they do. Noteworthy studies of media producers living, working, and making decisions in their native habitats have suggested that "the audience" is a socially constructed idea that workers in the culture industries define as they go about making media content.[1] Sometimes these estimations of "the audience" involve uncertain, varying interpretations of who audience members are and what sorts of content they prefer, suggesting that "the audience" may exist more in the imaginations of producers than in actual "reality".[2] In other words, audiences may not actually be getting "what they want" from producers, but content may instead be based merely on the best guesses of audience demand that producers can muster.

However, whether these imaginings come close to approximating actual audiences or not, "the audience" does indeed matter for producers and their work.[3] Production studies conducted in a number of commercial culture industries show how producers try to understand audience characteristics and tastes, and how they come up with explanations for why particular kinds of content resonate with audiences.[4] In the Hollywood film industry, studio executives and others who make decisions about particular films depend on their own hunches about what will "work" with moviegoers, much as they have continued to rely on audience research for many decades.[5] Accordingly, producers generate knowledge about audiences, ideas that may work as implicit explanations for why decisions about content should be made in a particular manner.[6]

Given the broad importance of audience knowledge for media production, it becomes similarly important to understand how it is that producers generate this knowledge. In other words, how exactly do producers create knowledge about their audiences? And how is this audience knowledge made out of the relationships that producers attempt to form with their audiences? Theoretically speaking, this question has existed for some time. Assessing ideas that existed about the producer–audience relationship in 1950s Hollywood, Herbert Gans noted the following divide: "Some critics have suggested that Hollywood products are so similar that the audience has no real choice, but must passively accept what is offered. Others have argued the opposite, that the moviemakers are virtually passive, and give the people what they want."[7] Many contemporary theoretical perspectives today conceptualize the producer–audience relationship along a similar set of divides, variously seeing both producers and audiences as "passive" in relation to each other. A further distinction is how producers are seen in varying degrees of proximity to audiences, as either opposite the audiences they are trying to understand or thoroughly a part of them. Dominant theoretical perspectives in production studies land at different points along these continua.

On one side of this divide are production studies that draw from neoclassical economics. In Waterman's *Hollywood's Road to Riches*, for example, the development of Hollywood film studios into the large, profitable multimedia enterprises that they are today is seen as stemming from producers' ability to recognize new aspects of "innate" audience demand.[8] According to this model, producers behave rationally in figuring out markets and tastes that objectively exist. They work opposite of their audiences, as passive entities that are only limited by the informational problems they might have in uncovering what audiences "really" want. Other important approaches, some of them very different from neoclassical economics, also carry with them similar assumptions about the producer–audience relationship. Media effects research, for example, tends to analytically separate producers and audiences, generally seeing producers as active senders of content and audiences as passive recipients.[9]

On the other side of the coin, and from other perspectives, producers are conceptualized as fully a part of their audiences. Pierre Bourdieu's "field theory" suggests that producers are "homologous" with their audiences, sharing the same intuitive sensibilities and tastes as those who consume their content.[10] Accordingly, producers are cut from the same "habituses" as their audiences, and enter the "field of cultural production" to produce content that intuitively resonates with both audiences and the producers themselves.[11] Here, the notion of "habitus" refers to common outlooks that people have for understanding and evaluating cultural products, outlooks which are usually rooted in social class experience. The "field of cultural production" refers to how cultural products (including movies and television) are arrayed along a continuum from most legitimate to least legitimate, from "high" culture to "low culture." In Bourdieu's analysis, producers are intuitively drawn to producing cultural forms that most resonate with their own experiences. In this way, producers and audiences are bound by their shared aesthetic sensibilities. For media scholars working in other traditions as well, the products of the "culture industries" are as much a product of a larger hegemonic order as they are productive of this order. As Todd Gitlin puts it:

> Commercial culture does not manufacture ideology; it relays and reproduces and processes and packages and focuses ideology that is constantly arising from both social elites and from active social groups and movements throughout the society (as well as within media organizations and practices).[12]

In this light, producers and audiences may share similar ideological perspectives on media content, a common understanding of the world which would be difficult to fundamentally challenge.

In this chapter, I offer an additional vantage point on the producer–audience relationship. Instead of conceptualizing producers as either opposite their audiences or thoroughly a part of their audiences, I show how producers can occupy a kind of liminal space (or gray area) between their statuses as "removed producers" and "audience members." Using the case of contemporary film industry professionals working in Hollywood, I highlight the work that producers do to understand audiences in their own everyday professional lives. Herein, many producers actively attempt to cultivate sharper "gut" instincts about what movie audiences will like by engaging in activities that audiences are thought to engage in. This involves producers "taking the role of the other" to attempt to understand audiences as *they* are thought to see the world.[13] Film industry professionals accomplish this within the overlapping spaces between their work and private lives, such that their private lives come to be seen as having instrumental value.

To make this argument, I went to places where I could observe and listen to how producers in the Hollywood film industry conceived of their relationship to their audiences, and how this relationship to "the audience" became salient in their everyday lives. Over the course of a year, I enrolled in several classes on the motion picture business offered through major film and business schools in the Los Angeles area. These courses were taught by various studio executives who were veterans in Hollywood, and were designed to introduce an interdisciplinary class of aspiring professionals in the film industry (most of them MBA and law students, but also some film students) to various aspects of the entertainment business. These classes allowed me to see how experienced members of the business attempted to teach initiates about how the film industry's production culture operated—the sort of activity that Emerson et al. identify as a key "moment of meaning" in ethnographic research.[14] The classroom settings operated as what John Caldwell refers to as an industrial "contact zone," serving as an important symbolic space for self-reflection within the film industry.[15] Second, I worked as an intern at a market research firm for many days over the course of two months, learning about how movie marketers made audience knowledge for film studios and how their everyday lives as audience researchers helped inform this work.

This approach fits with a recent ethnographic turn in sociological studies of media production. As Laura Grindstaff shows in her study of TV talk-show production, ethnographic insights enable researchers to see not only how producers talk, but also how they *act*.[16] While access to actual settings of commercial media production often remains difficult (as Grindstaff and others attest), participant-observation is capable of revealing important "backstage" elements of production cultures. As a part of this, researchers who place themselves in actual settings of production are able to see taken-for-granted assumptions that are embedded in production routines. Interview data can also become more valuable when it is first informed by ethnographic data, as producers' explanations of "how things work" can be more precisely contextualized using this strategy. This was the overall approach I used as I conducted this research project inside the Hollywood motion picture industry.

Film Industry Professionals Experiencing Social Distance from Movie Audiences

Gil Cohen,[17] a former studio head turned consultant who taught one of the courses I observed on the film business, spends much of his time flying in planes. He talks of frequent business trips to New York, trips to various parts of Europe, and occasional trips to India. Cohen is a gifted storyteller who thrives on entertaining students as much as instructing them, and tells stories about being seated in first class next to celebrities from the entertainment industries and professional sports. During the middle of one class session, he takes a cell phone call from a well-known movie star, much to the class's amusement. One of my fellow students later tells me that in a previous semester, Clint Eastwood had called. Gil, like other executives I had met, is also very coy about how much he gets paid, mocking the paycheck he received from the business school for teaching our class, saying sarcastically, "Oh, I got a raise." He later tells us with a wide smile on his face that, "We all get paid too much," referring to himself and his fellow Hollywood executives.

When it comes to the question of audiences, Gil frequently speaks of how "we" (meaning the entertainment industry at large) are out of touch with what audiences want, despite "our" best guesses. He is also fond of telling us that, "We live west of La Brea and east of the Hudson" or that "we live in towers in New York and L.A. and have no idea what's going on." On one occasion, he characterizes the problem of figuring out the tastes of motion picture audiences as follows:

> We are spending a billion dollars a year as an industry throwing wet paper towels at the ceiling. And when they by chance stick, we try to figure out what

it was. Did we ball it correctly? Was it wet enough? Was the temperature of the room right? We don't know ... And that's why you see this herd mentality, where if something works, we all think it was because of the particular thing that got thrown.

For Gil Cohen (one of a handful of people in the industry who has been responsible for "greenlighting" films), the process of making decisions about films, of calling the shots on which film projects to "greenlight" and which projects to shelve, is ultimately a hapless one. For all the money that the Hollywood film industry invests in researching and marketing motion pictures, much of the effort, according to Gil, still turns on how well he and his fellow executives are able to put their finger on the popular *Zeitgeist*—a challenge that Cohen saw as being all but impossible from the vantage point of an office tower in New York or Los Angeles.

Many of the film industry professionals that I spoke with and observed described a similar sense of social distance from the motion picture audience at large. The question was as follows: How could "we," who live substantially different lives in "Hollywood" than those in the rest of the country (much less the world), possibly understand what sorts of movies people will want to see? This sense of social distance from "the audience" broke down along two lines of thought. One was a kind of class-consciousness that held that Hollywood insiders were separated from the generalized audience for Hollywood films by virtue of their income and higher cultural status. The other source of social distance involved the notion that Hollywood was its own geographically cloistered enclave, separated from middle America by the Hollywood subculture.

Many of the executives and marketers I heard speak in classes described their personal incomes with an air of cockiness. Perhaps this cockiness stemmed in part from the fact that the class audience was a group of students and the speaker was held as an expert within that context. But there was also a sense of pride in how speakers talked about their incomes, alluding to it as a kind of marker of success within their business. One marketing executive described how his professional success in the industry had led to the establishment of a profitable company that had been bought by a large media conglomerate. After describing this, he made a half-joking aside, saying, "Yeah, my kids will never have to work." Another executive, who dealt with the home exhibition market, alluded to his success in the industry when he was talking about movie piracy. He told of how, given that a significant amount of his work involved stemming the flow of pirated movies, he had banned CD burners from his home because he did not want his kids using them to illegally copy movies—on principle. To our class's laughter, he imitated the conversation he had with his children, in which he explained his reasoning for banning CD burners and the risks to his livelihood that were posed by piracy: "Daddy makes his living off of protecting intellectual property. Do you like your big house in Southern California? Do you like living on an acre of land? Well, guess what? We're moving to Crenshaw Blvd."[18] The racist overtone to this comment was clear, as Crenshaw Blvd. is widely identifiable as a predominantly African American area of Los Angeles. I speculated over the extent to which the executive felt as though our class was a safe space to joke in this manner, as the students in the class were overwhelmingly white (and none were African American).[19]

While executives sometimes joked about their success in the industry and their financial standing, these facts simultaneously introduced problems when it came to understanding audience tastes. Some studio executives spoke of how "Hollywood" was lifestyles apart from its audiences. One executive captured this sense of separation during a discussion on the adoption of new home exhibition/gaming platforms, telling us:

> You and I don't count. We make too much. Median income in the US is about $36,000. These people don't have all the fancy toys. For them, you have to remember, it's like, "We ain't got no stinking PS1, PS2, or PS3" [referring to Sony's Playstation 3]. We don't count. We're in the upper strata.

In another example, during a class session in which we had been talking about DVD purchases at discount retailers like Wal-Mart, one executive made an aside about people who bought clothes there: "Nobody actually goes to Wal-Mart to buy clothes, do they? Who in this room has actually bought clothes from Wal-Mart? Eek!" Thus, many industry professionals were aware of themselves as having consumption habits that were markedly different from those of the American movie audience at large. At times, Gil Cohen would describe this social distance in terms of the difference between "red states" and "blue states," frequently describing the "blue state" audiences as more educated and more affluent than those in "red states." This too served as a "symbolic boundary" for producers, distinguishing them from their audience in terms of tastes rooted in social class differences.[20] "America has a totally ambivalent relationship with Hollywood," Cohen said. "Where is the movie business? LA and New York. They are blue states." Thus, movies that work in "blue states" might not work in "red states." But being able to sense this gap might become difficult from one's vantage point as a member of the socioeconomic elite.

Film industry professionals also spoke of their social distance from their audience in terms of their cloisteredness in the Hollywood milieu. Many producers told of how they felt the movie industry was its own subculture that encouraged a kind of "groupthink," providing little exposure to the outside world. One former studio executive reflected on this set of problems during an interview when I asked him about how he mapped audience tastes, back when his job was to choose which projects to greenlight:

> It was difficult. I was living in Sherman Oaks, California. I was eating in restaurants where a significant proportion of the people were working in the film business, or [were] lawyers, accountants, doctors, or investment bankers. I wasn't exactly in the broadest spectrum of society.

Given that social networks largely consisted of other people working in "the industry," it was similarly hard to gain a deep "feeling" for what audiences were like. Overall, these ideas of social distance from film audiences played a crucial role spurring industry professionals to seek better ways of guessing about audiences.

Producers Cultivating a "Gut" Instinct and Taking the Role of the Audience

In her classic ethnography of Hollywood in 1950, Hortense Powdermaker noted that Hollywood studio executives prided themselves on being "showmen gifted with special intuitive powers, who do not need to plan, and think, and work hard, as presumably do the heads of factories turning out automobiles and prefabricated houses".[21] Powdermaker went on to observe that this "intuitive" ability was a prized attribute of movie executives, even though movie executives did in fact work and plan just as other captains for industry did at the time.[22] The notion of "instinct" continues to be an important one in explanations that many Hollywood executives have for why they make the decisions that they do. This is so despite an extensive investment into commercial audience research on the part of the studios.[23] One interviewee, a high-ranking executive at a major studio, dismissed "scientific" research on audience tastes as, at best, "directional." He insisted that successfully choosing which movies to send into production was still primarily "a gut game." Executives might rise and fall on the basis of the quality of their instincts, on their knack for choosing commercial hits and failures.

Given that anxieties about the quality of one's "gut" instinct were often rooted in fears that one was socially distant from the tastes of typical audience members, many of the producers I spoke with and observed described how they attempted to put themselves in closer proximity to real audience members in order to sharpen their instincts. By taking the role of different audience members thought to be important to the Hollywood movie business, producers thought that they might be able to escape the narrow perspectives allowed by virtue of their socioeconomic standing and their cloistered life in Hollywood's subculture. For these producers, personal life and work overlapped in a workaholic frenzy. But it was not only that work took away from producers' personal lives, but also that their personal lives informed them in their professional capacities as the predictors of popular taste. In this way, the personal lives of producers came to have instrumental value because they could help producers take the role of movie audiences.

Hollywood producers found professional value in their personal lives in a couple of important ways. One useful kind of audience perspective came from producers' children. As many working in Hollywood attest, the youth market is an especially prized demographic for Hollywood studios to capture. An annual report released in 2006 by the Motion Picture Association of America (MPAA) concluded that nearly half of all annual theatrical admissions came from audiences ages 12–29, and that teenagers aged 12–17 constituted a full 20 percent of ticket sales.[24] Executives establish clout within studios by making pictures that "hit" this strategically important young demographic, in part because this shows that they are on top of ever-evolving popular tastes. Here, producers' own children may help provide information about tastes in movies that are deemed youthful. One studio executive I interviewed, in response to my question on how he stayed on top of popular taste, put it as follows: "I'll tell you how it's done for a majority of people: kids. Your kids, your nephews, your nieces, your cousins. Watching what they're doing, watching how they're doing it, watching where they're doing it." He went on to tell a story of how his preteen son had once helped call a sleeper hit. He recalled this as follows:

> Many years ago, I had three children. My son was in middle school, so he had to be around 11 or 12 years old. And a guy came to me and said, "listen, I've got this movie that we're making, and I want you [name of studio] to pick it up. And it's going to do a lot of business. It's a wonderful movie. It's live action." And I said, "OK, how much?" And he said, "You could have all the worldwide rights for $7 million." I said, "OK" and he brought me some stuff from the movie, some stuffed animals, and he brought me a little promo tape, like three minutes long. So, first I went and I showed it to my staff, and they all looked at it, and they said, "What are you crazy? This is horrible! We don't want to do this. This is not good." So I took it home and called my son into the room, and said "Son, I want you to see this." I put it into the machine and I played it, and he was like "Aw, dad this is great! You gotta' get this! The kids love this!" And I said, "Really?" And he said, "Oh yeah, this is the hottest thing goin', dad. You gotta' pick this up. This is gonna' do a lot of business!"

On his son's advice, the executive then took the movie back to his staff and other executives, but they collectively decided to pass on buying the film—even though the executive I interviewed thought it might be a good bargain. The executive eventually revealed the punch line of this story, which was that the film had been

Teenage Mutant Ninja Turtles (1990), which had an eventual US box office gross revenue of $135 million.[25] Much to his dismay, his son had been right and professional executives had been wrong. To this day, he acknowledged that he continues to rely on the advice of children in his family, which now includes his grandchildren:

> Now one of the things that's happening to me is my grandkids are coming along, and I watch what they're into, and I see the things they're into, what they love to do, what they don't love to do, and where they spend their time. And you start to say, "OK, let me start listening to them."

Other professionals in the film industry whom I spoke with told of how their children also helped inform their "gut" instincts about motion picture audiences. Martha, a marketer I worked with as a participant-observer, told me how she was her company's expert in marketing movies to children because she was one of a relatively few researchers who had young children of her own. She described how she had a deep knowledge of what sorts of films her children responded to, but also what sorts of strategies and popular culture characters her own children might respond to. For other movie marketers, one's children might help interpret audience data. One marketing executive I interviewed, in a discussion on what lay behind teenage movie attendance, told me: "I actually have a teen. And, you know, her use of movies is not really a movie, but to hang out with friends. She'll actually get to a movie late, they'll stay a short time and then they'll leave …" Thus, for this marketing executive, having a teenage daughter contributed to a more nuanced understanding of what drives teenagers to go to theaters, helping him see teenage attendance as more of a social event than something driven by interest in a film itself.

Another important way in which the Hollywood professionals I talked to attempted to gain audience perspective was by purposefully engaging with popular culture. This often became a part of work as well, done specifically to get inside the audience's worldview—even though producers might have had limited personal interest in the kinds of popular culture they had to become familiar with. Getting a sense of "what was going on" led many executives I interviewed to turn to popular publications as a summary of what was of concern within the popular mind. One top executive working at a major studio spoke to this when I asked him whether or not it was challenging to stay on top of popular taste. He responded:

> No, I think when you're in these jobs, part of what you do is you read a lot of magazines. You have people who feed you a lot of popular culture and things that are going on in the world. So to be good at your job you really do have to know what's going on out in the world.

Another former top executive I interviewed recalled the importance of reading popular publications and watching television when he was deciding which movies to greenlight:

> When I was doing it, I was reading three newspapers a day, probably six or seven magazines on a regular basis, and watching television. You know, trying to be as worldly as one could be, without having your mind become completely numb. But even still, I knew that all of that experience was very limited.

Working within a world in which it was difficult to fully grasp what the rest of the country might want to see thus proved to be an ongoing challenge for executives, perhaps one that could only be partially met by becoming a voracious consumer of popular publications and television.

Other elements of this strategy for maintaining a sharp sense for popular taste involved measures that were more directly related to the movies: namely, going to movies. Gil Cohen told our class that he used to require his junior executives to go to movies on their own. He recalled how one of these fellow executives had come to him with ticket stubs, asking if the studio would reimburse him or her for this expense. Cohen seemed incredulous that a fellow executive would fail to "get" the importance of putting oneself in a theater with actual audiences. He exclaimed, "If you're in the movies, go to the movies!" Various executives also regarded audience test screenings as very important for this reason as well. In addition to providing valuable statistics on the reaction of audiences to a particular movie, test screenings were said to help executives "feel" an audience. Also, by repeatedly watching movies with test audiences and then comparing how these subjective "feelings" of the audience stacked up against real numbers, some executives thought that they could sharpen their "gut" instincts more generally.

Conclusion

Like other chapters in this volume, the case of Hollywood film professionals developing their instincts shows the value of grounded approaches to studying media production. Where it is possible to conduct this kind of research, grounded ethnographic and interview evidence is capable of improving models of popular culture production, giving more nuance to key concepts and assumptions. The case I present here complicates implicit assumptions held by many models of media production that see producers as either opposite and separate from their audiences *or* as organic members of audiences. Instead, as the case of contemporary Hollywood moviemakers suggests, producers attempt to occupy a space that is somewhere between real film audiences and the cloistered studio lots, trendy restaurants, and glamorous Beverly Hills homes that make up "Hollywood."[26] In doing so, producers attempt to partially overcome their perceived limitations as inhabitants of an elite habitus.

Additionally, this chapter furthers understandings of what "instinct" is in culture industries like Hollywood filmmaking. One story that producers themselves tell when talking about "instinct" is that it is an innate gift. Accordingly, some gatekeepers of popular culture simply have a "golden touch" in choosing hits. However, my interviews and observations also suggest that many see "gut instinct" as something that is malleable and improvable. Furthermore, my data suggest that these "instincts" need not simply come from one's work within a particular industry. Instincts about popular tastes may also be rooted and justified through producers' everyday lives, in the overlapping spaces between "professional" and "personal."

Finally, my observations and interviews are suggestive for our theories of popular culture production more generally. In particular, this study shows how micro-level social phenomena can inform producers' common sense understandings of what sorts of products will "work" with audiences. While production studies emanating from economics and organizational science often emphasize the importance of "risk aversion" in explaining how decisions about commercial media are made, this study points to how producers' family lives or leisure activities may serve as mediating factors in helping them understand what ideas are in fact "risky." As such, these smaller worlds that producers inhabit may be important sources of both continuity and change in deciding how popular culture looks and sounds.

Notes

1   Todd Gitlin, *Inside Prime Time* (Berkeley and Los Angeles: University of California Press, 1983); Muriel Cantor, *The Hollywood TV Producer: His Work and His Audience* (New York: Basic Books, 1971).

2   Cantor, *The Hollywood TV Producer*.

3   James S. Ettema and D. Charles Whitney, eds., *Audiencemaking: How the Media Create the Audience* (Thousand Oaks and London: Sage Publications, 1994).

4   See, for example, Jarl A. Ahlkvist and Robert Faulkner, "'Will This Record Work for Us?': Managing Music Formats in Commercial Radio," *Qualitative Sociology* 25 (2002): 189–215; Arlene Dávila, *Latinos, Inc.* (Berkeley and Los Angeles: University of California Press, 2001); Laura Grindstaff, *The Money Shot: Trash, Class, and the Making of TV Talk Shows* (Chicago: University of Chicago Press, 2002); Joshua Gamson, *Freaks Talk Back: Tabloid Talk Shows and Sexual Nonconformity* (Chicago and London: University of Chicago Press, 1998).

5   Robert Marich, *Marketing to Moviegoers: A Handbook of Strategies Used by Major Studios and Independents* (New York and London: Elsevier, 2005); Leo Handel, *Hollywood Looks at Its Audience: A Report of Film Audience Research* (Urbana-Champaign: University of

Illinois Press, 1950); Susan Ohmer, *George Gallup in Hollywood* (New York: Columbia University Press, 2006).

6   Paul Espinosa, "The Audience in the Text: Ethnographic Observations of a Hollywood Story Conference," *Media, Culture & Society* 4, no.1 (1982): 77–86.

7   Herbert J. Gans, "The Creator–Audience Relationship in the Mass Media: An Analysis of Movie Making," in *Mass Culture: The Popular Arts in America*, eds. Bernard Rosenberg and David Manning White (Glencoe, IL: The Free Press, 1957), 315–324.

8   David Waterman, *Hollywood's Road to Riches* (Cambridge, MA and London: Harvard University Press, 2005).

9   Jennings Bryant and Dolf Zillman, eds., *Media Effects: Advances in Theory and Research* (Mahwah, NJ: Lawrence Erlbaum Publishers, 2002).

10   Pierre Bourdieu, *The Field of Cultural Production: Essays on Art and Literature* (New York: Columbia University Press, 1993).

11   Rodney Benson and Erik Neveu, eds., *Bourdieu and the Journalistic Field* (Malden, MA: Polity, 2005); Pierre Bourdieu, *Outline of a Theory of Practice*, trans. Richard Nice (Cambridge: Cambridge University Press, 1977); see also Sherry Ortner's chapter in this volume, which underscores the fact that Hollywood's independent film producers today are from the same "knowledge classes" as their target audiences.

12   Todd Gitlin, "Prime Time Ideology: The Hegemonic Process in Television Entertainment," *Social Problems* 26 (1979): 253.

13   George Herbert Mead, *Mind, Self, and Society*, ed. Charles W. Morris (Chicago: University of Chicago Press, 1934).

14   Robert M. Emerson, Rachel I. Fretz, and Linda L. Shaw, *Writing Ethnographic Fieldnotes* (Chicago: University of Chicago Press, 1995).

15   John Caldwell, *Production Culture: Industrial Reflexivity and Critical Practice in Film and Television* (Durham, NC and London: Duke University Press, 2008).

16   Laura Grindstaff, *The Money Shot: Trash, Class, and the Making of TV Talk Shows* (Chicago: University of Chicago Press, 2002).

17   Real names of all informants have been changed to protect their confidentiality.

18   Crenshaw Blvd. is a major strip in Los Angeles that runs through relatively less affluent South Central Los Angeles.

19   Due to its particular demographic composition, the classes I observed seemed to support the idea that those working in the film industry were socially distant from audiences (insofar as they were less diverse than the general population). In addition to the students being overwhelmingly white, all of the instructors in the courses I attended were white men.

20   Daniel Weber, "Culture or Commerce? Symbolic Boundaries in French and American Book Publishing," in *Rethinking Comparative Cultural Sociology: Repertoires of Evaluation in France and the United States*, eds. Michèle Lamont and Laurent Thévenot (Cambridge, UK: Cambridge University Press, 2000); Michèle Lamont, *Money, Morals, and Manners: The Culture of the French and American Upper-Middle Class* (Chicago: University of Chicago Press, 1992).

21   Hortense Powdermaker, *Hollywood: the Dream Factory: An Anthropologist Looks at the Movie-Makers* (Boston: Little, Brown and Company, 1950), 93.

22   Ibid.

23   Robert Marich, *Marketing to Moviegoers: A Handbook of Strategies Used by Major Studios and Independents* (New York and London: Elsevier, 2005); Janet Wasko, *How Hollywood Works* (Thousand Oaks and London: Sage, 2003).

24 Motion Picture Association of America, "The 2005 Movie Attendance Study," http://
www.mpaa.org (accessed June 21, 2006).
25 International Movie Database, "Teenage Mutant Ninja Turtles," http://www.imdb.com/
title/tt0100758/business (accessed September 16, 2008).
26 Nick Couldry, *The Place of Media Power: Pilgrims and Witnesses of the Media Age* (London:
Routledge, 2000).

Chapter 15

Lights, Camera, but Where's the Action?

Actor-Network Theory and the Production of Robert Connolly's *Three Dollars*

Oli Mould

In Hollywood, filmmaking is dominated by a number of large production studios that have placed increasing emphasis upon contract and freelance labor since the end of the studio era.[1] Feature film production in many other countries and cities relies even more extensively on impermanent self-employed freelance workers that are less integrated into the long-range business plans of the major studios/distributors. American economist Jeremy Rifkin remarks, "every film production brings together a team of specialised production companies and independent contractors, each with its own expertise, along with the talent.[2] Together, these disparate parties constitute a short-lived network enterprise whose lifespan will be *limited to the duration of the project*."[3] The project-based nature of employment in this industry is hence comprehensive, with very few large film producing firms, formulating what has been coined a "cottage economy."[4]

Noting this mode of production, this chapter will show, through a project-based case study of *Three Dollars* (an Australian feature film directed by Robert Connolly) how Actor-Network Theory (ANT) can be employed to describe this project-based mode of film production that is sensitive to the freelance workers enrolled within it. The development of ANT in the social sciences literatures has offered scholars an alternative to Marxist approaches of media industry analysis. That is, ANT describes and prioritizes *action* of production work activities and relationships over *structure* of the industry's institutions and economies. This chapter therefore explores the potential of ANT as a research language for the film industry by highlighting how some of the nuances of ANT emerge through the case study of *Three Dollars*; and, by noting the research on this according to several key authors, how ANT differs from other theoretical approaches to media production.

Essentially, employing ANT frees the researcher/author from the conceptual straightjacket imposed by top-down, grand, determining metanarratives (such as capitalism, economy, culture, globalization and so on), and helps detail the processes which construct and maintain the dynamic behaviors of the production networks in question. ANT is therefore often articulated as a "flat" or "horizontal" concept, in opposition to "top-down" approaches that have been utilized traditionally in fields such as cultural geography. Hence, the case study presented in this chapter will highlight the actions and practices of those people (and in some cases, the things) involved in the production of the film. In this way, we will be able to uncover what it is that is done in these projects, how they are maintained over a given time period, and which of them are (un)productive. In other words, to quote one of the "godfathers" of ANT, the French anthropologist and social theorist Bruno Latour, ANT "lead(s) you backstage and introduce(s) you to the skills and knacks of practitioners, it also provides a rare glimpse of what it is for a thing to emerge out of existence by adding to any existing entity its time dimension."[5] As a result, the case study will provide the qualitative data in rich, descriptive detail, and throughout these discussions, ANT will be used as a language to highlight how a focus on *action* over *structure* allows us to explore project-based film production in an alternative, more "horizontalized" way than has previously been offered by other approaches to media industry analysis.

ANT Terminology

In order to proceed, it is necessary to first highlight four key terms used in ANT and ANT-inspired research, and they must be clearly defined as they relate to media production studies: actant, enrolment, black-boxing, and practice. While this is in no way an exhaustive list of the key ANT vernacular, these terms provide the fundamental concepts that are deployed in the *Three Dollars* case study that follows, and provide the basics of understanding of the "actor" and "network" (and the hyphen) in Actor-Network theory.

Actant(s)

Humans in ANT are commonly referred to as actors (and so from henceforth in this chapter, I shall use the term "actor" in the ANT meaning of the word, not to denote a dramatic actor on film or television). Actant is the collective term for either a human *or* nonhuman entity that can be involved in the network. For example, the power inherent in a camera or piece of the set can be just as forceful or power-inherent as the verbal or gestural directions from a director (which would themselves not be possible without inhuman actants, namely the camera, video-assist monitor, megaphone or even the director's chair). If we follow Latour, every action in the production of media that is carried out by a human actor (the director, DP, gaffer, editor) therefore "ends up in the action of a nonhuman" (camera movement, lighting schemes, digitized footage). For this reason, Bruno Latour argues that the responsibility for any given action in production lies with both human and nonhuman actants.[6] The ability that an actant has to "operationalize" this kind of network on the set is known as agency, which, said in another way, is the "force" used to create the network as the actants in it act.

Enrolment

This process of "enrolment" is fundamental to ANT as the term refers to how the web of actants, or network, in a given production is lengthened or extended. Enrolment in the network involves actants who use their agency in two particular ways—as *"intermediaries"* and *"mediators."* The difference between the two functions is slight, but important in terms of understanding the mechanics of the network. An intermediary transports meaning without deformation (e.g., a DVD), so identifying its inputs on the network equates to identifying its outputs. Mediators, on the other hand, cannot be identified this singularly, as they might count for one, for nothing, for several, or for infinite outputs. Indeed, for mediators in a network, "their input is never a good predictor of their output; their specificity has to be taken into account every time."[7] Therefore, mediators are, more often than not, the people in the network, but they could be an intricate piece of machinery which requires constant "tinkering," such as the camera or postproduction software. The terms "intermediary" and "mediator" are therefore terms signifying the relative effect of actants over the project. They can enrol other actants into their network, and this is how "power" is therefore achieved.[8]

Black-boxing

In research, ANT considers all aspects of the network that can affect the direction, characteristics, and behavior of the network. When a part of the network becomes self-contained and ineffectual then it can be considered "black-boxed." The classic example offered in many ANT texts is that of the human body—in that the inner goings-on of the human body are only considered when it breaks down. To "black-box" is to effectively convert the inner workings of a human into an intermediary, in that its overall agency has no effect on the network. "Black-boxing" facilitates the studying and description of networks as it allows the researcher or author to gloss over certain aspects of the network without having to detail the many nuances inside the black box. However, if that "black box" is to break down, then it will change the development of the network (and become akin to a mediator described above) and hence will require description.

Practice

ANT takes scholarship past the constraints of ontologically established spatial boundaries and views the world as a construction made up of connections established by the "doing" of actants. Practice, therefore, is essentially that "doing" that makes up the construction. Space is hence constructed through the practices of actor-networks. Within this scheme, the "spatial variation" is what Michael Serres and Latour[9] talk of when they offer the analogy of the handkerchief; when spread out, you can see certain fixed distances, but when crumpled up these two distances are suddenly close, even superimposed. This "crumpling" forms a mesh of networks (much like the production of a feature film), and the production would incorporate many actants from differing locations, whose actions constitute the timing and spacing of the network, all folded in with the others to produce not simply one time and space, but a multitude of contemporaneous space-time topologies.[10] Practice is often used in conjunction with other different yet related terms such as performance, action, behavior, or doing.

* * * *

Armed with knowledge of the fundamental language of ANT, it can therefore be highlighted throughout the discussion of the production and distribution of *Three Dollars*. In this way, the practices of the actants will be explored through the qualitative data presented, and the project itself can "tell the story" of project-based production, rather than reverting to a "top-down" metanarrative articulation which, as we have seen, ANT offers an alternative to.

Three Dollars Case Study

Arena Films, which is based in the Surry Hills area of Sydney, Australia, produced the film *Three Dollars* in 2005. *Three Dollars*, originally a novel by Elliot Perlman published in 1998, tells the story of one man's downward spiral to homelessness. Juxtaposed with his material vagrancy, his fluctuating personal relationships give him a feeling of hope and satisfaction at the finale. As well as my own personal interviews with Robert Connolly and other key actors in the filmmaking process, my research involved accessing a plethora of published work on *Three Dollars*, including newspaper and magazine articles, websites, radio and television programs that could be used as data sources, as well as watching the film itself.

Three Dollars is directed by Robert Connolly, who is a Sydney-based feature film director and producer, co-founder of Arena films and Footprint films, a graduate from a Sydney film school and an Australian Film Institute (AFI) award winner. When writing the screenplay for the film, he sought the help of the novel's author Perlman, and together they wrote the screenplay, for which they won the AFI award in 2005. As Connolly explains, the screenplay differs in chronology from the novel, but still retains all the critical narrative and character elements:

> I think *Three Dollars* was a different, tougher nut to crack [than his previous film *The Bank*] in that respect, because the politics of Elliot's novel are much

clearer and we were very keen not to be didactic. So there was a common level of discussion amongst the entire creative ensemble I work with about how we were going to sneak this one under the radar.[11]

The story of *Three Dollars* revolves around a single character, Eddie, played by David Wenham, and was filmed in Melbourne, despite Arena films being based in Sydney. Perlman, who lives in Melbourne, explains how he became enrolled into the production network by visiting Sydney:

They flew me to Sydney for a while and we had a series of meetings over four days, this was the beginning of it. And I walked into the room with a document that I'd prepared. I'd essentially condensed 380-something pages of the novel into around 40 or 50 pages, so that every single thing that happened was there in point form, cross-referenced to the page in the novel … And Robert walked into the room with a series of cards, I think they were different coloured cards, and he divided the story into three acts, a different colour for each act. And although I had met him before, I didn't know him all that well and it was the first time we'd actually talked about the work and how we were going to structure the film.[12]

This process shows how the script is an intermediary, coming to existence through the association of Connolly, Perlman, and the novel. Also, it could be argued that Perlman has had to reopen the black box of the novel, to revisit the structure and content of the story. As the film differs in chronology to the book, there has been a reworking of the narrative in order to become a feature film. When there is a screen adaptation of a novel, there remain very few instances where the story in the novel is not changed in some way, but the degree to which this happens can be seen as the degree to which the original novel is the opening of a black box. In this case, it was Connolly and Perlman in conjunction that completely reworked the novel itself, adapting the narrative to suit the big screen.

Once the script had been finalized, there then began a process of pitching the script to various institutions to acquire financing. Connolly explains:

So in the development stage, networks would involve dealing with agents, negotiating, our lawyers, funding bodies to raise finance, with a video distribution—we work with the company in Melbourne called Madhouse— although having said that we doubled our money with a special program at the Australian Film Council (AFC), so we deal with the AFC and the Film and TV office (FTO). Because we were shooting in Melbourne and Victoria, we contacted Film Victoria as well. During that development stage, acquiring the rights for the project … often may involve international communication, someone like David [Wenham] had an American agent, and when we are in the financing stage we have our relationships directly with financiers, the Film Finance Corporation (FFC), state agencies, video distribution, Dendy Cinemas to secure a theatrical release, and Dendy were involved in the release of the film internationally, kind of broadening out.[13]

The enrolment of various institutions in both Sydney and Melbourne can be viewed as a process of lengthening the actor-network, enrolling actants from other cities, thereby associating the cities together through the project—in this case the development of finances for the film. When a Sydney-based filmmaker is looking to make a film, the financing provides a common stumbling block, with many firms struggling to obtain sufficient funds to make the film that they have in mind. So the differing amounts of institutions and distribution firms that were contacted (enrolled) by Robert Connolly show that he had applied for a multitude of financing options. He contacted the AFC, the FFC, video distributors, and Dendy Cinemas and each contributed capital toward the production of the film. Once the money had been raised, the process of recruiting the filmmakers began. Connolly follows, "Then in production, we set up a whole new set of complex relationships, casting agents, you really end up broadening your production and postproduction networks."[14]

The enrolling of key crew members and actors in this type of production (actor-network) is more reliant on the relationships that Connolly had than in a production with a larger budget, as he had almost complete creative control over the final film. For instance, he used David Wenham for the main role, an actor he has worked with on all three of his previous films—*The Bank* in 2001, *The Boys* in 1998, and *Roses are Red* in 1995—as they have a strong working relationship. The cast and crew numbers are small and there are fewer departments than on Hollywood films, which is in part due to the intimacy required by the director, but also due to the lack of finance with which to employ a larger crew. For many films made by Sydney-based filmmakers (and indeed in other cities around the world where the budgets for their films are relatively small), there is an ethos, a general filmmaking philosophy of subsistence filmmaking. The small crew means that the production of the film is more intimate, with a greater degree of creative control at the hands of the director than there would be on a production with more executive producers. However, this increased creative control is malleable, as proved to Connolly by the 10-year-old actor playing Eddie's daughter Abby in the film.

I remember on set there's a scene where she [Abby] has come back from hospital and she says, "I was on a bed with wheels on it in the hospital," and her grandmother says, "That must have been fun," and Johanna says, "No, everyone had them." And on set I said to Johanna [who plays Abby], "Look maybe in this next take could you show a bit more attitude towards your grandmother, you know, that you're a bit frustrated she'd ask you such a dumb question." And Johanna thought about it and she turned to me and said, "I don't think my character would be rude to her grandmother." And I felt this crew of 40 people looking at me going, "The kid's right, how's the director going to handle this?" It was quite daunting.[15]

It could be said in ANT terms, then, that Johanna is a mediator, changing the outcome of the product through her practice. This effect is opposed to (for example) the light used to illuminate her during a shot, since the light as an intermediary rarely changes its outputs beyond off and on (unless of course it malfunctions, in which case the light becomes an actor-network of electrical parts—the black box of the light is opened up).

Once the shooting period was completed on *Three Dollars*, the film and recordings from the production sets and locations were transferred and forwarded to the image and sound editors so that the next phase, editing or postproduction could begin. On this project, postproduction was conducted not in Sydney but in Melbourne because, as Connolly explains, "It's not done on a cost basis, it is done on a relationship basis. Nearly everyone that I have mentioned, it is an ongoing relationship."[16] Again, the nature of the connections is portrayed as a relationship, not simply a question of which firm will be the cheapest, and the work was conducted by a company that Connolly trusted and knew could do the job that was up to the standards that he required. In ANT terms, his gambit short-circuits the network when Connolly contacts people he trusts, thereby cutting out the practice of finding the cheapest, best, most reliable postproduction provider. This process of trust is crucial when casting; indeed, one of the actors in the film, Sarah Wynter, working on an Australian film for the first time suggested "they work in a way that's very collaborative, but not to the point where I felt like an outsider. I was very welcomed."[17]

Three Dollars initially received limited distribution throughout Australia, and was released in an arthouse cinema chain, Dendy Cinemas (as one of the original financers of the film, Dendy secured cinematic distribution rights to the film). The other areas of distribution (regional and international markets, as well as the various TV and electronic media outlets) are owned by the original firm. Arena films produced the film, and Footprint films, which has ancillary markets for video and pay-TV, provided the Australian distribution rights. Many films produced by domestic filmmakers open in arthouse cinemas such as the Dendy cinema chain, which has locations in Sydney (Newtown and Circular Quay areas), Melbourne, Brisbane, and Byron Bay (all of which are nonhuman actants, essential to the success of the film). There are very few national cinema chains (the largest being Village Roadshow, Hoyts, and Greater Union) that will screen Australian-made films because the fees charged by the larger cinema chains are unaffordable to local filmmakers. With fees upward of AU$1 million, Australian independent films have to rely on ratings in the preliminary weeks in the arthouse cinemas. If strong enough, the larger cinema chains will then start to show these films. The arthouse cinema chains are thus very important to the distribution of the films made by Sydney filmmakers, and as such, their importance to the network of not only this production, but also most independently produced films in Australia, is crucial. This is why Connolly embarked on a vigorous marketing campaign which saw him visit Darwin, Cairns, and Byron Bay in three consecutive days in order to promote the film to local cinemas, to the local press, and to television stations.[18] If a film is successful enough to make the transition to national release (as was the case with *Three Dollars*) the arthouse cinemas lose out on their exclusive rights.[19] The Dendy cinema in Newtown (an inner-city suburb of Sydney) was the first cinema to show *Three Dollars* as it suited the particular market that the manager was looking for. However, once the film "went national," the audiences then began to watch the show at the larger cinema chains rather than the Dendy cinema in the Newtown inner-city suburb of Sydney.

The type of distribution a particular film receives can also play an important role in the financial and critical success of a film. The Cinema Release Calendar (CRC) is an important force in the distribution business as it largely determines when a particular film is going to be released. Studios that make a film for a particular audience, for example a Pixar animated film aimed predominantly at families, may decide to hold off release to the next school holiday as a distribution strategy. Hollywood majors, with their integrated production and distribution facilities, can "date dump," meaning that they can release a number of their own films on a particular date in order to reduce competition.[20] The CRC can be used as another example of the importance of nonhuman actors in the networks of film distribution, so incorporating and accounting for the CRC in the ethnography again highlights the role that nonhuman actants (in this case, an industry-wide scheduling protocol) can perform in the spacing and timing of the film industry's distribution and exhibition practices.

Once the film had been released and run its course of show times in the various cinema chains that Connolly managed to secure, it was released as a DVD, its rights sold to television networks to air it. In general, once this practice is underway, it could be argued that the film itself is an intermediary. While it may be experienced as a different product depending on where it is viewed (an arthouse cinema, multiplex, or on a DVD player at home), the actual product itself (i.e., the frame-by-frame procession of images) rarely changes form as it is passed around the network (unless there are director's cuts or different versions of the same film). While the medium is altered by the technological differences involved in the transfer of content, unless the film is subtitled or dubbed, then the DVD version is essentially the same film that might air on television. Then, the translation would occur through the enrolment of the film into other "areas," such as the sound system or quality of television used to view it, the purpose for which it is being viewed, and the social, cultural and personal makeup of the audience.

Hence, the final film product functions as an actant-network. The film is also a black box of associations that has been "opened-up" through this case study, something that an ANT approach to a case study has allowed. There are obviously many other interrelated actors and institutions that could have been articulated in this project-based case study. The network would extend, for example, to the locales used for shooting, the extras, the lawyers, the agents, the projectionists who work at the cinemas. The list could be literally endless. Opening up the black box of *Three Dollars* in this way shows how, as researchers, we can gain a better insight into those practices that are successful, and those that are not so successful. Describing the action of the humans and nonhumans in the network allows for this, as it provides the reader with a better and more nuanced understanding of the processes involved that develop and maintain the film production networks.

That's a Wrap

This chapter has argued that production research using an ANT-inspired methodology can serve as a crucial tool for analyzing and understanding the more intricate, project-based and temporary aspects of the film industry. This is because ANT ties together and considers the differing moments, times, and spaces of a specific production in a single study, *as a networked whole*. Succeeding at this sort of "project ecology" in the context of production studies, Latour asks us to "tell a story" through empirical description and ethnographic research.[21] This project-based research methodology allows researchers to examine the film industry through various techniques, including photographic ethnographies, filmic ethnographies, time-space budget diaries and so on. Such techniques are relevant because they deliberately highlight the "messiness" and complexities of the actor-networks of film production.[22] Using ethnographies as a methodological technique resonates with ANT, as they allow for more *relational* data to be gathered,[23] more descriptive accounts of practice, and therefore more information regarding how spaces (and timings) of networks are created.

ANT, while being criticized in some quarters for downplaying particular human traits (such as emotion and feelings[24]) can provide a crucial methodological language for not just researching the film industry, but for studying project-based industrial organization as a whole. Moreover, the creative industries in general, unlike other heavy industries, are characterized by project-based labor[25] and as ANT provides a more functional "way in" to researching this mode of operation, the coupling of the two (i.e., ANT research into the cultural industries) promises to become increasingly productive in social science and humanities inquiry.

Notes

1 The major studios, for example, include: Universal, Twentieth Century Fox and others. See Allen Scott, *On Hollywood* (New York: Princeton University Press, 2005) for a comprehensive overview of the so-called "majors."

2 See Jeremy Rifkin, "When Markets Give Way to Networks," in *The Creative Industries*, ed. John Hartley (Oxford: Blackwell, 2005), 363. The quote contains my emphasis.

3 This project-based mode of production is described and examined as "migratory production churn" and a "nomadic labor system" in John Caldwell, *Production Culture* (Durham, NC: Duke University Press, 2008), 113–119.

4 See, for example, Helen Blair, "'You're Only as Good as Your Last Job': The Labour Process and Labour Market in the British Film Industry," *Work, Employment and Society* 15, no. 1 (2001): 149–169; Malcom Long, "Solving Box Office Blues: Australia Needs More Working Dogs," *Australian Financial Review*, February 24, 2005, 44; Galina Gornostaeva, "The Film and Television Industry in London's Suburbs: Lifestyle of the Rich or Losers' Retreat?" *The Creative Industries Journal* 1, no. 1 (2008): 47–71.

5 See Bruno Latour, *Reassembling the Social: An Introduction to Actor-Network-Theory* (Oxford: Oxford University Press, 2005), 88.

6 There has been an advancement of the nonhuman debate by Heike Jöns who suggests that there is a "complex trinity of actants" that forms a continuum ranging from immaterial entities, through dynamic hybrids to material entities; see Heike Jöns, "Dynamic Hybrids and the Geographies of Technoscience: Discussing Conceptual Resources beyond the Human/Non-human Binary," *Social & Cultural Geography* 7, no. 4, (2006): 573.

7 Latour, *Reassembling the Social*, 39.

8 John Allen, "The Whereabouts of Power: Politics, Government and Space," *Geografiska Annaler B* 86, no. 1 (2004): 19–32. Forms of enrolment include "problematization," which is the identification of a network goal; and "interessement" which is "the group of actions by which an entity … attempts to impose and stabilize the identity of other actors it defines through problematization." Quoted from Michelle Callon, "Some Elements of a Sociology of Translation: Domestication of the Scallops and the Fishermen of St. Brieuc Bay," in *Power, Action and Belief: A New Sociology of Knowledge*, ed. John Law (London: Routledge and Kegan Paul, 1986), 208.

9 Michael Serres and Bruno Latour, *Conversations on Science, Culture and Time* (Ann Arbor: University of Michigan Press, 1995).

10 Jonathan Murdoch, "The Spaces of Actor-Network Theory," *Geoforum* 29, no. 4 (1998): 357–374.

11 Michelle Dawson, "Interview with Robert Connolly," *Byron Shire News*, June 21, 2005, 5.

12 *ABC: At the Movies*, July 1, 2005.

13 Robert Connolly, interview with the author, May 11, 2005.

14 Ibid.

15 Ibid.

16 Ibid.

17 Quote from Sarah Wynter in Sacha Molitorisz, "It's All About the Buck," *Sydney Morning Herald*, April 22, 2005.

18 Dawson, "Interview with Robert Connolly," 5.
19 Ibid.
20 Mark Sarfarty, interview with the author, June 2, 2005.
21 On "project ecologies," see Gernot Grabher, "Learning in Projects, Remembering in Networks? Communality, Sociality and Connectivity in Project Ecologies," *European Urban and Regional Studies* 11, no. 2 (2004): 103–123. For discussion of necessity of "story-telling", see Latour, *Reassembling the Social*.
22 John Law, *After Method: Mess in Social Science Research* (London: Routledge, 2004).
23 Harold Bathelt and Jonathan Glucker, "Toward a Relational Economic Geography," *Journal of Economic Geography* 3 (2003): 117–144.
24 Eric Laurier and Chris Philo, "The Region in the Boot: Mobilising Lone Subjects and Multiple Objects," *Environment and Planning D: Society and Space* 21, no. 1 (2003): 85–106.
25 Kate Oakley, "Not So Cool Britannia," *International Journal of Cultural Studies* 7, no. 1 (2004): 67–77.

Chapter 16

"Both Sides of the Fence"

Blurred Distinctions in Scholarship and Production (a Portfolio of Interviews)

John T. Caldwell

This final chapter examines scholar-practitioners who "work both sides of the fence" in production studies. To address practical questions of methodology readers may have from the wide-ranging studies in this book, I hope to consider three individual scholars who pursue industry fieldwork at the same time they maintain production identities. This includes questions about: gaining access to closely guarded communities; the impact of professional identities on types of disclosure in the field; and the "trade-offs" scholar-practitioners make to pursue work on production. I am particularly interested in the extent to which fieldwork interactions enable or discourage researchers from maintaining independent critical arguments about their human subjects, and how "insider" technical knowledge might provide additional skills capable of cutting through the industry's carefully maintained layers of promotional flak. All ethnography involves scholar-informant "exchanges," but researching corporate, proprietary production worlds requires considerable negotiation if the scholar hopes to move beyond the tired forms of deference the trade and popular press typically grant industry. The intimate working knowledge of production processes of the three individuals featured in the following portfolio of interviews pushes them beyond the sometime rudimentary questions that scholars with little direct knowledge of film/television raise. Yet "straddling the fence" also forces them to regularly negotiate both their access *and* their critical distance from those granting access.

The relationship between the academic ethnographer and the human subject has a long and complicated history.[1] The production studies traditions mapped in this volume traverse the same slippery trajectory, in terms of who is "inside" and who is "outside" of the industry being studied. Powdermaker set the methodological bar high by arguing that she did not have a screenplay in her back pocket (that is, unlike others, had no vested interest in "making it" in the industry). By contrast, her predecessor Leo Rosten worked as a screenwriter before he began his sociological study of Hollywood. Yet this "insider" status was conveniently elided from his major 1941 book on Hollywood, which he sold to readers based on the quantitative scale of his largely interview- and survey-based study.[2] Much later, Justin Wyatt leveraged his experience as a studio marketing executive into a key scholarly book on "high-concept" marketing. Horace Newcomb wrote screenplays before *The Producer's Medium*. Barry Dornfeld worked as a documentary producer before his important ethnographic study in public television. Vicki Mayer and Laura Grindstaff both crossed over as assistants in the community-video and talk-show research that they completed. Sherry Ortner's invitation to behind-the-scenes observation led to work as an "extra" on the set. Whereas the above-the-line affinities of Rosten, Newcomb, and Wyatt positioned them to access executive levels in Hollywood, the cultural margins and industrial "borderlands" that I have worked on as a scholar/independent-producer have meant that my access and affinities have primarily been with below-the-line craft workers. This is probably because I have found it much easier, and honest, to "talk shop" to camera operators and editors than to decipher the often impenetrable and scripted flak with which producers and executives now mechanically "spin" scholars and journalists.

My book *Production Culture* argued, in part, that a range of distinctions between production and audiences have largely collapsed; and second, that the cultural borders between the industry and the "outside" have become more permeable, extensive, and traversable (for aspirants and scholars alike). These recent changes have created practical opportunities to access and research production. Industry now continuously researches and "theorizes" about itself, and hosts "summits," think-tanks, and conferences to debate cultural, technological, and aesthetic trends. It also involves journalists, and scholars through faculty "internships," partnerships, technology beta-testing, and consultancies. "Nonprofit" groups and foundations support film/television industry initiatives through the guises of "education" and "cultural legacy." Rather than "public intellectuals" we might consider participants in these contact zones "industrial intellectuals"—with all of the problematic implications that such a shift in rhetoric entails. These wide-ranging industry/academic interactions today mean that some scholars now function more as "observational participants" (who fulfill industrial roles) than as "participant-observers" (the traditional academic model).

Clearly, distinctions between "industry" and "academia" are no longer as certain as they once were, and this impacts how scholars gain access to industry. One of the defining contradictions of contemporary media that I have detailed elsewhere is the public promotion of greater industrial access alongside vigorous new legal actions to police and shut access down.[3] On the one hand, outsourcing and decentralizing production and the growth of channels and technical platforms have increased the demand for employees. On the other hand, university human subjects rules, corporate policies, and employer nondisclosure agreements together make production harder to study and less open to fieldwork. Despite this double bind, five factors provide increased opportunities for fieldwork as institutional barriers have gotten more complicated. First, many of our students and alumni now work in the cultural industries, providing opportunities for access. Second, industry values our ethnically and culturally diverse graduates to exploit increasingly diverse, global, multichannel niche markets.[4] Third, industry considers various universities and film schools as direct training grounds for future culture and media trendsetters; and once these are professionals, they frequently return to our campuses as guest speakers and even faculty members. Fourth, historically, industry controlled production knowledge by distributing it across organized crews and segregated departments.[5] Today, greater premium is placed on the technical and conceptual "multitasking" skills that younger workers bring organizations. When craft unions no longer control and "ration out" technical/aesthetic knowledge, the "production of knowledge" *about production* becomes more unruly and democratic—displacing the controlled "re-production of knowledge" of earlier, longstanding studio–labor collusions. Finally, as public education funding dries up, many universities and corporations seek "public–private partnerships." Justified as a way to financially prop up the failing public sector, such things frequently convert universities into inexpensive "corporate farm-systems" that provide cheap labor, unpaid interns, brainstorming, and R&D for the creative industries. This churn across institutional borders offers clear opportunities for scholars willing to jump into the interchanges and "contact zones" that result.[6]

The following interviews consider how professional identities impact production culture research, and vice versa. Each offers practical insights on method gained from doctoral dissertation research and fence-straddling fieldwork on the "craft association," gendered "assistanting," and the "writers' room" respectively.

Paul Malcolm, "The Craft Association"

Paul Malcolm worked as a journalist and associate film editor for *LA Weekly* for ten years, where he contributed regular reviews, interviews, and "on-the-set" pieces. He has since worked as the Membership and Special Projects Coordinator for the Visual Effects Society (VES) in Los Angeles. This enabled him to pursue the fieldwork featured in this interview, and serves as the basis for his UCLA dissertation *World of Effects: The Craft and Culture of Visual Effects Production in the Digital Age*. He currently programs films for the Los Angeles Film Festival and the UCLA Film and Television Archive.

Can you summarize your research fieldwork?

I have been observing visual effects production both "on the set" and "on the desktop" at various digital visual effects companies. At the VES, I was responsible for planning programming, including its Festival of Visual Effects [VFX], awards show, and seminars and panel discussions to update members on rapidly changing

VFX techniques. I also attended board meetings and "Think Tank Dinners," where industry leaders candidly discussed issues they faced as either independent contractors or company heads and how the VES could better serve as an advocate … within the film industry as a whole. These were key sites for both industry networking and contestation between the different VES factions that struggled to reach consensus about contentious industry issues, including runaway production, unionization and standardization of visual effects credits. They provided a wealth of information for follow-up interviews with key industry players as well as context for "reading between the lines" of trade journal reporting meant for public, industry consumption.

What distinctive insights do you think your background has given your fieldwork?

In a story about "working-class Hollywood" for *LA Weekly*, I found myself on the set of *NYPD Blue* in 1998 watching the show's long-time gaffer, Michael Katz, at work. Katz was trying to set the lighting for a close-up of an African American actor appearing on that week's show. As Katz checked his light meter in front of the actor's face, the actor joked to Katz, "Make sure I get my stop" meaning his "f-stop." Katz instantly realized what the actor was referring to and suddenly the two of them were talking about race, cinematography and Hollywood's long history of mis-lighting for darker skin. Katz assured the actor that he would get his stop, but it "would never make up for all the times when you were lit at 1.85." It was one of those revelatory moments when I realized that academic discussions of representation had a practical counterpart that occurred on the production set where the numbers on a light meter could reveal as much as the deftest theoretical turn. Even more importantly, it revealed that some, perhaps small, but still crucial decisions about representation were being negotiated well below the radar of some overarching ideological apparatus between a bit-player and below-the-line worker just talking on the set. I carried this knowledge with me into my academic career and quickly recognized other parallels between academic discussions and the production practices I had observed. I didn't feel that academia was "getting it wrong" but rather that accessing production cultures and practices could complement and deepen academic analysis of the production of meaning.

There were early, and sometimes hard, lessons I learned as a journalist earning the trust of my subjects—including a keen awareness that this trust was always conditional. I had several introductory phone calls with Katz and spent several hours interviewing him before he asked permission for me to come to the set. (He was nervous about how it would look to other members of the cast and crew for a journalist to be paying so much attention to him over other contributors higher up the pay scale.) I felt that we had developed a certain rapport—I had done my research and was as unobtrusive as possible while he worked—but whatever trust I had earned was instantly threatened the second I asked him about his exchange with the African American actor. Katz immediately resisted my attempt to read anything into the exchange beyond the fact that he was just doing his job, trying to get the best shot. Most professional actors, black or white, he explained, knew something about lighting and the levels that best suited their particular skin tones. That was all it was. The idea that this moment might be situated within a larger institutional history of Hollywood racism and representation was not an idea he was willing to entertain. In seeking "verification" for my reading of the exchange from my subject, I ended up raising suspicions about my motives.

Have you discovered any practices on the "inside" that scholars have been "wrong" about?

One of the first questions I was asked by the VES staff and members was whether I knew the difference between special and visual effects.[7] Whether or not I could articulate this distinction was an important test of my seriousness for many of the visual effects artists I've met. To give the wrong answer or express confusion would have been to label myself an unserious fan or, even worse, an Ivory Tower Intellectual. They had a point. Too often I've seen academic scholars elide the difference between special and visual effects when discussing the aesthetics and meaning of Hollywood effects films, in general. For working visual effects artists, it would be akin to ignoring the difference between a location shoot and a stage set.

Does wearing "two hats" ever create problems in your worker interactions?

While my "doubled-identity" was not announced at larger private and public VES events, such as Board of Directors meetings, most members I had regular contact with were aware of it. They often jokingly referred to me as "Doctor Malcolm" in reference to my academic pursuits. In terms of my interaction with practitioners on the set or during interviews, once I had gained the initial trust of my subjects, they almost invariably proved extremely open, helpful and encouraging.

What situations offer the best opportunities for useful professional disclosures?

Formal interviews have been invaluable but they have their limitations. Especially when one is dealing with more senior practitioners, producers, supervisors, etc., who may have more experience dealing with the media and the press. Once the tape recorder is on, or the notebook out, they can tend to fall back into safe, canned responses that require follow-up questions and a little coaxing to break down. The most fruitful, revealing situations are small group settings, whether on the set or in VES planning meetings. In these settings, practitioners are more likely to engage in a natural parlance and camaraderie, even if they never fully lose awareness that an outside observer is present. Practitioner interactions here are often rife with jokes, shared references and anecdotes that can prove incredibly rich for later interpretation.

Has fieldwork given you insights that contradict producer explanations?

VFX artists and companies still tend to publicly embrace their craft's traditional associations with "magic" and "magicians." Recently, this rhetoric of the VFX artist-as-magician—capable of making anything possible in their struggle to get work from studios—has started to crack. Behind the scenes, VFX supervisors complain that boasts of unlimited capabilities have actually encouraged a willful and dangerous ignorance on the part of producers and directors. Taking visual effects artists "at their word," studio producers don't want to know how the "trick" was done … because ignorance allows them to keep demanding bigger and better rabbits to be pulled out of the digital hat, on less and less time and money. In many ways, visual effects practitioners find themselves in a position of having to undo an image of their creation. One VFX supervisor explained: "In our earnest desire to get a seat at the 'Adult table' of the business, we have been engaged in a thirty-year publicity campaign to make everyone aware of what we do and how we do it," he said.[8] "In this process we have focused on the success stories and hidden away the terrible truth of how we got to those successes … Most directors and producers … are not at all aware of how time and hands-on intensive the process really is. What we need to do is … begin telling the painful truth."[9] Traditional craft explanations are colliding with severe new economic realities. This requires that crafts-workers find new ways of identifying and explaining themselves, to survive in negotiations with studio producers.

Have institutional factors constrained what you are able to study?

Where I have requested access to VFX facilities to observe work being done, it has always been granted. While confidentiality agreements have come up in discussions, I have not yet been asked to sign any kind of official document, although I expect I might be in the future. The biggest limitations I expect to face as I turn to expand my "on-the-set" fieldwork is the fact that so many VFX-heavy Hollywood productions are shot outside of Los Angeles, often in Canada. In this case, the economic realities of the industry present something of a problem for my personal economic reality.

Any troubling ethical issues about getting your research published?

I refer to the frank and candid information acquired at high-level industry meetings as "deep background" research. While it will inform further research and writing, I will not reference quotes or sources directly unless I receive subsequent permission from that source. When I can confirm information from another source who will go on the record, I will reference that source only. Ultimately, I plan to present all relevant sections of my dissertation to the VES Executive Director. I feel I have an obligation to seek his comments and allow him an opportunity to point out potentially sensitive information.

Any advice for young scholars about access?

I think I got lucky with the VES. Starting as an unpaid intern then working my way to a paid, full-time position, I earned my subjects' trust faster than if I'd approached them cold. I had built up a track record of trust and reliability among the Society as someone who was working on behalf of visual effects artists, an impression that they seemed to carry over rather naturally to my research. In a sense, my subjects never felt that I wanted more from them than what I was asking. They recognized that I wasn't looking for a job in the industry and I think that has helped me to gain and keep their trust.

Erin Hill, "Hollywood Assistanting"

Erin Hill worked as an assistant to writers, directors, and producers at various film and television companies including Jerry Bruckheimer Films (*Pirates of the Caribbean*, *Pearl*), Hofflund/Polone (*Curb Your Enthusiasm*, *Panic Room*, and *Gilmore Girls*), and Shukovsky English Entertainment (*Murphy Brown*, *The Women*), and as a freelance story analyst for studios and production companies. She is currently completing a doctoral dissertation in Cinema and Media Studies at UCLA, and continues her work as a story analyst, film industry blogger, and participant in the channel 101 underground filmmaking community.

Can you summarize your research?

My research concerns various historically low-status "women's jobs" in film and television production that, despite the industry's claims that the playing field has been leveled for women, are still feminized and/or female-dominated. At present I'm attempting to explain this gendered present not only through interviews and research in the present, but also through an archival examination of Hollywood's gendered past, from the 1910s—when the studios and their systems of production were forming—to the studio system that had more fully developed by the 1930s and '40s.[10]

What insight has your background given to your fieldwork?

I worked at a number of assistant desks over the years, which not only exposed me to a wide variety of film/television work (casting, research, development, writers' assistant duties, event planning, production management, office management, and film budgeting, to name a few) but also a number of major Hollywood players and their wildly divergent office environments. I've been curious about gender's function in the spaces where media are made ever since the first day ... As a kind of low-status jack-of-all-trades, first out of necessity and later by choice for my research, this curiosity has remained a constant and provided a through-line for my academic inquiries.

Have you discovered any practices on the "inside" that scholars have been unaware of?

Absolutely. Much of my research focuses on areas where little academic study has been made (relatively low-status film/TV jobs that are gendered female), so the biggest challenge I face is not correcting anything that any scholar has gotten "wrong," but making practices and trends known to academia in a way that isn't simple description and that sheds light on the larger systems that produced them.

But more generally, since I was inside before I was outside, I think much of my work, especially early on, was a knee-jerk reaction to the way that academia has often approached media production in the past, sometimes simply looking at the finished film or television text to draw conclusions about how it was made. This approach is understandable in some cases, because the lack of access to information about the production process experienced by many academics can be frustrating, and even when access is granted, the complexity of that production process can be daunting. So it may seem more manageable to create and impose one's own interpretation on that process in the same way one would interpret the meaning of a text. But deciding why [director] Howard Hawks made a certain shot a certain length or cut from one angle to another without taking into account any of the myriad production variables that would have contributed to that decision is, in my mind, not terribly useful either to an understanding of his films or of how they were made.

Off-screen, Hollywood filmmaking also runs on myths, which help to organize and distribute a hundred years of accumulated industrial wisdom. So the best way to understand individual choices is to understand the system of myths and shared industrial wisdom which is in place for any given production and which comes from all the productions before it. I have to do this for my work, since there are not only no books or major articles written on below-the-line women workers in film history, but also few onscreen "texts" to analyze in which I could point to any one decision as theirs. But even in the case of major films by major directors, I think that looking at this larger system of industrial myths governing film production can only enhance our understanding of media texts, whether we're looking at them as art or as cultural objects.

Does wearing "two hats" ever create problems in your worker interactions?

The academic hat is always problematic. Just as academia doesn't always understand the industry, the industry doesn't always understand academia. For example, the people I interview are often cautious initially, because they think that my research is going to be published a week later in a major outlet, when really it may be months or years to publication for mostly scholarly consumption. Also they don't trust me if they think I'm an academic only and therefore an outsider, since outsiders don't know the rules of the industry. I tend to warm up with chit-chat about experiences, companies or colleagues we have in common to put them at ease and show them that I "get it." I suppose my last statement also hints at the other potential problem of wearing two hats: over-rapport, or identifying with my subjects to the point that it could affect the work. So I try to negotiate the space between academia and industry so that I'm never fully in one camp or the other.

What situations offer good opportunities for useful professional disclosures?

Coffee shops and bars are not great, since they're loud and distracting, and since everyone in this town thinks that everyone else is listening to what they're saying. People's homes work better. I interviewed one subject who I could tell wanted to open up to me about something, but who didn't feel safe until she'd moved the interview to her bedroom and closed the door so that her roommate couldn't hear what she was saying. She'd had an experience that had led to her career being badly damaged because of a superior's behavior, and wouldn't have spoken about it in a place that felt any less safe.

Has fieldwork given you insights that contradict producers' explanations?

I recently conducted forty or so interviews with assistants. When I asked the ones who were newest to the industry and earning the least money if they thought they should make more money, they almost all answered that that question wasn't really answerable since the system "is the way it is," that there was no way for them to make more money, and that they were paying their dues and therefore supposed to be enduring low pay in order to gain access to higher levels. Yes, there are really small companies with tight budgets that can't afford to pay more than $400/week, but at most companies this isn't true at all, which is obvious when incoming executives at the same companies negotiate for huge salaries. The industrial mythology of dues-paying is in place to keep workers at low salaries from demanding more.

Any ethical issues before publishing your research?

When I speak to a subject I take great pains to make sure that (a) I'm accurately contextualizing what they've said and understanding what they meant, and (b) they're protected if they're not in positions of power. For these reasons I usually send them drafts of what I'm writing so that they can look over their statements and the text surrounding them. I've never changed an argument or conclusion I've made based on a participant's reaction to a draft, but I have revised when I've misinterpreted a quote or included a detail that might compromise the anonymity of a low-status worker. A colleague once told me he conducted interviews with co-workers in the office environment with his industry "hat" still on in an attempt to get them to forget they were speaking on the record and then didn't allow them to see their quotes before they were published. I found that approach very troubling.

Any advice for young scholars about access?

The best advice I can give to anyone studying production cultures is to get an entry-level job related to the part of production in which they're interested and work at it for six months. An assistant job, whether in development or on a set, can provide the foundation for understanding what, how, and why things happen, in a specific labor sector and in the industry in general. My work as an assistant also taught me everything I needed to know about gaining access to other industry workers, from how to make first contact to how to address workers of varying status levels once access was granted … Spending time in LA, NY, and a few other production centers and working and socializing in them is the best way to truly understand them. If that's not possible, there are a lot of industry-related message boards and websites that might be studied, with extra attention paid to any arguments or flame wars that occur, since online dust-ups between film and television workers are becoming more and more frequent, and a lot gets explained there out of sheer desire to win a public argument. Trade papers and journals, industry job lists, books by film and television workers ..., as well as how-to manuals, DVD extras and fictionalized accounts of the industry are all good places to look as well, and should definitely be thoroughly examined before any interviews with film workers are conducted, since a lack of preparation is an easy way to either take up precious interview time with elementary questions or turn off an interview subject completely. As is the case when getting a new job, the best preparation is apprenticing, but if that's not possible, there are other sources of information to be mined.

Felicia D. Henderson, "The Writers' Room"

Felicia D. Henderson is a primetime drama and comedy writer, and now a media studies scholar pursuing fieldwork and dissertation research at UCLA on the television "writers' room."[11] Her credits include: *The Fresh Prince of Bel Air* (writer), *Moesha* (writer/co-producer), and *Sister, Sister* (writer/co-executive producer), *Gossip Girl* (writer/co-executive producer), *Everybody Hates Chris* (consulting producer), and J. J. Abrams' series *Fringe* (writer/co-executive producer). She was the creator/executive producer of the longrunning, critically acclaimed, award-winning Showtime series *Soul Food*.

Can you summarize your research?

My research explores the television writer's workspace—usually a conference room—called "the writers' room" or simply "the room." In general, my goal is to define the "culture of performance" that inhabits the writers' room, which I argue is crucial to television comedy and drama making. With this project I hope to better define the collective and "situational authorship" birthed in a staged environment long before studios, networks, directors, crews, and actors ever become part of the process. This includes investigating how gender, race, and class figure into the rules, roles, and rituals that inhabit the writers' room.[12]

Your background before starting scholarly research?

In the early 1990s I was awarded an NBC Fellowship because the television networks were actively recruiting MBA students interested in TV management. After graduating, I landed my first job as a "creative associate," a management trainee of sorts, which gave me my first exposure to primetime series marketing, on-air promotions, publicity, and how half-hour comedies were developed (created). That initial exposure to scripts led to my interest in writing. I would read the scripts that writers turned in and comment to my boss, the vice-president of comedy programs, that what I was reading didn't seem particularly difficult to write. He finally challenged me to stop critiquing the scripts and write one of my own. I did. That script led to my acceptance into the Warner Bros. Writers' Workshop—a very competitive writer's boot camp.

Did this background impact your choice of research topics?

I executive produced *Soul Food* while completing my screenwriting MFA. I remember sitting in a critical studies course and hearing a student (who didn't know I was associated with the show) criticize *Soul Food* for missing opportunities to break with traditional depictions of women, given that the show starred three black women. The student went on to say that she doubted that there were any women of power behind the scenes of the show and then further criticized the show from a feminist theory point of view. It was a moment I will never forget. How was it possible that my goal—a goal I was confident I was attaining—of depicting race and gender from an atypical, enlightened, point of view, was not being communicated to this female student? (After beginning the doctoral program and reading much Stuart Hall, I understood encoding and decoding in a very personal way.)[13] This experience solidified my interest in critically examining my professional endeavors. From that moment, I knew that scholarship would benefit if those that worked behind the scenes became involved in critically interrogating production culture. Equally important, however—given media's power to influence society—is the need for the creative industry to consider itself critically. Hopefully, scholars and professionals can fill the unfortunate gap in their two-way relationship with constructive dialogue.

Have you recognized practices on the "inside" that scholars have been unaware of or "wrong" about?

As I became a scholar, I was immediately frustrated by some of the scholarly work about how television is produced; especially the pervasiveness of a "film studies" approach to television. One film-centric example is the privileged position that scholars typically assign to directors and producers. This assignment of authority absolutely holds for film. However, it is increasingly clear (not just from observing the production process but also from widely available items such as DVD "behind the scenes" bonus materials) that writers now function as the creative heads in television. I am intrigued by why researchers pay little attention to writers, but much to producers. Writers usually take on the title of "producer" as they are promoted through the ranks of the writing staff, yet their primary responsibilities still revolve around their roles in writing and managing the story. To talk of creative agency or power in television today means to pay particular attention to the writer-producer hybrid. Yet some scholars ignore the writer's side of the "hyphenate," and continue to conflate power with a non-writing producer function.

Additionally, much attention is being paid to "convergence culture" as television goes digital. Yet scholars have focused less on how digital convergence has changed the practical ways that television is produced, and by whom. A variety of new trends—the shuffling of executives to better accommodate a series' Internet presence; the addition of "New Media Consultants" as part of writing staffs; the development of comic books based on the series before the series premieres on television; Nielsen Media Research's factoring of viewership statistics for episode downloads for MP3 and PC viewing; and the growth of product placement relationships that include agreements with corporations to integrate their products into storylines—are all areas of scholarship yet to be mined.

Does wearing "two hats" ever create problems in your professional interactions?

I decided to write a critical essay about *Grey's Anatomy*, which is celebrated as the standard for progressive multiculturalism and color-blindness. Oddly, the series manages to be both culturally and racially inclusive while somehow ignoring both culture and race. Network diversity executives, civil rights organizations, and my industry friends consider it primetime television at its best. I argued that this drama exemplified the use of race as a floating signifier, even as the updated, stereotypical trope *superspade* now wears scrubs. My black professional colleagues reacted to my proposed scholarly critique with shock and dismay. How could I be critical of series creator, Shonda Rhimes? They reminded me that as one of so few black executive producers/showrunners, and as the number one show on television, this is a "win" for all of us. Despite my assurances that my views were not a personal attack on Rhimes, that I admire her and her accomplishments, and enjoy watching the show every week, the close-knit group of black executives and writers, of which I am one, were offended. As one friend said, "Oh I get it now. You want to suggest that the images of the black doctors on *Grey's Anatomy* are problematic so you can be legitimate with those scholarly types you hang out with now."[14]

What situations offer good opportunities for useful disclosures?

In terms of spaces/contexts that have proven to be the least helpful, I still find network presidents to have responses that are the most managed. Perhaps because they spend too much time dealing with the press in protective soundbites, it's nearly impossible to get them to drop the façade. Also, given their schedules, they are almost always only available on the telephone or with a trip to his/her office. There is very little hope of getting them to open up, when they're sitting in the corporate environment that reminds them of their responsibilities and their means of dealing with media and press.

Has fieldwork given you insights that contradict producer explanations?

One central feature of writers' room culture is how the room of writers is "cast" (or how writers are hired on writing staffs). My research demystifies writer-casting practices to illuminate how these rituals impact the authoring process. Much of what happens in the creation of weekly storylines has very little to do with the actual writing of scripts. The human interactions in writers' rooms are forms of collective authorship because the sociocultural dynamics there heavily influence the narrative that finds its way to the page, and eventually to the screen.

Casting writers' workspaces is a very complex undertaking, and so is studying it. Most writer/executive producers, when interviewed, say they hire writers based on their writing "talent"—not on the staff "role" they will perform. Such producers seldom detail the reasons, beyond subjectively determined exceptional writing skills, that writers are hired. Being privy to inside company information or writers' room activities, however, undercuts this standard producers' explanation. Writing staffs work together an average of ten to sixteen hours per day; many high-paid writers are under contract deals with studios and if their ideas don't make it to air, they are farmed off on writing staffs to "work off" their highly paid contracts; very junior writers (called staff writers) and trainees are very inexpensive on the budget and therefore two or three writers at this lower level may be hired to save money "at the top" of the writing staff; the studio or network might place another executive producer level writer as a partner for the executive producer of record because the latter is known for being a great writer, but poor manager. In other words, there are many nonaesthetic reasons a writer might be chosen for a writing staff that go far beyond the "most talented" rhetoric inherent in those "we've got the best writing staff in television" soundbites trotted out for the trade press.

Have institutional factors constrained your study?

A lot of the people I worked with in my early career have gone on to become executives who remember me and are willing to speak with me. Over the years, I have made many contacts through the writing staffs I worked on. Because they, for the most part, consider me one of them, they are willing to talk to me. Others are frequently willing to speak with me because they either are familiar with the current series I'm working on or they or someone they're close to are big fans of the show. Or, quite frankly, they think I can do something for them—get their significant other an audition or an agent, for instance. From an economic point of view, my study is impacted because I am holding a full-time job and can only do most of my interviews and independent observations when the show I'm working on is on spring/summer hiatus.

Notes

1 This ranges from early assumptions in the social sciences, derived from the physical sciences, about the need to maintain controlled distance and objectivity in survey research and social settings. It also includes the tradition of participant-observation that came to define anthropology, where relationships between analyst and indigenous subject became a fundamental matter of public concern. Poststructuralists like James Clifford and George Marcus subsequently turned the still-identifiable subject–object distinctions of participant-observation on their head. By shifting from ethnography-as-observation to ethnography-as-a-textual practice, their "reflexive" turn greatly complicated the relationships between ethnographer and human subject in fieldwork, making indigenous informants co-authors and authors of ethnographies, among other things.

2 Only later, as John Sullivan points out in this book, did Rosten admit that his earlier experience as a screenwriter gave him crucial forms of access.

3 John Caldwell, *Production Culture: Industrial Reflexivity and Critical Practice in Film and Television* (Durham, NC: Duke University Press, 2008), 339–343.

4 The need for more niche content means that recruited employees need to be more conversant in the history and implications of cultural identities and trends, competent in aesthetic analysis and self-monitoring, and thus capable of *marketing* their company's different products effectively.

5 The generational shifts, ageism, and lowered barriers for entry discussed above have also undercut the studios' longstanding ability to "bunker" these conventions about "how media are made" away from the public and aspirants.

6 For a more detailed examination of these industry-academic "contact zones," see John Caldwell, "Industrial Geography Lessons: Socio-Professional Rituals and the Borderlands of Production Culture," in *MediaSpace: Place, Scale, and Culture in a Media Age*, eds. Nick Couldry and Anna McCarthy (New York: Routledge, 2004).

7 Malcolm: "The difference is that special effects can be filmed through regular photographic means on set in front of the camera, pyrotechnics and make-up being classic examples, while visual effects require special photographic means to produce and are often produced, whether through optical printers or, now, digital compositing, in post-production. Models and miniatures straddle the line, being both practical (in front of the camera on a set) while requiring special photographic techniques to shoot and insert into the final image, but are considered visual effects in the industry."

8 This statement was made by Jeffrey A. Okun, VFX supervisor and Chairman of the Board of the VES.

9 Malcolm: "Where and how that discussion about the painful truth takes place, is one of the questions the industry now faces. In 2007, the VFX industry was shocked when one of its leading companies and practitioners, ILM and visual effects supervisor John Knoll,

went public in the pages of *Variety* with the near disastrous postproduction crunch on *Pirates of the Caribbean 3: At World's End*. Knoll's revelations were intended as a wake-up call to the industry that budgets and schedules were being so closely cropped, it was only a matter of time before a VFX-heavy tent pole release missed its opening day because of impossible producer demands. At the same time, the article underscored demands on the part of VES member companies, including ILM, that the "honorary" Society needed to act more like a trade organization as conduit for industry complaints, so that individual companies would not appear to be biting the hand that feeds them.

10 Hill: "This studio period and the classes of women workers it created are the focus of my dissertation. Their examination, it is hoped, will both add to an understanding of how women were pushed out from behind the camera during the studio era—a question which is the primary focus of much current research into feminist film history—and bring to light the importance to the Hollywood filmmaking process of the work of the millions of women who were working in Hollywood as readers, researchers, assistants, script supervisors, casting directors, etc., when those were the only jobs open to them."

11 Henderson: "In television, unlike film, those who are responsible for dialogue are simply called 'writers' not 'screenwriters'—including those who write comedy, drama, animation, soap operas, game shows, or reality television."

12 Henderson: "Given my production background, my research is deeply reflexive, and is both an 'auto-ethnography' and a study of the writing staff as culture."

13 Stuart Hall, "Encoding/Decoding," in *Culture, Media, Language: Working Papers in Cultural Studies, 1972–79*, eds. Stuart Hall et al. (London: Hutchinson, 1980), 128–138.

14 Henderson: "This insult led to my defiance. I wrote and presented that paper. Yet when given the opportunity to publish it, I didn't feel so defiant, and ultimately decided not to publish it … Rhimes is a very important writer/executive producer at a major network that I someday hope to work at … I did not feel proud of this decision. But I rationalized it. I was a working television writer and that's what paid the bills. My creative and critical halves battled, the creative side won. This is a challenge I continue to struggle with."

Select Bibliography

Agee, James and Walker Evans. *Let Us Now Praise Famous Men*. Boston: Houghton Mifflin, 1941.

Ahlkvist, Jarl A. and Robert Faulkner. "'Will This Record Work for Us?': Managing Music Formats in Commercial Radio." *Qualitative Sociology* 25 (2002): 189–215.

Alexander, Alison, James Owers, Rodney A. Carveth, C. Ann Hollifield, and Albert N. Greco, eds. *Media Economics: Theory and Practice*. Mahweh, NJ: Lawrence Erlbaum, 2004.

Anderson, Benedict. *Imagined Communities: Reflections on the Origin and Spread of Nationalism*. London: Verso, 1983.

Andrejevic, Mark. *Reality TV: The Work of Being Watched*. New York: Roman and Littlefield, 2004.

Auletta, Ken. *Three Blind Mice: How the TV Networks Lost Their Way*. New York: Random House, 1991.

Bagdikian, Ben. *The New Media Monopoly*. Boston: Beacon Press, 2004.

Banks, Miranda J. *Bodies of Work: Rituals of Production and the Erasure of Film/TV Production Labor*. PhD diss., University of California, Los Angeles, 2006.

Bart, Peter and Peter Guber. *Shoot Out: Surviving Fame and (Mis)fortune in Hollywood*. New York: The Berkley Publishing Group, 2002.

Beaty, Bart and Rebecca Sullivan. *Canadian Television Today*. Calgary: University of Calgary Press, 2006.

Beck, Ulrich. *Power in the Global Age*. Translated by Kathleen Cross. Cambridge, UK: Polity, 2005.

Bedell, Sally. *Up the Tube: Prime Time TV and the Silverman Years*. New York: Viking Press, 1981.

Benson, Rodney and Erik Neveu, eds. *Bourdieu and the Journalistic Field*. Malden, MA: Polity, 2005.

Bielby, William T. and Denise D. Bielby. "Organizational Media of Project-Based Labor Markets: Talent Agencies and the Careers of Screenwriters." *American Sociological Review* 64, no. 1 (1999): 64–85.

Biskind, Peter. *Easy Rider, Raging Bulls: How the Sex-Drugs-and-Rock 'n Roll Generation Saved Hollywood*. New York: Simon and Schuster, 1998.

———. *Down and Dirty Pictures: Miramax, Sundance, and the Rise of Independent Film*. New York: Simon and Schuster, 2004.

Boltanski, Luc and Eve Chiapello. *The New Spirit of Capitalism*. Translated by Gregory Elliott. London: Verso, 2005.

Born, Georgina. *Uncertain Vision: Birt, Dyke and the Reinvention of the BBC*. London: Vintage, 2005.

Bourdieu, Pierre. *Outline of a Theory of Practice*. Translated by Richard Nice. Cambridge: Cambridge University Press, 1977.

————. *Distinction: A Social Critique of the Judgement of Taste*. Translation by Richard Nice. Cambridge, MA: Harvard University Press, 1984.

————. *The Logic of Practice*. Translated by Richard Nice. Stanford: Stanford University Press, 1990.

————. *The Field of Cultural Production: Essays on Art and Literature*. Edited by Randal Johnson. New York: Columbia University Press, 1993.

Brantlinger, Patrick. "A Response to Beyond the Cultural Turn." *The American Historical Review* 107, no. 5 (2002): 1500–1511.

Brenton, Sam and Reuben Cohen. *Shooting People: Adventures in Reality TV*. London and New York: Verso, 2003.

Brookey, Robert Alan and Robert Westerfelhaus. "The Digital Auteur: Branding Identity on the *Monsters, Inc.* DVD." *Western Journal of Communication* 69, no. 2 (2005): 109–128.

Brown, Les. *Televi$ion: The Business Behind the Box*. New York: Harcourt Brace Jovanovich, 1971.

Bryant, Jennings and Dolf Zillman, eds. *Media Effects: Advances in Theory and Research*. Mahwah, NJ: Lawrence Erlbaum Publishers, 2002.

Burawoy, Michael. *Manufacturing Consent: Changes in the Labor Process under Monopoly Capitalism*. Chicago: University of Chicago Press, 1979.

————, Joseph Blum, Sheba George, Zsuzsa Gille, Teresa Gowan, Lynne Haney, Maren Klawiter, Steven Lopez, Seán Riain, and Millie Thayer, eds. *Global Ethnography: Forces, Connections and Imaginations in a Postmodern World*. Berkeley: University of California Press, 2000.

Byers, Michele, ed. *Growing Up Degrassi: Television, Identity and Youth Cultures*. Toronto: Sumach Press, 2005.

Caldwell, John Thornton. *Televisuality: Style, Crisis, and Authority in American Television*. New Brunswick, NJ: Rutgers University Press, 1995.

————. "Industrial Geography Lessons." In *MediaSpace: Place, Scale and Culture in a Media Age*, edited by Nick Couldry and Anna McCarthy, 163–188. New York and London: Routledge, 2004.

————. "Cultural Studies of Media Production: Critical Industrial Practices." In *Questions of Method in Cultural Studies*, edited by Mimi White and James Schwoch, 109–153. Malden, MA: Blackwell, 2006.

————. "Critical Industrial Practice: Branding, Repurposing, and the Migratory Patterns of Industrial Texts." *Television & New Media* 7 (2006): 99–134.

————. *Production Culture: Industrial Reflexivity and Critical Practice in Film and Television*. Durham, NC: Duke University Press, 2008.

Callon, Michel. "Some Elements of a Sociology of Translation: Domestication of the Scallops and the Fishermen of St. Brieuc Bay." In *Power, Action and Belief: A New Sociology of Knowledge*, edited by John Law, 196–233. London: Routledge and Kegan Paul, 1986.

Cantor, Muriel G. *The Hollywood TV Producer: His Work and His Audience*. New York: Basic Books, 1971.

———. "Review: The Perils of Prime-Time Politics." *Contemporary Sociology* 13, no. 4 (1984): 417–419.

——— and Cheryl Zollars, eds. *Current Research on Occupations and Professions: A Research Annual, 8*. Greenwich, CT: JAI Press, 1993.

Carey, James. *Communication as Culture*. New York: Unwin Hyman, 1989.

Carter, Bill. *Desperate Networks*. New York: Doubleday, 2006.

Casagrande, Joseph B. *In the Company of Man: Twenty Portraits by Anthropologists*. New York: Harper & Row, 1964.

Charters, W. W. and Motion Picture Research Council. *Motion Pictures and Youth, a Summary*. New York: The Macmillan Company, 1933.

Collins, Felicity and Terese Davis. *Australian Cinema after Mabo*. Cambridge: Cambridge University Press, 2004.

Cornea, Christine. *Science Fiction Cinema: Between Fantasy and Reality*. Edinburgh and New Brunswick, NJ: Edinburgh University Press and Rutgers University Press, 2007.

Couldry, Nick. *The Place of Media Power: Pilgrims and Witnesses of the Media Age*. New York and London: Routledge, 2000.

———. *Media Rituals: A Critical Approach*. New York and London: Routledge, 2003.

Crane, Diana. *The Production of Culture: Media and Urban Arts*. Edited by Garth S. Jowett. Vol. 1, *Foundations of Popular Culture*. Newbury Park, CA: Sage, 1992.

Crewe, Ben. *Representing Men: Cultural Production and Producers in the Men's Magazine Market*. New York: Berg, 2003.

D'Acci, Julie. *Defining Women: Television and the Case of Cagney & Lacey*. Chapel Hill, NC: University of North Carolina Press, 1994.

———. "Nobody's Woman? Honey West and the New Sexuality." In *The Revolution Wasn't Televised: Sixties Television and Social Conflict*, edited by Lynn Spigel and Michael Curtain, 72–93. New York: Routledge, 1997.

———. "Cultural Studies, Television Studies, and the Crisis in the Humanities." In *Television after TV: Essays on a Medium in Transition*, edited by Lynn Spigel and Jan Olsson, 418–446. Durham: Duke University Press, 2003.

Dávila, Arlene. *Latinos, Inc.* Berkeley and Los Angeles: University of California Press, 2001.

Denzin, Norman K. and Yvonna S. Lincoln, eds. *Handbook of Qualitative Research*. Thousand Oaks, CA: Sage Publications, 2000.

DiMaggio, Paul. "Cultural Entrepreneurship in 19-Century Boston: The Creation of an Organizational Base for High Culture in America." *Media, Culture & Society* 4, no. 1 (1982): 33–50.

Dornfeld, Barry. *Producing Public Television, Producing Public Culture*. Princeton: Princeton University Press, 1998.

Doucet, Andrea. "'From Her Side of the Gossamer Wall(s)': Reflexivity and Relational Knowing." *Qualitative Sociology* 31, no. 1 (2008): 73–87.

Dubrofsky, Rachel. "The Bachelor: Whiteness in the Harem." *Critical Studies in Media Communication* 23, no. 1 (March 2006): 39–56.

du Gay, Paul, Stuart Hall, Linda Janes, Hugh Mackay, and Keith Negus. *Doing Cultural Studies: The Story of the Sony Walkman*. London: Sage, 1997.

du Gay, Paul and Michael Pryke. "Cultural Economy: An Introduction." In *Cultural Economy: Cultural Analysis and Commercial Life*, edited by Paul du Gay and Michael Pryke, 1–20. London: Sage, 2002.

Dunne, John Gregory. *The Studio*. New York: Vintage Books, [1968] 1998.

Dyer, Richard. *Stars*. London: British Film Institute, 1979.

Elliott, Philip. *The Making of a Television Series: A Case Study in the Sociology of Culture*. Edited by Jeremy Tunstall. London: Constable, 1972.

Emerson, Robert M., Rachel I. Fretz, and Linda L. Shaw. *Writing Ethnographic Fieldnotes*. Chicago: University of Chicago Press, 1995.

Espinosa, Paul. "The Audience in the Text: Ethnographic Observations of a Hollywood Story Conference." *Media, Culture & Society* 4, no. 1 (1982): 77–86.

Ettema, James S. and D. Charles Whitney, eds. *Audiencemaking: How the Media Create the Audience*. Thousand Oaks, CA and London: Sage Publications, 1994.

Federal Writers' Project. *These Are Our Lives*. Chapel Hill: University of North Carolina Press, 1939.

Feuer, Jane, Paul Kerr, and Tise Vahimagi, eds. *MTM: 'Quality Television.'* London: British Film Institute, 1985.

Fisher, Melissa S. and Greg Downey, eds. *Frontiers of Capital: Ethnographic Reflections on the New Economy*. Durham, NC: Duke University Press, 2006.

Fisk, Catherine. "Authors at Work: The Origins of the Work-For-Hire Doctrine." *Yale Journal of Law and the Humanities* 15 no. 1 (2003): 1–70.

Fiske, John. *Television Culture*. London and New York: Methuen, 1987.

Flew, Terry. *Understanding Global Media*. Hampshire, UK: Palgrave Macmillan, 2007.

Foucault, Michel. *Discipline and Punish: The Birth of the Prison*. New York: Vintage, [1975] 1995.

Friedman, James, ed. *Reality Squared: Televisual Discourse on the Real*. New Brunswick, NJ: Rutgers University Press, 2002.

Gamson, Joshua. "Stopping the Spin and Becoming a Prop: Fieldwork on Hollywood Elites." In *Studying Elites Using Qualitative Methods*, edited by Rosanna Hertz and Jonathan B. Imber, 83–93. Thousand Oaks, CA: Sage, 1995.

————. *Freaks Talk Back: Tabloid Talk Shows and Sexual Nonconformity*. Chicago: University of Chicago Press, 1998.

Gans, Herbert J. "The Creator-Audience Relationship in the Mass Media: An Analysis of Movie Making." In *Mass Culture: The Popular Arts in America*, edited by Barnard Rosenberg and David Manning White, 315–324. Glencoe, IL: The Free Press, 1957.

Garnham, Nicholas. "Political Economy and Cultural Studies." *Critical Studies in Mass Communication* 12, no. 2 (1995): 62–71.

Gerbner, George. "Communication and Social Environment." *Scientific American* 227 (1972): 153–160.

Giles, David. "The Quest For Fame." In *The Celebrity Culture Reader*, edited by P. David Marshall, 470–486. New York and London: Routledge, 2004.

Ginsberg, Faye. "Ethnography and American Studies." *Cultural Anthropology* 21, no. 3 (2006): 487–495.

————, Lila Abu-Lughod, and Brian Larkin, eds. *Media Worlds: Anthropology on New Terrain*. Berkeley and Los Angeles: University of California Press, 2002.

Gitlin, Todd. "Prime Time Ideology: The Hegemonic Process in Television Entertainment." *Social Problems* 26 (1979): 251–266.

————. *Inside Prime Time*. New York: Pantheon Books, 1983.

Goldman, William. *Adventures in the Screen Trade: A Personal View of Hollywood and Screenwriting*. New York: Warner Books, 1983.

Goldsmith, Ben and Tom O'Regan. *Cinema Cities, Media Cities: The Contemporary International Studio Complex*. Brisbane: AFC/Australian Key Centre for Cultural Studies and Media Policy, 2003.

————. *The Film Studio: Film Production in the Global Economy*. Lanham: Rowman and Littlefield, 2005.

Gomery, Douglas. *The Hollywood Studio System: A History*. London: British Film Institute, 2005.

———— and Benjamin M. Compaine. *Who Owns the Media?: Competition and Concentration in the Mass Media Industry*. Hillsdale, NJ: Lawrence Erlbaum, 2000.

Gough-Yates, Anna. *Understanding Women's Magazines*. London: Routledge, 2002.

Gramsci, Antonio. *Selections From the Prison Notebooks*. Translated by Quintin Hoare and Geoffrey Nowell-Smith. New York: International Publishers, 1972.

Grindstaff, Laura. *The Money Shot: Trash, Class, and the Making of TV Talk Shows*. Chicago: University of Chicago Press, 2002.

———— and Joseph Turow. "Video Cultures: Television Sociology in the 'New TV' Age." *Annual Review of Sociology* 32 (2006): 103–125.

Gusterson, Hugh. *Nuclear Rites: A Weapons Laboratory at the End of the Cold War*. Berkeley, CA: University of California Press, 1996.

————. "Studying Up Revisited." *Political and Legal Anthropology Review* 20, no. 1 (1997): 114–119.

Gwenllian-Jones, Sara and Roberta Pearson. *Cult Television*. Minneapolis: University of Minnesota Press, 2004.

Hamilton, Marci. "Commissioned Works as Works Made for Hire Under the 1976 Copyright Act: Misinterpretation and Injustice." *University of Pennsylvania Law Review* 135 (1987): 1281–1320.

Handel, Leo. *Hollywood Looks at Its Audience: A Report of Film Audience Research*. Urbana-Champaign, IL: University of Illinois Press, 1950.

Hannerz, Ulf. *Foreign News: Exploring the World of Foreign Correspondents*. Chicago: University of Chicago Press, 2004.

Hartley, John, ed. *Creative Industries*. Malden, MA: Blackwell, 2005.

Havens, Timothy. "Universal Childhood: The Global Trade in Children's Television and Changing Ideals of Childhood." *Global Media Journal* 6, no. 10 (2007), http://lass.calumet.purdue.edu/cca/gmj/sp07/gmj-sp07-havens.htm.

————, Amanda D. Lotz, and Serra Tinic. *Critical Media Industry Studies: A Research Approach*. Unpublished manuscript.

Hearn, Alison. "'John, a 20-year-old Boston Native with a Great sense of Humor': On the Spectacularization of the 'Self' and Incorporation of Identity in the Age of

Reality Television." In *The Celebrity Culture Reader*, edited by P. David Marshall, 618–633. New York and London: Routledge, 2004.

Herd, Nick. *Chasing the Runaways: Foreign Film Production and Studio Film Development in Australia 1988–2002*. Sydney: Currency House, 2004.

Hesmondhalgh, David. *The Cultural Industries*. London and Thousand Oaks, CA: Sage, [2002] 2007.

———. "Politics, Theory and Method in Media Industries Research." In *Media Industries: History, Theory, and Methods*, edited by Jennifer Holt and Alisa Perren, 245–255. Malden MA: Blackwell.

Hill, Annette. *Reality TV: Audiences and Factual Television*. London and New York: Routledge, 2005.

Hills, Matt. "Defining Cult TV: Texts, Inter-texts and Fan Audiences." In *The Television Studies Reader*, edited by Robert C. Allen and Annette Hill, 509–523. New York and London: Routledge, 2004.

Himpele, Jeff D. "Arrival Scenes: Complicity and Media Ethnography in the Bolivian Public Sphere." In *Media Worlds: Anthropology on New Terrain*, edited by Faye Ginsburg, Lila Abu-Lughod, and Brian Larkin, 301–316. Berkeley and Los Angeles: University of California Press, 2002.

Hirsch, Paul. "Cultural Industries Revisited." *Organization Science* 11, no. 3 (2000): 356–361.

Hochschild, Arlie Russell. *The Managed Heart: Commercialization of Human Feeling*. Chicago: University of Chicago Press, 1983.

———. *The Commercialization of Intimate Life*. Berkeley and Los Angeles: University of California Press, 2003.

Horkheimer, Max and Theodor W. Adorno. *The Dialectic of Enlightenment*. London: Continuum, [1947] 1976.

Hull, Geoff. *The Recording Industry*, 2nd ed. New York: Routledge, 2004.

Jenkins, Henry. *Convergence Culture: Where Old and New Media Collide*. New York and London: New York University Press, 2006.

———, Tara McPherson, and Jane Shattuc, eds. *Hop on Pop: The Politics and Pleasures of Popular Culture*. Durham, NC: Duke University Press, 2002.

Jensen, Joli. "An Interpretive Approach to Culture Production." In *Interpreting Television: Current Perspectives*, edited by William Rowland and Bruce Watkins, 98–118. Beverly Hills: Sage, 1984.

Johnson, Catherine. *Telefantasy*. London: British Film Institute, 2005.

Johnson, Richard. "What is Cultural Studies Anyway?" *Social Text* 16 (1986): 38–80.

Johnson-Smith, Jan. *American Science Fiction TV: Star Trek, Stargate and Beyond*. London: I.B. Tauris, 2005.

Jones, Janet Megan. "Show Your Real Face: A Fan Study of the UK Big Brother Transmissions." *New Media & Society* 5 (2003): 400–421.

Jöns, Heike. "Dynamic Hybrids and the Geographies of Technoscience: Discussing Conceptual Resources Beyond the Human/Non-Human Binary." *Social & Cultural Geography* 7 no. 4 (2006): 559–580.

Jowett, Garth. *Film: The Democratic Art*. Boston: Little, Brown & Co., 1976.

————, Ian C. Jarvie, and Kathryn Fuller. *Children and the Movies: Media Influence and the Payne Fund Controversy*. New York: Cambridge University Press, 1996.

Katz, Elihu. "Review: *Inside Prime Time*." *The American Journal of Sociology* 90, no. 6 (1985): 1371–1374.

Lamont, Michèle. *Money, Morals, and Manners: The Culture of the French and American Upper-Middle Class*. Chicago: University of Chicago Press, 1992.

Landman, Jane. *'The Tread of a White Man's Foot': Australian Pacific Colonialism and the Cinema, 1925–1962*. Canberra: Pandanus, 2006.

Latour, Bruno. *Reassembling the Social: An Introduction to Actor-Network-Theory*. Oxford: Oxford University Press, 2005.

Law, John. *After Method: Mess in Social Science Research*. London: Routledge, 2004.

Lazere, Donald. "TV Hegemony." *Journal of Communication* 34, no. 2 (1984): 170–172.

Lent, John. "Overseas Animation Production in Asia." In *Animation in Asia and the Pacific*, edited by John Lent, 239–245. Bloomington: Indiana University Press, 2001.

Levine, Elana. "Toward a Paradigm for Media Production Research: Behind the Scenes at *General Hospital*." *Critical Studies in Media Communication* 18 (2001): 66–82.

————. "National Television, Global Market: Canada's *Degrassi: The Next Generation*." *Media, Culture & Society*, forthcoming.

Levinson, Richard and William Link. *Stay Tuned: An Inside Look at the Making of Prime-Time Television*. New York: St. Martin's Press, 1981.

Lipset, Seymour Martin. *Continental Divide: The Values and Institutions of the United States and Canada*. New York: Routledge, 1990.

Lotz, Amanda D. "The Promotional Role of the Network Upfront Presentations in the Production of Culture." *Television & New Media* 8, no. 1 (2007): 3–24.

————. *The Television Will Be Revolutionized*. New York: New York University Press, 2007.

Mackey, Eva. *The House of Difference: Cultural Politics and National Identity in Canada*. London: Routledge, 1999.

Mander, Jerry. *Four Arguments for the Elimination of Television*. New York: Harper, 1981.

Marc, David and Robert J. Thompson. *Prime Time, Prime Movers: From 'I Love Lucy' to 'L.A. Law'—America's Greatest TV Shows and the People Who Created Them*. Boston and London: Little, Brown and Company, 1992.

Marich, Robert. *Marketing to Moviegoers: A Handbook of Strategies Used by Major Studios and Independents*. New York and London: Elsevier, 2005.

Mayer, Vicki. "Guys Gone Wild? Soft-Core Video Professionalism and New Realities in Television Production." *Cinema Journal* 47, no. 2 (2008): 97–116.

Mazzarella, William. *Shoveling Smoke: Advertising and Globalization in Contemporary India*. Durham: Duke University Press, 2003.

McCarthy, Anna. *Ambient Television: Visual Culture and Public Space*. Durham, NC and London: Duke University Press, 2001.

McCarthy, Cameron, Aisha Durham, Laura Engel, Alice Filmer, Michael Giardina, and Miguel Malagreca, eds. *Globalizing Cultural Studies: Ethnographic Interventions in Theory, Method and Policy*. New York: Peter Lang, 2007.

McChesney, Robert W. *The Problem of the Media: U.S. Communication Politics in the 21st Century*. New York: Monthly Review Press, 2004.

McGregor, Gaile. "*Stargate* as Cancult: Ideological Coding as a Function of Location." In *Reading Stargate SG-1*, edited by Stan Beeler and Lisa Dickson, 154–167. London and New York: I.B. Tauris, 2006.

McLellan, David. "Economic and Philosophical Manuscripts (1844)." In *Karl Marx: Selected Writings*, 2nd ed. Edited by David McLellan. Oxford: Oxford University Press, 2000.

Meehan, Eileen. "'Holy Commodity Fetish, Batman!': The Political Economy of a Commercial Intertext." In *The Many Lives of The Batman: Critical Approaches to a Superhero and His Media*, edited by Roberta E. Pearson and William Uricchio, 47–65. New York: Routledge, 1991.

Merton, Robert. *Social Theory and Social Structure*. New York: Free Press, 1968.

Miege, Bernard. *The Capitalization of Cultural Production*. New York: International General, 1989.

Miller, Tony, Nitin Govil, John McMurria, and Ting Wang. *Global Hollywood 2*, London: British Film Institute, 2005.

Mills, Charles Wright. *The Power Elite*. New York: Oxford University Press, 1956.

Moeran, Brian. "Tricks of the Trade: The Performance and Interpretation of Authenticity." *Journal of Management Studies* 42, no. 5 (2005): 901–922.

Moore, Candace. "Having it All Ways: The Tourist, the Traveler, and the Local in *The L Word*." *Cinema Journal* 46, no. 4 (Summer 2007): 3–23.

Motion Picture Association of America. *The 2005 Movie Attendance Study*, www.mpaa.org.

Murdoch Jonathan. "The Spaces of Actor-Network Theory." *Geoforum* 29, no. 4 (1998): 357–374.

Murray, Susan and Laurie Ouellette, eds. *Reality TV: Remaking Television Culture*. New York: New York University Press, 2004.

Nader, Laura. "Up the Anthropologist—Perspectives Gained from Studying Up." In *Reinventing Anthropology*, edited by Dell H. Hymes, 284–311. New York: Pantheon Books, 1969.

————. "Controlling Processes: Tracing the Dynamic Components of Power." *Current Anthropology* 38 (December 1997): 711–737.

Newcomb, Horace and Robert S. Alley. *The Producer's Medium: Conversations with Creators of American TV*. New York: Oxford University Press, 1983.

————. and Amanda D. Lotz. "The Production of Media Fiction." In *A Handbook of Media and Communication Research*, edited by Klaus Bruhn Jensen, 62–77. New York: Routledge, 2002.

Obst, Lynda. *Hello, He Lied—and Other Truths from the Hollywood Trenches*. New York: Broadway Books, 1997.

Ortner, Sherry B. *Anthropology and Social Theory*. Durham, NC: Duke University Press, 2006.

Parks, Lisa and Shanti Kumar, eds. *Planet TV: A Global Television Reader*. New York: New York University Press, 2002.

Paul, Alan and Archie Kleingartner. "Flexible Production and the Transformation of Industrial Relations in the Motion Picture and Television Industry." *Industrial and Labor Relations Review* 47, no. 4 (1994): 663–678.

————. "The Transformation of Industrial Relations in the Motion Picture and Television Industries: The Talent Sector." In *Under the Stars: Essays on Labor Relations in Arts and Entertainment*, edited by Lois Gray and Ronald Seeber, 156–180. Ithaca: ILR Press, 1996.

Peterson, Richard A. "The Production of Culture: A Prolegomenon." In *The Production of Culture*, edited by Richard A. Peterson, 7–22. Beverly Hills, CA: Sage, 1976.

————. "Five Constraints on the Production of Culture: Law, Technology, Market, Organizational Structure and Occupational Careers." *Journal of Popular Culture* 16, no. 2 (1982): 143–152.

———— and Narasimhan Anand. "The Production of Culture Perspective." *Annual Review of Sociology* 30 (August 2004): 311–334.

Powdermaker, Hortense. *Hollywood the Dream Factory*. New York: Little, Brown & Company, 1950.

————. *Stranger and Friend: The Way of an Anthropologist*. New York: W.W. Norton & Company, 1966.

Rabinow, Paul. *Making PCR: A Story of Biotechnology*. Chicago: University of Chicago Press, 1996.

Raphael, Chad. "Political Economy of Reali-TV." *Jump Cut* 41 (1997): 102–109.

Rifkin, Jeremy. "When Markets Give Way to Networks." In *The Creative Industries*, edited by John Hartley, 361–373. Malden, MA: Blackwell, 2005.

Robben, Antonius C. G. M. "Ethnographic Seduction, Transference, and Resistance in Dialogues about Terror and Violence in Argentina." *Ethos* 24, no. 1 (1996): 71–106.

————. *Political Violence and Trauma in Argentina*. Philadelphia: University of Pennsylvania Press, 2005.

———— and Jeffrey S. Sluka, eds. *Ethnographic Fieldwork: An Anthropological Reader*. Malden, MA: Blackwell, 2007.

Roshco, Bernard. "Inside Prime Time." *Social Forces* 64, no. 3 (1983): 827–828.

Ross, Andrew. *No Respect: Intellectuals and Popular Culture*. London: Routledge, 1989.

Ross, Lillian. *Picture*. Cambridge, MA: Da Capo Press, [1952] 2002.

Rosten, Leo C. *The Washington Correspondents*. New York: Harcourt Brace, 1937.

————. "A 'Middletown' Study of Hollywood." *The Public Opinion Quarterly* 3 (1939): 314–320.

————. *Hollywood: The Movie Colony, the Movie Makers*. New York: Harcourt Brace, 1941.

————. *The Many Worlds of Leo Rosten; Stories, Humor, Social Commentary, Travelogues, Satire, Memoirs, Profiles, and Sundry Entertainments Never Before Published; with a Special Introduction, Background Notes, Revelations and Confessions, All Hand-written and Themselves Worth the Price of Admission*, 1st ed. New York: Harper & Row, 1964.

Rothenbuhler, Eric and Mihai Coman, eds. *Media Anthropology*. Thousand Oaks, CA: Sage, 2005.

Ryan, Bill. *Making Capital from Culture: The Corporate Form of Capitalist Cultural Production*. Berlin: Walter de Gruyter, 1992.

Salamon, Julie. *The Devil's Candy: The Bonfire of the Vanities Goes to Hollywood*. Boston: Houghton Mifflin, 1991.

Schatz, Thomas. *Boom and Bust: The American Cinema in the 1940s*. New York: Charles Scribner's Sons, 1997.

Seiter, Ellen. *Television and New Media Audiences*. Oxford: Oxford University Press, 1999.

Serres, Michel and Bruno Latour. *Conversations on Science, Culture and Time*. Ann Arbor, MI: University of Michigan Press, 1995.

Shields, Stephanie. *Speaking from the Heart: Gender and the Social Meaning of Emotion*. Cambridge, UK: Cambridge University Press, 2002.

Shohat, Ella and Robert Stam. *Unthinking Eurocentrism: Multiculturalism and the Media*. New York and London: Routlege, 1994.

Sito, Tom. *Drawing the Line: The Untold Story of the Animation Unions from Bosko to Bart Simpson*. Lexington, KY: University Press of Kentucky, 2006.

Spigel, Lynn. *Make Room for TV: Television and the Family Ideal in Postwar America*. Chicago: University of Chicago Press, 1992.

Stahl, Matthew. "Non-Proprietary Authorship and the Uses of Autonomy: Artistic Labor in American Film Animation, 1900–2004." *Labor: Studies in Working-Class History of the Americas* 2, no. 4 (2005): 87–105.

Stewart, Johanna F. "The Freelancer's Trap: Work for Hire Under the Copyright Act of 1976." *West Virginia Law Review* 86 (1984): 1305–1316.

Straubhaar, Joseph D. *World Television: From Global to Local*. London and Thousand Oaks, CA: Sage, 2007.

Sullivan, John L. "Marketing Creative Labor: Hollywood 'Making of' Documentary Features." In *Knowledge Workers in the Information Society*, edited by Catherine McKercher and Vincent Mosco, 69–83. Lanham, MD: Lexington Books, 2007.

Tinic, Serra. *On Location: Canada's Television Industry in a Global Market*. Toronto: University of Toronto Press, 2005.

Traube, Elizabeth G. *Dreaming Identities: Class, Gender and Generation in 1980s Hollywood Movies*. Boulder: Westview Press, 1992.

———. "Introduction." In *Making and Selling Culture*, edited by Richard Ohmann, xi–xxiii. Hanover: Wesleyan University Press, 1996.

Tuchman, Gaye. *Making News: A Study in the Construction of Reality*. New York: Free Press, 1978.

Tunstall, Jeremy. *The Media Are American: Anglo-American Media in the World*. New York: Columbia University Press, 1977.

———. *The Media Were American: US Mass Media in Decline*. New York: Oxford University Press, 2008.

Turner, Graeme. "Celebrity, the Tabloid, and the Democratic Public Sphere." In *The Celebrity Culture Reader*, edited by P. David Marshall, 487–500. New York and London: Routledge, 2004.

Turow, Joseph. "Learning to Portray Institutional Power: The Socialization of Mass Media Organizations." In *Organizational Communication: Traditional Themes and New Directions*, edited by Robert McPhee and Phillip Tompkins, 211–234. Beverly Hills: Sage, 1985.

———. *Media Systems in Society: Understanding Industries, Strategies, and Power*, 2nd ed. New York: A.B. Longman, 1997.

Vachon, Christine with Austin Bunn. *A Killer Life: How an Independent Film Producer Survives Deals and Disasters in Hollywood and Beyond*. New York: Simon and Schuster, 2006.

Wasko, Janet. *How Hollywood Works*. Thousand Oaks, CA and London: Sage, 2003.

Waterman, David. *Hollywood's Road to Riches.* Cambridge, MA and London: Harvard University Press, 2005.

Weber, Daniel. "Culture or Commerce? Symbolic Boundaries in French and American Book Publishing." In *Rethinking Comparative Cultural Sociology: Repertoires of Evaluation in France and the United States*, edited by Michèle Lamont and Laurent Thévenot, 127–147. Cambridge, UK: Cambridge University Press, 2000.

Whitney, D. Charles and James S. Ettema. "Media Production: Individuals, Organizations, Institutions." In *A Companion to Media Studies*, edited by Angharad Valdivia, 157–186. Oxford: Blackwell, 2003.

Wilson, Pamela. "Jamming Big Brother: Webcasting, Audience Intervention, and Narrative Activism." In *Reality TV: Remaking Television Culture*, edited by Susan Murray and Laurie Ouellette, 323–343. New York: New York University Press, 2004.

List of Contributors

Miranda J. Banks is an Assistant Professor in the Department of Visual & Media Arts at Emerson College. Her research focuses on Hollywood's creative and craft guilds and unions. Her current book project is a history of the Writer's Guild of America. She has written for *The Journal of Popular Film and Television*, *Television & New Media*, and *Flow*, and for the anthologies *Teen Television* (McFarland, 2008) and *Garb: A Fashion and Culture Reader* (Pearson Prentice Hall, 2008). She received her PhD from the Department of Film, Television, and Digital Media at UCLA in 2006.

John T. Caldwell is Professor of Cinema and Media Studies at UCLA. His books include *Production Culture: Industrial Reflexivity and Critical Practice in Film and Television* (Duke UP, 2008), *Televisuality: Style, Crisis, and Authority in American Television* (Rutgers UP, 1995), *Electronic Media and Technoculture* (edited, Rutgers UP, 2000), *New Media: Theories and Practices of Digitextuality* (edited with Anna Everett, Routledge, 2003). He is also the producer/director of the award-winning documentary films *Rancho California (por favor)* (2002), and *Freak Street to Goa: Immigrants on the Rajpath* (1989). His productions have been screened at various film festivals in North America and Europe, and broadcast on public television in the US and Australia. His creative work has also received awards and grants from the National Endowment for the Arts, the Illinois Arts Council, and the Regional Fellowships of the AFI/NEA.

Christine Cornea is a Lecturer with the School of Film and Television at the University of East Anglia. Christine has published extensively on science fiction, including her book *Science Fiction Cinema: Between Fantasy and Reality* (co-published by Edinburgh UP and Rutgers UP, 2007). Recently, Christine also edited and wrote the introduction for "In Focus: The Practitioner Interview," *Cinema Journal* 47, no. 2 (2008): 117–123, and *Genre and Performance: Film and Television* (Manchester UP, 2009). She is working on a further monograph project, currently entitled: *Post Apocalypse on the Small Screen*.

Laura Grindstaff is an Associate Professor of Sociology at UC Davis. She directs the Consortium for Women and Research, and is an active member of the Graduate Group in Cultural Studies. She teaches and writes about American popular culture. Her first book, *The Money Shot: Trash, Class, and the Making of TV Talk Shows* (University of Chicago Press, 2002), received the Distinguished Scholarship Award from the Pacific Sociological Association and the Culture Section Book Prize from the American Sociological Association. Her second book, in progress, is an ethnographic study of cheerleading in/as American culture.

Jane Landman is a Senior Lecturer at Victoria University in Melbourne, where she teaches media studies in the School of Communication and the Arts. Her research interests include the history of Australia's cinematic engagement with western Pacific states, and contemporary television drama. She is the author of *'The Tread of a White Man's Foot': Australian Pacific Colonialism and the Cinema* (Pandanus Press, 2006).

Elana Levine is Associate Professor in the Department of Journalism and Mass Communication at the University of Wisconsin-Milwaukee. She is the author of *Wallowing in Sex: The New Sexual Culture of 1970s American Television* (Duke University Press, 2007) and co-editor of *Undead TV: Essays on Buffy the Vampire Slayer* (Duke University Press, 2007). She has published articles in such journals as *Critical Studies in Media Communication*, *Television & New Media*, *Media, Culture & Society*, and *Feminist Media Studies*, as well as contributing chapters to numerous edited collections.

Amanda D. Lotz is Associate Professor of Communication Studies at the University of Michigan. She is the author of *Redesigning Women: Television after the Network Era* (University of Illinois Press, 2006) and *The Television Will Be Revolutionized* (New York University Press, 2007).

Denise Mann, MFA/PhD, Associate Professor and head of the UCLA Producers Program, is the author of *Hollywood Independents: The Postwar Talent Takeover* (University of Minnesota Press, 2008) and co-editor of *Private Screenings: Television and the Female Consumer* (University of Minnesota Press, 1992). She has published chapters in several anthologies, including Jeremy G. Butler, ed., *Star Texts: Image and Performance in Film and Television* (Wayne State Press, 1991) and Daniel Bernardi, ed., *Different Visions, Revolutionary Perceptions: Race, Gender and Sexuality in the Work of Contemporary Filmmakers* (University of Texas Press, forthcoming). Mann served as an associate editor on *Camera Obscura* for six years (1986–1992). She is a frequent guest lecturer on the topic of contemporary Hollywood media industry practices at the Tokyo IFF, Shanghai IFF, Beijing

Broadcasting Institute, Shanghai University, Paris 1 Sorbonne-DESS, and Institut National de L'Audiovisuel (INA).

Vicki Mayer is an Associate Professor and Chair of the Department of Communication, Tulane University. A participant-observer of interpretative communities of media consumers and producers, she is the author of *Producing Dreams, Consuming Youth: Mexican Americans and Mass Media* (Rutgers UP, 2003) and *Below the Line: Producers and Production Studies in the New Television Economy* (Duke UP, forthcoming). She has also published in journals in communication, film and television studies, and sociology, and sits on the editorial board of *Critical Studies in Media Communication*.

Candace Moore is a PhD candidate in Cinema and Media Studies at UCLA, where her work focuses on queer representation in television. Moore's articles have appeared or are forthcoming in: *Reading 'The L Word': Outing Contemporary Television* (I.B. Tauris, 2006), *Televising Queer Women* (Palgrave MacMillan, 2008), *Cinema Journal,* and *GLQ.* Moore has also published extensively as a film and television critic for *Girlfriends Magazine, Curve,* and AfterEllen.com.

Oli Mould is a post-doctoral research fellow currently at the University of the Arts London. His research to date has engaged with the film and television production industry of the city of Sydney, relating it to the broader themes of urban theory and world city network analysis. A scholar of economic geography, his academic interests also include urban theory, the creative industries of architecture and music, city branding including the use and symbolism of signature architecture, as well as more theoretical ideas of poststructuralism and Actor-Network theory.

Sherry B. Ortner is Distinguished Professor of Anthropology at UCLA. Her most recent books are *Anthropology and Social Theory: Culture, Power, and the Acting Subject* (Duke University Press, 2006) and *New Jersey Dreaming: Capital, Culture, and the Class of '58* (Duke University Press, 2003).

Matt Stahl is an Assistant Professor in the Faculty of Information and Media Studies at the University of Western Ontario. He has published in *Popular Music,* the *Journal of Popular Music Studies,* and *Labor: Studies in the Working-Class History of the Americas,* as well as the collection *Bad Music: The Music We Love to Hate* (Routledge, 2004) and *The Media and Social Theory* (Routledge, 2008). His research interests include the social relations of cultural production and the representation of these relations in popular media. Of special analytical interest are the ways in which the politics of authorship, alienation, and autonomy in cultural production highlight the links between the neoliberalizing political economy and liberal society's founding tension between democracy and the employment relation. Matt Stahl is currently writing a book about the politics of cultural work, tentatively titled *That "Feeling" of Revolution: Autonomy, Property, and Popular Music Making*.

John L. Sullivan is an Associate Professor in the Department of Media and Communication at Muhlenberg College in Allentown, Pennsylvania. He received his PhD in Communication in 2000 from the Annenberg School for Communication at the University of Pennsylvania. His research interests include the history of media production studies, the formation and implementation of US media policy, and the institutional constructions of audiences. He has published in journals such as *Communication Research* and *Communication Law & Policy*, and has recently published a chapter entitled "Marketing Creative Labor: Hollywood 'Making of' Documentary Features" in *Knowledge Workers in the Information Society*, edited by Catherine McKercher and Vincent Mosco (Lexington Books, 2007). He is currently writing a textbook on media audiences for Sage Publications.

Serra Tinic is an Associate Professor of Media Studies in the Department of Sociology at the University of Alberta, Canada. Her research focuses on critical television studies and media globalization. She is the author of *On Location: Canada's Television Industry in a Global Market*. She has published in a range of scholarly anthologies and journals including *Television and New Media*, *Journal of Communication*, *Social Epistemology*, and *The Velvet Light Trap*. She is currently working on a book project, *Trading in Culture: The Global Cultural Economy of Television Drama*.

Stephen Zafirau is a Visiting Assistant Professor in the Department of Communication at Tulane University. He recently completed his doctoral work at the University of Southern California, where his dissertation research focused on how knowledge of American movie audiences is socially constructed within the everyday worlds in which Hollywood moviemakers live and work. A recent article stemming from this project appears in the journal *Qualitative Sociology*.

Index